W9-CBR-245

Hogs Wild

Hogs Wild

SELECTED REPORTING PIECES

Ian Frazier

Farrar, Straus and Giroux   New York

Farrar, Straus and Giroux
18 West 18th Street, New York 10011

Grateful acknowledgment is made to *The Atlantic Monthly, Mother Jones, The New Yorker,* and *Outside* magazine, where these pieces first appeared, in slightly different form.

Grateful acknowledgment is made for permission to reprint excerpts from the lyrics of *The Lonesome Death of Hattie Carroll* by Bob Dylan, copyright © 1964, 1966 by Warner Bros. Inc.; renewed 1992 by Special Rider Music. All rights reserved. International copyright secured. Reprinted by permission.

Library of Congress Cataloging-in-Publication Data
Frazier, Ian.
  [Essays. Selections]
  Hogs wild : selected reporting pieces / Ian Frazier. — First edition.
    pages   cm
  ISBN 978-0-374-29852-4 (hardback) — ISBN 978-0-374-71353-9
  (e-book)
  I. Title.

PS3556.R363 A6 2016
814'.54—dc23
                                                          2015036372

Designed by Jonathan D. Lippincott

Our books may be purchased in bulk for promotional, educational, or business use. Please contact your local bookseller or the Macmillan Corporate and Premium Sales Department at 1-800-221-7945, extension 5442, or by e-mail at MacmillanSpecialMarkets@macmillan.com.

www.fsgbooks.com
www.twitter.com/fsgbooks • www.facebook.com/fsgbooks

1   3   5   7   9   10   8   6   4   2

Contents

Hogs Wild

By the Road

It was the winter that Bernhard Goetz shot the four guys on the subway. The "subway vigilante," as news stories called him, had just surrendered to police, and everybody had an opinion about what he did and whether he was wrong or right. I was living in northwest Montana, in a house on the side of the Swan Mountains, as far up as you could go before national-forest land. Past the Swan range, behind the house, began the Bob Marshall Wilderness, one of the largest national-wilderness areas in the lower forty-eight states. At the foot of the mountains was the valley of the Flathead River. From clear across the valley you could see the light above our garage door.

When I moved to Montana from New York, I'd thought I was going back to some earlier and better version of America, to an Ansel Adams photograph suspended in time. Of course, Montana isn't like that, nor (as far as I know) is anywhere else. Nowadays, the particular nuttiness of the age surges everywhere instantly, like a magnetic field. Sometimes half the drop-offs at local U-Haul rental places come from California, and whenever upheaval happens there—an earthquake, a riot—the number of refugees seems to go

up. A lot of people in Montana aren't so much living there
as they are not living somewhere else.

That winter, the Bernhard Goetz winter, it really snowed.
A hard snowfall makes you feel excited and cozy for only
about ninety minutes, I found; after that, it becomes irri-
tating, then worrisome, then alarming, and so on, sometimes all the way to panic. Writing, with its limitations at
expressing tedium, can't accurately convey the feeling of
watching a steady, hard, unpicturesque, windless snowfall
come down for days at a time. Snow piled high on our front
deck and on our roof. Sometimes the roof's snow mass,
warmed underneath by the heat it was insulating, would
slide down until it met the snow heap on the deck and then
freeze there, shutting off the front of the house like a security gate. The driveway to that house was two hundred yards
long and included a switchback. I kept it shoveled through
the first several snowfalls, but then gave up. Getting it
plowed cost more than I could afford, so my wife and I
began parking our cars at a wide part of the road about a
quarter mile downhill. One of our neighbors, a man named
(let's say) Len Dodd, parked his car there, too. Len Dodd had
moved here from Southern California, where he had been
a policeman. He had been inspired to move by various
long-cultivated dislikes and resentments, combined with a
general expectation of coming apocalypse. He talked about
these topics in a manner that managed to be tight-lipped
and loquacious at the same time. He was short and stocky,
with a bristly mustache and narrow eyes, and he often wore
a billed cap of a wild, vivid paisley pattern that suggested
the scrambled contortions of the thoughts inside.

Len Dodd thought that the subway vigilante was great.
He talked about him often, said that Goetz had taught the
punks of the world a lesson, hoped that now more people
would start carrying concealed weapons on the subway,

etc. I was still young enough and game enough to argue. One afternoon, we were standing by our cars for a moment before setting out on the long trudge to our houses, and Len Dodd said that Goetz had to shoot the guys, because they were threatening him and they were armed. I said that they weren't "armed"; they had screwdrivers. He said that those weren't ordinary screwdrivers, they were *sharpened* screwdrivers. I said—I had just read an article discussing the subject—that the screwdrivers weren't sharpened. Len Dodd gave me a narrow, in-the-know look, lowered his voice, and said, "That's not what *I* heard."

I looked down the road and up it. Repeated plowings had left the snow berms so high that the tire-packed track in between was like a bobsled run with white walls taller than a person. Snow had fallen the night before, reburdening the trees all the way to the crest of the Swans, whose topmost spruces and pines stood minutely whitened against the sky like fine-edged crystals of frost on a windowpane. The muffling of new snow added an extra hush to the woods' usual silence, and the painfully cold air carried no smell but that of the gigantic blankness of the Bob Marshall Wilderness beyond. Not even a deer had ventured up here for months. Len Dodd's gaze became more intense, as if to convey a hidden truth to me by mental telepathy. "Where did you hear that, Len?" I asked.

December 22, 2003

Hungry Minds

The Church of the Holy Apostles, at the corner of Twenty-eighth Street and Ninth Avenue in Manhattan, is a church only two-sevenths of the time. The other five-sevenths—every weekday including holidays, no exception made for weather, fire, or terrorist attack—it is the largest soup kitchen in New York City. It serves an average of about twelve hundred meals a day, though the number often spikes higher; on a recent Columbus Day, the number of meals served was 1492. As a church, Holy Apostles is a not large and not wealthy parish in the Episcopal Church's Diocese of New York. As a soup kitchen, it has lasted for more than twenty-five years, since back in the first Reagan administration, and has served more than six million meals.

I know about the soup kitchen because I am one of the teachers of a writers' workshop that meets there after lunch on Wednesdays in the spring. I started the workshop fourteen years ago, with the help of a grant. I wanted to do something with the soup kitchen because I admired the people there and the way it is run and the whole idea of it. There are so many hungers out there; the soup kitchen deals, efficiently and satisfyingly, with the most basic kind. I consider it, in its own fashion, a work of art.

To walk into the church while lunch is going on is to enter one of the city's defining public spaces. The building, which turned 160 this year, was declared a New York City Landmark in 1966. It has a high, arched cathedral ceiling supported by cylindrical pillars that rise to Tuscan-style groined arches. Natural light comes into the nave through tall and narrow stained-glass windows whose age and artistry make them rarities in themselves. But as for traditional church fanciness, that's about it. Most strikingly, the church has no pews. From the baptismal font, at the back of the church, to the steps of the altar, ninety feet away, no pews or carpet or other fixtures interrupt an open expanse of stone tiles, whose foot-polished smoothness suggests a dance studio or the floor of Grand Central.

People who work for the soup kitchen set up round dining tables and metal folding chairs in the main part of the church every lunchtime. The soup-kitchen guests wait in line on the sidewalk outside, receive meal tickets, file through the serving stations in the Mission House adjoining the church, fill their trays, come into the church, sit down, and eat. The meal, which lasts from ten thirty to twelve thirty, takes place in a murmur of dining noises sometimes accompanied by music on the church's piano or organ beneath (if the day is sunny) shafts of stained-glass light. Most guests finish eating in twenty minutes or half an hour and are on their way. Formerly, when the church was not used for dining, you ate in a smaller room in the Mission House and had to be finished in seven and a half minutes. Now you can take your time.

To let all the soup-kitchen guests know that our writers' workshop exists, I sometimes sit during lunch with a hand-lettered sign and a stack of flyers at a little table right by the exit door. Often, I have to clip a pen to the flyers and tape the sign to the table so they won't blow away in the cold drafts from the door. For the two hours I'm there, the stream of people does not stop. Preceding me in the exit line might be tables for representatives of housing advocacy groups, drug- and alcohol-counseling services, domestic-abuse shelters, or (a few years back) Charles, the Condom Man, who passed out free condoms for AIDS prevention with a carny barker's spiel. Because I'm nearest the door, many people wait a moment at my table before heading out into the cold, where some of them will be continuously until they return for lunch the following day.

Some ask about the workshop; most do not. They set their paper cups of hot coffee or tea next to the flyers, along with the orange or the piece of bread they were given on the way out, and they button up, pull their caps over their ears, put on gloves if they have them, retie the bags or parcels they brought, and kind of hunch down into themselves, getting ready for the city again.

On really chilly days, they might spend a long time on these details before they go. And then sometimes, after half an hour or so, the same person is again at my table, again buttoning up for outdoors. That means the person waited in line, filled his tray, ate, and then went through the process over again. There's no rule against going back for seconds; the soup kitchen never turns anybody away. On occasion, I've noticed people who have passed by three or even four times—have eaten that many lunches, in other words. The soup kitchen portions are generous, and the menu for each lunch has been designed to provide a person with enough calories to last twenty-four hours. Most people who eat at the soup kitchen look like anybody. If you sat across from them on the subway, you would never guess how hungry they were.

But there are a lot of hungry people in New York City. Talking about hunger and being hungry are two different things; talk can wait for a convenient moment, but when you're hungry, you're hungry right now. Many people on the streets of New York are hungry right now. Every year, the city has been getting hungrier. The New York City Coalition Against Hunger estimates that 1.3 million New Yorkers can't afford to buy enough food for themselves and their families all the time. That works out to about one person of every six in the city.

••

Once when I was sitting at my table by the door, a tall, thin, long-faced black man with deep-set eyes made deeper looking by the hood of his dark sweatshirt stopped at my table. As he was adjusting his clothing for outside, he looked at my sign. "Writers' *work*-shop!" he said, in a tone indicating that he was not impressed by the idea.

"Yes, we meet every Wednesday at twelve thirty in the narthex, that little room in the front of the church. Would you like to join?" I asked.

"Uh-uh, no," he said. "I ain't doin' no writers' workshop. I *done* that shit before."

"Really? You were in a writers' workshop before?"

"Hell yes, I was. And my teacher was a better writer than *you*."

"Oh? What writer was that?"

"John Cheever."

Apparently, the guy had been in a workshop that Cheever taught at the prison in Ossining, back in the seventies. I had met Cheever once, and the guy and I talked about him for a while. I asked the guy what he had learned from the workshop with Cheever, and he said, "Cheever, you understan', he was a brilliant writer. When he wrote something, he always had two things going on at a time. He told us, when you writin', you got this surface thing, you understan', goin' on up *here*"—he moved his left hand in a circle with his fingers spread apart, as if rubbing a flat surface—"an' then once you get that goin' on, now you got to come *under* it"—he brought his right hand under his left, as if throwing an uppercut—"come *under* this thing here that's goin' on up here, you understan'. That was how John Cheever said you write.

"John Cheever had that writers' workshop at Ossining," he continued, "and later he wrote a book about the prison, *Falconer,* and it was a number one bestseller. I ain't in that book. He got a bestseller from the workshop, and I didn't get shit. I ain't doin' writers' workshops no more."

Most of the people I met were less skeptical. When they saw my sign, they stopped to talk, their lunch having put them in a narrative mood. Almost everybody who talked to me said they had some amazing stories to tell if they could only write them down. Many said that if their lives were made into books, the books would be bestsellers. Some few had written books about their lives already, and they produced the manuscripts from among their belongings to show me. If you take any twelve hundred New Yorkers, naturally you'll find a certain number of good musicians, skilled carpenters, gifted athletes, and so on; you'll also come up with a small percentage who can really write. Lots of people I talked to said they were interested in the workshop; a much smaller number actually showed up. Some attended only one session, some came back year after year. In all, over fourteen years, maybe four hundred soup-kitchen guests have participated.

When I think of them, who stands out? There was Sundance, a hobo, who wrote about etiquette in hobo camps and told me where to go in the Newark train yards if I wanted to hop long-distance freight trains; and David, a bicycle messenger, who wrote a fast-paced poem about his job, titled "In Flight"; and a guy whose name I've forgotten who tried to sell stolen watches in class; and Wendy-Anne, who always wore a white bonnet and who was trying to regain ownership, she said, of her ancestral property in France; and Jay, a soup-kitchen volunteer, who wrote interestingly about the history of this neighborhood, Chelsea, and about a dollar store accessible to wheelchairs; and Roger, a former MTA employee, who came to a class, slept for a while with his head on the table, then sat bolt upright and shouted, "I need some guidance!"; and Ted, who had been a merchant seaman and wrote about being in a bar fight while the song "I've Got a Tiger by the Tail" played on the jukebox; and Donald, a regular in the early years, who penned a book-length memoir about being homeless entirely in blue ballpoint using large block capitals, because of his poor eyesight, and who had an article about the workfare program published on the op-ed page of the *Times*; and Charles, a bearded, wild-haired fellow, who said he preferred sleeping outside and resented being picked up in the protective sweeps the cops conducted on cold nights, and who, when I asked where he was sleeping now, replied, "the Italian embassy."

And William, who wrote about an intergalactic battle among God, various superheroes, and the Alcoholics Anonymous Higher Power; and Tory, whose hilarious piece about her brief stint as a contest-winning backup dancer for Lionel Richie and the Commodores always brought down the house at our public readings; and Carol, who wore a different hat every day and wrote a great piece about a memorial service at St. Mark's in-the-Bowery when Allen Ginsberg died; and Ron, who after a few years in the workshop began to write his own column for a men's magazine; and John, who after many years of faithful attendance called the church in 2007 to say he couldn't come to the workshop that spring because he was in Antarctica; and Joe, whose stories about his heart attack encapsulated fear in the night; and Norm, a dedicated poet, who wrote a poem titled "On Achieving Section 8 Housing"; and Jeff, who disappeared one year and returned the next saying that he had been traveling internationally as a player on a homeless men's soccer team (a claim that turned out to be true); and Nelson, who wrote tantalizingly short pieces and then came back, years later, all smiles, having found a job and his own apartment, and brought a camera and took photographs of everybody.

Listing all the writers I remember would take pages. We welcome everybody who wants to attend, with a very few exceptions. Once, I was sitting at the table by the exit with Bob Blaisdell, a teacher and writer who has taught in the workshop since the beginning, when a nattily dressed man with a West Indian accent approached us and asked if we would like him to come to the workshop and write about the nine people he had killed in Jamaica. The man posed the question with a big smile, made more striking by his gold inlays, which had been set in a line rising diagonally across his upper front teeth. I admired Bob for replying that, no, we did not want him to come and write about the nine people he had killed in Jamaica.

Every class, we met in the narthex at twelve thirty, passed out pens and notebooks, and gave optional topics for that session's writing. Proven topics have been "How I Came to New York," "If I Hadn't Seen It, I Wouldn't Have Believed It," "Shoes," "The Other Me," and "My Best Mistake." A few topics we've had to retire because they're too fraught; "My First Love," for example, was producing too many wrenching tales of first encounters with drugs and alcohol. In each session, people would write for about forty-five minutes. Then we would read the pieces out loud. All the writers were usually kind in listening to and criticizing one another; the common decorum of group-therapy sessions seemed to apply here, and, besides, we were in a church.

Once in a while, classes could be pretty tense nonetheless. Flare-ups occurred over things as simple as one guy picking up another guy's pen by mistake. The jumpiest times in the class were in 2002 and 2003, after the United States had invaded Afghanistan and then Iraq. I recall a day when Charles, the guy who slept at the Italian embassy, brought in a copy of the *Post* with the headline KABULLSEYE! above a target circle superimposed on a photo of a recently bombed building in Kabul. The headline got us all so jangled we could hardly sit still to write. For people like those in the workshop group, many of whom have pulled their lives together only by means of routine and self-restraint and talking things through, the sight of their own government glorying in chaos shook the ground under their feet.

In the workshop's fourteen years, several participants have died. Pierce, a tall, white-haired man with bushy black eyebrows, was a volunteer at the soup kitchen. Almost every piece he wrote centered on the most important moment in his life—when he attempted suicide by jumping into the East River. After police pulled him out, he quit drinking; many of his pieces ended, "One day at a time." A few years ago when the workshop reconvened, we learned that Pierce had died of a heart attack not long before. Janice, a stylish, gentle woman in her mid-fifties, also died of heart trouble. At one of our public readings, Janice wore a copper-colored fuzzy sweater and an off-green head scarf and held the whole church silent with a story about the death of her young son. Now Janice's daughter, Thyatira, sometimes attends the workshop, and brings her four-year-old daughter, Janyah. They are the only multigenerational participants we've had so far.

Clarence, a middle-aged Jamaican, always spoke slowly and precisely and wore a jacket and tie. He used to write minisermons on quotations from the Bible. When he had written a lot of these pieces, I asked if he wouldn't like to branch out, try some memoir or just describe what he did that day. He politely ignored me. After a few years, he stopped coming and we heard no more about him. Then, in the fall of '02, city employees got in touch with one of the workshop teachers, the poet Susan Shapiro, to say that Clarence had died (another heart attack); searching his belongings for information about next of kin, they had found her business card in his wallet. Evidently no kin were ever located; Clarence was buried in the potter's field.

Susan often handed out her business cards in the workshop, worked with writers outside of class, and helped them get published in newspapers and magazines. Susan knows hundreds of people in the city and throughout publishing and talks so fast she says ten words for every one of mine. In 2004, she co-edited (with the Reverend Elizabeth Maxwell, the associate rector of Holy Apostles) an anthology of writing from the workshop. The book, called *Food for the Soul*, is dedicated to Pierce, Janice, and Clarence. The money it earned—some thousands of dollars—mostly went to the contributors, who got a hundred dollars each. A few of the contributors also appeared on the *Today* show and National Public Radio.

I have been part of the workshop almost every year, with a couple of interruptions when my family and I lived in Montana. After four years out there, we moved back east, to New Jersey. One Sunday soon after we returned, I took my daughter into Manhattan to go to museums and reacquaint her with the city generally. She was in fifth grade and curious about everything. At the end of the day, as we were standing in line at the Port Authority waiting for our bus back to the suburbs, a man who had been in the writers' workshop came walking down the line. At each person he stopped and tried to sell a copy of *Street News*. He was wearing layers of semidisintegrating clothes and he had his hair in short, multidirectional corkscrew dreadlocks. Most of the people he went up to did the usual thing of recoiling slightly and looking away. When he got to us, he recognized me, and we began to talk. I asked how he was doing and he said pretty well—he had written a piece for *Street News* and it had been published recently. He asked if the workshop would be starting again soon, and I said it would, and he said he'd be there. I bought a copy of *Street News* for myself and another for my daughter and said I'd see him in the spring, and we got on our bus. When we arrived home, my wife asked my daughter how she had liked the city. "It was pretty good," she said. "Not much happened. At the bus station, we ran into a friend of Daddy's."

• •

Suddenly, the clouds begin to fly backward very fast, like the view out the window in that movie *The Time Machine*, and then they come to a stop and slowly move forward again. It is 1836. Chelsea—the future neighborhood of the Church of the Holy Apostles—is mostly fields. Squatters who have recently emigrated from England and Ireland live along the marshy shoreline of the Hudson River. Some young people who attend St. Peter's Episcopal on Twentieth Street visit this district and are appalled by the condition of the immigrants and especially by that of their "neglected and isolated" children. To help them, these young people start a Sunday school. With $750 of their own and their friends' money, they erect a schoolhouse on Thirty-sixth Street between Eighth and Ninth Avenues. Many people start to attend informal services there on Sundays. Soon the Episcopal Diocese of New York decides that the Sunday school has enough congregants to become an official parish of the church.

A local landowner gives four lots for construction of a church across from his estate on Ninth Avenue. The church's founders decide what it will be called. An architect named Minard LeFever, who has designed other churches in the city, is hired. His usual style, the Gothic Revival, he forgoes in this instance, opting instead for a pared-down version of Tuscan design combined with disparate Italianate elements and incorporating a steeple more than twice the height of the church itself. The building is finished early in 1848. The first service in the building is held in February 1848. North and south transepts, added 1858, enlarge the structure to its final size. In its stylistic eclecticism combined with simplicity, Holy Apostles is a typical church of the American frontier.

The neighborhood swirls around the church like a slow-moving tornado. In 1850, a "pestilence"—probably cholera—hits the area, and the church cares for the sufferers and holds seventy funerals. Rich people begin to move to Chelsea from downtown, and the church's finances improve. In 1871, the Ninth Avenue elevated train brings its cinders, smoke, and noise to right above the church's front yard. The church sues the el for damages and eventually wins a few thousand dollars. Upper Fifth Avenue becomes fashionable, rich people move out of Chelsea, and the church's finances decline. Waves of immigrants from eastern and southern Europe come to New York City. By and large, they don't join Protestant churches, and those churches begin to close. Holy Apostles hangs on. For years at a time, the church gets by only with the help of contributions from Trinity Episcopal, on Wall Street.

Reformers like Jacob Riis speak at Holy Apostles. In the early 1900s, the church inclines to the leftist, progressivist beliefs of the Social Gospel, an affinity that will go on. Still, its congregation is never large. Money remains a problem. Somehow, the church stays open through mixed fortunes during war, depression, and war. Its steeple keeps wanting to fall over and must be shored up, expensively. In the twenties, there is a fire. In 1940–41, the Ninth Avenue el is torn down, to the church's relief. After the Second World War, congregants to whom the pastor had sent long letters while they were away in the service drift from the church. Highrise apartment buildings erected by the International Ladies' Garment Workers' Union for moderate-income people fill the sky above the steeple on several sides. The church looks to the neighborhood for new members and finds some, mostly West Indian and American black people.

Rectors at Holy Apostles come and go. Its first rector, Foster Thayer, quits over the issue of rented pews. In many of the city's churches, families pay rent for their private pews. Thayer thinks that's unchristian and that all pews should be free. The vestry, or church's officers, appreciate his point, but they also have construction loans to pay off. After quitting, Thayer moves to Vermont and soon leaves the ministry entirely. Other Holy Apostles ministers work themselves to exhaustion, take leaves of absence for their health, never return. One or two hold up fairly well. Lucius A. Edelblute, the wartime letter writer, serves from 1918 to 1950. In 1949, he writes the church's centennial history.

In the sixties, the church becomes a center for left-wing causes, especially opposition to the war in Vietnam. A minister in the seventies welcomes gays and lesbians to Holy

Apostles, then decides they must allow Jesus to cure them of their sexual feelings. Turmoil follows. The congregation goes into a decline. The church has no full-time rector from 1975 to 1978.

By 1980, the church is one of the oldest buildings on Ninth Avenue. Its membership has dwindled to about 125. Basically, it's dying. Its roof, still the original slate, needs replacing. Leaks have damaged the ceiling, now in danger of falling in. Repairs to the roof would cost half a million dollars. The Right Reverend Paul Moore, Episcopal bishop of New York, wants to close the church and consolidate its congregation with St. Peter's. Ronald Reagan is elected president. Government money to help the poor is cut, fewer people have public housing, Chelsea's single-room-occupancy hotels close. Homelessness becomes a visible New York City problem. Often, people knock on the church's doors asking for help.

Father Rand Frew, the church's new, young minister, suggests to the congregation that the church should start a soup kitchen. Father Frew thinks big and has a gift for starting programs. His previous church was in Las Vegas; perhaps a bit of gambling instinct is involved in this idea. The congregation wonders where it will come up with the huge amount of money a daily soup kitchen requires, but it gives the okay. The consensus is that if Holy Apostles is going out of business anyway, it might as well do some good before it does.

Father Frew finds $50,000 and donors of surplus food. He rounds up a head chef, cooking supplies, volunteers. On the soup kitchen's first day, October 22, 1982, it serves about thirty-five meals. Starting then, it establishes its policy of being open every weekday. Its numbers of guests—from the beginning, the people it serves are referred to as guests—increase. Now the problem of repairing the church's roof and ceiling has been simplified: donors who would never contribute to save a dilapidated church with a shrinking congregation are more willing to give to a historic church with a well-run and rapidly growing soup kitchen. More money comes in and the church borrows half a million for the roof repair.

By the mid-eighties, nine hundred or more guests are having lunch at the church's Mission House every day. By 1990, the repairs to the roof are almost done. On April 9, workmen up in the roof beams accidentally start a small fire with an acetylene torch. They put the fire out, they think. In the afternoon at quitting time, the workmen leave. A few hours later, the church is holding evening services in the narthex when someone sticks his head in the door and says, "Your church is on fire." In minutes, the roof goes up in flames. The Fire Department comes and puts out the fire. Inside and out, the destruction is immense. Many of the irreplaceable stained-glass windows had to be broken to vent the gases from the fire. That night, the church is blackened, dripping, open to the sky. Nonetheless, the soup kitchen serves lunch in the undamaged Mission House the next day: a cold meal, owing to circumstances—macaroni-and-tuna salad, fruit, and juice. It feeds about 950.

The church has fire insurance. Repairs of the damage, including installing another new slate roof, fixing the ceiling, and assembling the fragments of the stained-glass windows, will cost about $8 million. By now, Father Frew has left, and the rector of the church and executive director of the soup kitchen is William Greenlaw, a manager whose skill with money has acquired him the nickname Father Greenbacks. He consults with Elizabeth Maxwell and the vestry, and they decide to plan the reconstruction so that the soup kitchen can expand into the church itself. What to do about the pews? Take them out—the church stopped renting them a century ago, no money will be lost—and keep the space open for dining. During services, the congregation can just as easily use folding chairs. Everybody agrees about this immediately.

Reconstruction takes four years. When all is finished and the first meal is served in the main church, the guests come in quietly with their trays, unsure about the protocol for eating in a church. Wendy Shepherd, the church's long-time administrative supervisor, watches them and worries that people won't be comfortable eating here, but in a few days the strangeness goes away. The *Times* reports that mid-nineteenth-century pews saved from the fire at Holy Apostles are for sale for $450 apiece at a public architectural salvage yard in Brooklyn. Somewhere, the shade of Foster Thayer smiles.

Today, the church, fully restored, remains the one unchanging landmark in Chelsea. To judge from a photograph of church and churchyard taken in 1880, the fire hydrant next to it on Twenty-eighth Street has also stayed the same.

• •

At night, people sleep on the E train as it makes its long run out into Queens and then back again to Manhattan. They sleep on the stairs of the Twenty-fifth Street entry to the E and C subway station at Eighth Avenue, or in the top stairwell of the building on Nineteenth Street where they once had an apartment, or under the hoardings at the back of the main Post Office building, or on the front steps of a church on Sixteenth, or under sections of the old elevated tracks near Tenth Avenue, or in the vestibule of a twenty-four-hour copy shop on Seventh, or somewhere else in Chelsea or farther away. People used to be able to sleep in Chelsea Park, across the street from the church, but now it and most other neighborhood parks are off-limits at night.

If you find a more official place to stay temporarily, it might be the Rescue Mission, on Lafayette Street, downtown (men only; cots), or the Bellevue Shelter, on Thirtieth (men only; couples assigned elsewhere), or one of the outer-borough shelters. Stays at drop-in centers, like the Oliveri Center, on Thirtieth (women only), or Open Door, on Forty-first, or Peter's Place, on Twenty-third (men and women fifty-five and over only), are intended to be shorter term. In most drop-in centers, you have to sleep sitting up in a chair, which can cause your legs to swell.

People planning to have lunch at the soup kitchen show up sometimes hours before the church is open in the morning. A few bring all they own loaded in shopping carts, wheeled garment racks, hand trucks, or the side baskets of bicycles. Their bundles are tied together with yellow nylon rope, cinched with bungee cords, taped with silver duct tape, or packed loose in double or triple plastic shopping bags. One older woman with a weathered face and long brown hair sometimes carries, close at hand among her bags, a big tube of sunblock. Now and then, the loads of belongings include those woven-nylon suitcases, white with broad plaid stripes, which are the people's luggage all over the world. During lunch, the shopping carts and other conveyances are parked in the churchyard, where someone from the soup kitchen keeps an eye on them.

Volunteers are asked to show up by 10:00 a.m. The soup kitchen needs at least forty volunteers to serve every meal. All kinds of people help out, but Manhattan retirees are usually the bulk of the volunteers. Some have been doing this almost since the soup kitchen began; Ilona Seltzer, a Chelsea resident, has been volunteering since 1985. School groups volunteer, and Sunday-school classes and Scout troops and the rabbis and members of Congregation Beth Simchat Torah (which holds its own services in the church on Friday evenings). Kim, a software designer from Orange County, California, volunteers when she's in the city visiting her aunt and uncle. Susan Sarandon and Tim Robbins, longtime Chelsea-ites, have volunteered. Senator Jeff Sessions (Republican of Alabama) and others of the Alabama delegation spent a morning working at the soup kitchen during the Republican National Convention in 2004. Senator Sessions used the photo opportunity that resulted to praise the soup kitchen as the sort of private initiative that naturally takes up the tasks our government should not do and should not have to do—an opinion with which everybody at the soup kitchen disagreed.

Clyde Kuemmerle, the soup kitchen's associate program director, signs in the volunteers and tells them what their jobs will be. Clyde, a bearded man in his early sixties, has a PhD in theater from the University of Minnesota, and in the past he worked on Broadway plays as a producer, which resembles his present occupation. He carries a walkie-talkie and runs the whole soup kitchen day to day. People sometimes yell at Clyde, but he has great equanimity. Plenty of soup kitchen guests carry a world of troubles with them, and they may fluctuate in their medications, and for these and other reasons some can be quick to get mad. During almost every lunch, somebody takes offense at somebody else, voices are raised, and people stand up and confront each other. Then Clyde and the employees who work on the floor—Harold McKnight and his brother Prince, Rodney Williams, Olimpo Tlatelpa, among others—come over and intervene. They step between the arguers, they remonstrate with them quietly, and soon the shouting dies down. The way they are completely firm and at the same time completely kind should be studied by the UN.

The soup kitchen's counseling trailer, which is in the

churchyard by the gate where the guests come in, is open five days a week before and after lunch. Jacqueline Mc-Knight, the soup kitchen's assistant counselor, whom everybody calls Jackie and who is married to Harold, handles the guests' problems with food stamps, disability payments, housing applications, medical referrals, etc. Now and then a person comes to the trailer who is in a crisis at that very moment. One December afternoon, a woman walked into Jackie's office while in the middle of labor. With no time to take her anywhere, Jackie sat her on a chair and called Linda Adams, who works in the church offices, and Clyde. Jackie and Linda comforted the woman and helped her with her breathing while Clyde put some coats on the floor and waited there for the baby. He was shaking because this experience was a first for him. Fortunately, EMS soon showed up, and the EMS guys performed the actual delivery.

The woman, a skinny white lady who had barely even looked pregnant, kept hollering that she didn't want the baby, that she had hoped to leave it in the soup-kitchen bathroom, and that Jackie and Linda could have it. On the spot, they told the woman they would take it. When the baby—a pink and healthy-looking girl—came out, the EMS guys said it was fine with them if Jackie and Linda took her; in fact, in their opinion, that would be a very good idea. First, however, the EMS guys had to follow procedure and take baby and mother to St. Vincent's Hospital. They did, and Jackie and Linda followed in a cab.

But at St. Vincent's the women were not allowed to see the baby, and though they persisted in trying to find out about her, neither Jackie nor Linda ever saw her again. Later, they heard that the baby had been adopted by a family where she had been sent for foster care. Jackie and

Linda both think of the little girl often and wonder how she's doing.

• •

To keep going, the soup kitchen needs $2.7 million a year. It spends more than $10,000 every operating day. For this church, whose congregation still has fewer than two hundred members, that's a lot. About 35 percent of the money needed comes from individual donors who send checks in response to direct-mail solicitations. That income rises and falls, but is generally dependable. Most of the rest comes from foundations and from the city, state, and federal governments, which tend to be less predictable.

Government money for the hungry is a small and ever-shifting stream, moved by political change. City funding disappears under sudden budget pressure, federal poverty funds administered by FEMA are cut 19 percent, and a farm bill gets stuck in Congress, with the result that government surplus food suddenly becomes less available. Keeping up with the veerings of government support is a scramble. As for foundations, they are well-intentioned and generous, but subject to moods. "Donor burnout" is one of those. Fashions in charitable giving also come and go. Recently, foundation charity has been more focused on "making a difference," an idea that works against the soup kitchen, which changes people from hungry to not, but invisibly. Also, foundation donors now like to talk about "measurable outcomes"—they expect recipients like the soup kitchen to single out the people who are helped and measure the improvement in those people's situations over time. Again, that's not something the soup kitchen, with the off-the-street population it serves, can easily do. In the past eighteen months, several major foundation donors have dropped out, and no replacements have been found. There's enough money for now, and for a while, but the future is unclear. The soup kitchen has been in this spot before.

Father Greenlaw, who has overseen the raising of all this money for twenty-five years, will retire at the end of July. He has served longer than any other Holy Apostles rector except Lucius Edelblute and Brady Electus Backus (1876–1901), and now he would like not to think about money so much. The twenty-five years have left him remarkably unworn; he has bright green eyes, a full head of hair, and a broad smile that alternates between seraphic and pained. In his quiet office on the third floor of the Mission House, he explains how much the soup kitchen depends on New York's Jewish community ("If the Jews of New York City stopped giving, we'd go out of business"), and how he's had no success raising money among red-state evangelical Christians, and how urban secular mailing lists like the list of subscribers to *The New York Review of Books* or of Channel Thirteen supporters or of members of the North Shore Animal League are much better places to find donors.

In talking about the soup kitchen, Father Greenlaw generally does not mention Jesus. That's only natural, given the ecumenical nature of the enterprise. Instead, he describes the work of feeding the hungry in terms that people are likely to agree on regardless of religious belief or unbelief. He talks about the joy of being alive in this sacred space, of sharing a meal with other people in a beautiful landmarked building, of seeing in the people who come to the soup kitchen "a window into what makes humanity human, into the deepest levels of being."

The soup kitchen never proselytizes or hands out religious literature. But in the church offices upstairs in the Mission House, the serene and genteel and somewhat fraught atmosphere of modern Episcopalianism prevails. There is, of course, the pervading aroma of coffee, the denomination's secular wine. Elizabeth Maxwell, whose fresh-faced good looks add emphasis to her strong preaching, has been with the church and the soup kitchen for nineteen years. Liz, as she's called, has done every job from big-dollar fund-raising to counseling to serving and cleanup; usually, every fourth Sunday she also delivers a sermon. In her work, she expects surprises and is undismayed by them. Once, she told me, she was in the trailer counseling a man who said he had been rejected by every homeless shelter he had gone to. She couldn't figure out why this should be, and, as she was puzzling it out, she saw a rustling in the guy's shirt, and then a large snake stuck its head from between two of his shirt buttons. The snake was his pet, and shelters don't allow pets. She persuaded the man to return the snake to the exotic-pet store where he got it.

When I pressed Liz about the specifically religious inspiration that applies here, she said, "Well, we do this because Jesus said to feed the hungry. There's no more to it than that. Jesus told us to take care of the poor and the hungry and those in prison. In Matthew 25 he says, 'As you have done to the least of these, you have done to me.' In all the intricacies of scriptural interpretation, that message—feed the hungry—couldn't be more clear. Those of us who worship at Holy Apostles feel we have a Sunday–Monday connection. The bread and wine of the Eucharist that we share with one another on Sunday become the food we share with our neighbors during the week. We believe that our job as Christians is to meet Jesus in the world. We meet him, unnamed and unrecognized, in the guests who come to the soup kitchen every day."

• •

After the last session of the writers' workshop every year, there's a public reading at the church. We put together an anthology of the best of or all of that year's work (typed into final form by our poet/typist, Alice Phillips), and then we get the anthology copied and spiral-bound at the same nearby copy shop in whose lobby one or two soup-kitchen guests sometimes spend the night. Participants read from a lectern up front, and the audience, which usually numbers about seventy-five or a hundred, listens on folding chairs.

Sometimes as many as eighteen or twenty people read their pieces. With that many, we try to keep each reading short, but things happen as they happen. The pieces range from poetry to personal history to novel excerpts to science fiction to exercises in Hegelian philosophy. We have an informal rule that the reader must only read, and not digress into impromptu explanations of what he or she is reading, but that rule is sometimes overlooked. On occasion, people have brought tape recorders to play music accompanying or introducing what they read. Sometimes people sing. Tory, the writer who did the piece about being a backup dancer for the Commodores, has a song she wrote about the soup kitchen. The sound of a single voice, singing or reading, as it rises to the vaulted beams of the church can lift you almost off the ground.

When the reading is over, everybody gets something to eat—there's a spread of sandwiches and soft drinks provided by the soup kitchen—and the writers and the audience mingle. The people who attend the reading may be Holy Apostles parishioners, soup kitchen donors, editors, arts administrators, students from other writing programs, clergy of various kinds, curious passersby. Soup-kitchen alumni from workshops in past years sometimes show up and fill us in on where they are and what they're doing now. Sometimes we talk about people from past workshops whom we haven't seen for a while, or about the ones who came only a few times and then were never seen again—names like Lisa, Wayman, Smokey, White Mike, Coleman, Rashid, Blue, Luis, Rosa . . . The alchemy of writing gives everybody who's been in the workshop an extra dimension: along with possessing a name and a face, each is also the particular person who wrote whatever. Somehow, writing even a few lines makes the person who does it more substantial and real. In geometric terms, it's like the difference between being a point and being a plane.

Usually, the reading is on a Wednesday evening in late May. With luck, the weather is mild, and the church's front doors are open. People arrive dressed up, and some of the soup-kitchen staff are in white shirts and black bow ties. The ambient New York City air comes in; you can imagine that the floor of the church, the pavement of Ninth Avenue, the asphalt in Chelsea Park, and the shiny surface of the Hudson River a few blocks away are all connected, one continuous terrestrial floor. As the evening advances and the sunset fades, the lights inside the church brighten. It's a benign time of day to be in a church, or any public space open to the evening. For a moment, the whole city seems to flow in with the air.

May 26, 2008

The One That Got Away

The police report listed the name of the deceased as Joseph Adam Randolph and his age as forty-eight. It did not mention the name he had given himself, Stealhead Joe. The address on his driver's license led police to his former residence in Sisters, Oregon, where the landlord said that Randolph had moved out over a year ago and had worked as a fishing guide. In fact, Randolph was one of the most skilled guides on the nearby Deschutes River, and certainly the most colorful—even unforgettable—in the minds of anglers who had fished with him. He had specialized in catching sea-run fish called steelhead and was so devoted to the sport that he had a large steelhead fly with two drops of blood at the hook point tattooed on the inside of his right forearm. The misspelling of his self-bestowed moniker was intentional. If he didn't actually steal fish, he came close, and he wanted people to hear echoes of the trickster and the outlaw in his name.

••

I spent six days fishing with Stealhead Joe in early September 2012, two months before he died. I planned to write a profile of him for *Outside* magazine and had been trying for a year to set up a trip. Most guides' reputations stay within their local area, but Joe's had extended even to where I live, in New Jersey. Somehow, though, I could never get him on the phone. Once, finding myself in Portland with a couple of days free, I drove down to Sisters in the hope of booking a last-minute trip, but when I asked for him at the Fly Fisher's Place, the shop where he worked, I was told, in essence, "Take a number!" Staffers laughed and showed me his completely filled-out guiding schedule on a calendar on an office door, Joe himself being unreachable "on the river" for the next x days.

The timing sorted itself out eventually. Joe and I spoke, we made arrangements to fish together, and I met him in Maupin, a small town on the Deschutes about ninety miles from Sisters. Joe had moved to Maupin for personal and professional reasons by then. On the day we met, a Sunday, I called Joe at nine in the morning to say I was in town. He said he was in the middle of folding his laundry but would stop by my motel when he was done. I sat on a divider in the motel parking lot and waited. His vehicle could be identified from far off. It was a red 1995 Chevy Tahoe with a type of fly rod called a spey rod extending from a holder on the hood to another holder on the roof like a long, swept-back antenna.

I have seen a few beat-up fishing vehicles and even owned one or two of them myself. This SUV was a beaut, and I chuckled in appreciation as Joe got out and introduced himself, and showed me its details. The Tahoe's color was a dusty western red, like a shirt that gets brighter as you slap dust off of it. (To maintain that look, he deliberately did not wash his vehicle, a girlfriend of Joe's would later tell me.) The grille had been broken multiple times by deer Joe had hit while speeding down country roads in predawn darkness in order to be on the water before everyone else, or returning in the night after other anglers had gone home. He had glued it back together with epoxy, and there was still deer hair in the mends.

Hanging from the inside rearview mirror was a large red-and-white plastic fishing bobber on a loop of monofilament line, and on the dash and in the cup holders were coiled-up tungsten-core leaders, steelhead flies, needle-nose pliers—"numerous items consistent with camping and fishing," as the police report would later put it. While Joe and I were admiring his truck, I didn't guess I was looking at the means he would use to take his life. He died in the driver's seat, which he pushed back into its full reclining position for the occasion. The report gave the cause of death as asphyxiation from carbon-monoxide poisoning.

• •

Something momentous always seems about to happen in canyon towns like Maupin, where the ready supply of gravity suggests velocity and disaster. Above the town, to the east and west, the high desert of central Oregon spreads its dusty brown wheat fields toward several horizons. Below the town, in a canyon that is wide in some places and narrow in others, forty-five hundred cubic feet per second of jade-colored river go rushing by. Four-hundred-some people live in Maupin in the winter; several thousand might occupy it on any weekend from June through Labor Day. People come to white-water raft, mainly, and to fish. Guys plank on bars in the wee hours, tequila shots are drunk from women's navels, etc. Sometimes daredevils pencil-dive from Maupin's one highway bridge; the distance between the Gothic-style concrete railing and the river is ninety-eight feet. They spread their arms and legs in the instant after impact so as not to hit the bottom too hard.

Maupin, an ordinary small western town to most appearances, actually deals in the extraordinary. What it offers is transcendence; people can experience huge, rare thrills around here. Fishing for steelhead is one of them.

Steelhead are rainbow trout that begin life in freshwater rivers, swim down them to the ocean, stay there for years, and come back up their native rivers to spawn, sometimes more than once. They grow much bigger than rainbows that never leave freshwater, and they fight harder, and they shine a brighter silver—hence their name. To get to the Deschutes from the ocean, the steelhead must first swim up the Columbia River and through the fish ladders at the Bonneville Dam and The Dalles Dam, massive power-generating stations that (I believe) add a zap of voltage to whatever the fish do thereafter. Some are hatchery fish, some aren't, but all have the size, ferocity, and wildness associated with the ocean. "Fishing for steelhead is hunting big game," says John Hazel, the senior of all the Deschutes River guides and co-owner of the Deschutes Angler, a fly shop in Maupin.

••

Steelhead are elusive, sometimes not numerous, and largely seasonal. They seem to prefer the hardest-to-reach parts of this fast, rock-cluttered, slippery, rapid-filled, generally unhelpful river. On the banks, you must watch for rattlesnakes. Fishing from a boat is not allowed. You wade deeper than you want, and then you cast, over and over. You catch mostly nothing. Casting for steelhead is like calling God on the telephone, and it rings and rings and rings, hundreds of rings, a thousand rings, and you listen to each ring as if an answer might come at any moment, but no answer comes, and no answer comes, and then on the 1,001st ring, or the 1,047th ring, God loses his patience and picks up the phone and yells, "WHAT THE HELL ARE YOU CALLING ME FOR?" in a voice the size of the canyon. You would fall to your knees if you weren't chest-deep in water and afraid that the rocketing, leaping creature you have somehow tied into will get away.

··

Joe's other nicknames (neither of which he gave himself) were Melanoma Joe and Nymphing Joe. The second referred to his skill at fishing for steelhead with imitations of aquatic insects called nymphs. This method uses a bobber or other floating strike indicator and a nymph at a fixed distance below it in the water. Purists don't approve of fishing this way; they say it's too easy and not much different from dangling a worm in front of the fish's nose. For himself, Joe believed in the old-time method of casting downstream and letting the fly swing across the current in classical, purist style. But he also taught himself to nymph, and taught others, and a lot of Joe's clients caught a lot of fish by this method. In one of Joe's obituaries, Mark Few—Joe's prized and most illustrious client, the coach of the highly ranked men's basketball team at Gonzaga University, whom Joe called, simply, "Coach," who liked to catch a lot of fish, and who therefore fished with nymphs—praised Joe's "open-mindedness" as a guide.

The nickname Melanoma Joe came from Joe's habit of fishing in board shorts and wading boots and nothing else. Most guides long-sleeve themselves and lotion and hat and maybe glove themselves, and some even wrap a scarf around their heads and necks and faces like mujahideen. Joe let the desert sun burn him reddish brown. Board shirts, T-shirt, sunglasses, baseball cap, flip-flops—that was his attire when we met. He grew up mostly in California and still looked Californian.

• •

He smoked three packs of Marlboros a day.

• •

For a guy as lost as Joe must have been, he gave off a powerful fatherly vibe. Even I was affected by it, though he was thirteen years my junior. An hour after we met, we waded out into the middle of the Deschutes in a long, straight stretch above town. The wading freaked me out, and I was frankly holding on to Joe. He was six-five, broad shouldered, with a slim, long-waisted swimmer's body. I wore chest waders, and Joe had put on his waders, too, in deference to the colder water. I held tightly to his wader belt. Close up, I smelled the Marlboro smell. When I was a boy, many adults, and almost all adult places and pastimes, smelled of cigarettes. Joe had the same tobacco-smoke aroma I remembered from dads of fifty years ago. I relaxed slightly; I might have been ten years old. Joe held my hand.

That day we were in the river not primarily to catch fish but to teach me how to cast the spey rod. I had been dreading the instruction. Lessons on how to do any athletic activity fail totally with me. Golf-coach reprimands like "You're not opening up your hips on the follow-through" fall on my ears as purest gibberish, speaking in tongues, like the lost language of a tribe of Israel that has been found again at Pebble Beach—

Where Joe was once a golf pro, by the way, as he told me in passing. The only athletic enterprises he had never tried, he said, were boxing and wrestling. Now he demonstrated to me the proper spey-casting method. Flourishing the rod through positions one, two, three, and four, he sent the line flying like a perfect tee shot down fairway one. From where we were standing, above our waists in water, it went ninety feet, dead straight. You could catch any fish in the river with that cast.

Regular fly-casting uses the weight of the line and the resistance of the air to bend the rod—or "load" it—so that a flick of the wrist and arm can release the tension and shoot the line forward. Spey-casting, an antique Scottish technique from the heyday of waterpower, uses a longer rod, two hands, and the line's resistance on the surface of the river to provide the energy. You lay the line on the water beside you, bring the rod up, sweep it back over the line against the surface tension, and punch it forward with an in-out motion of your top and bottom hands. The spey cast is actually a kind of water-powered spring. It throws line farther and better than regular fly-casting does, and because it involves no backcast it is advantageous in closed-in places like the canyon of the Deschutes.

..

If Joe showed any signs of depression in the first days we fished together, I did not notice them. Walking along the railroad tracks beside the river on our way to a good place to fish, he seemed happy, even blithe. As we passed the carcass of a run-over deer with the white of buzzard droppings splattered all around, he said, "I've been fly-fishing since I was eight years old. Bird hunting, too. My grandfather sent me a fly rod and a twelve-gauge shotgun for my eighth birthday, because he fished and hunted and wanted me to be like him. He was a Cajun from south Louisiana. His last name was Cherami. That was my mom's family, and my dad's family was also from the South, but they were more, like, aristocrats. My last name, Randolph, is an old Virginia name, and I'm actually a direct descendant of Thomas Jefferson. My dad's father is buried at Monticello."

We went down the riprap beside the tracks and held back the pricker bushes for each other. They were heavy with black raspberries; the smell in the cooler air by the water was like someone making jam. He stopped to look at the Deschutes before wading in. "This is the greatest river in America," he said. "It's the only one I know of that's both a great steelhead river and a blue-ribbon trout stream. The way I came to it was, I was married to Florence Belmondo. Do you know who Jean-Paul Belmondo is? Famous French movie actor? You do? Cool! A lot of people never heard of him. Anyway, Florence is his daughter. She's an amazing person, very sort of withdrawn in a group but warm and up for anything—like, she has no fear—and knockout beautiful on top of that. We met on a blind date in Carmel, California, and were together from then on. Flo and I got married in 2003, and we did stuff like stay at Belmondo's house in Paris and his compound in Antigua."

I looked at Joe, both to make sure he was being serious and to reexamine his face. I observed that he looked a bit like Belmondo himself—the same close-set, soulful eyes, big ears, and wry, downturned mouth.

Florence skis, Joe was a snowboarder. They began to visit central Oregon for the snow at Mount Bachelor, Joe discovered the Deschutes, Florence got him a guided trip on the river as a present, he fell in love with the river, they moved to Sisters, and she bought them a big house in town in 2005. "After I learned the river and started my own guiding, I think that was what created problems between Florence and me," Joe said. "Being a kept man sounds great, but it's really not. To be honest, there were other problems, too. So finally we divorced. That was in '08. We tried to get back together once or twice, but it didn't work out. Well, anyway—man, it was awesome being married to her. I'll always be grateful to her, because she's the reason I came here and found this river. And I have no desire to fish anywhere else but on the Deschutes for the rest of my life."

··

The railroad tracks we were walking on belong to the Burlington Northern and Santa Fe Railway. During the day, the trains sound their horns and rattle Maupin's stop signs and bounce echoes around the canyon. At night they are quieter; if trains can be said to tiptoe, these do. The rhythmic sound of their wheels rises, fills your ears, and fades; the silence after it's gone refills with the sound of the river. We were out in the night in Maupin a lot because first light and last light are good times to catch steelhead. It seems to me now that I spent as much time with Joe in the dark as I did in the light.

On my second night, he and I went to a fish hatchery downstream from town. We parked, zigzagged down a slope, passed dark buildings, crossed a lawn, and wrong-footed our way across the tracks, on whose curving rails the moon had laid a dull shine. After about a mile, we plunged through some alders and into the river and stood in the water for a long time waiting for dawn to start. This all felt a bit spooky and furtive to me.

My instinct, I later learned, was right. I had a fishing license, and Joe had licenses both to fish and to guide. He did not, however, possess a valid permit to be a fishing guide on the Deschutes. Two months earlier, he had left the Fly Fisher's Place in Sisters (actually, he had been fired), and thus he had lost the guiding permit that the shop provided him. His attempt to jury-rig a permit from a rafting guide's permit loaned to him by an outfitter in Maupin was not enough, because it allowed him to guide rafters but not anglers. Joe was breaking the law, in other words, and the consequences could be a fine of up to $2,500, a possible prison term, and the forfeit of his guiding license—no small risk to run.

On some evenings, after fishing, Joe and I went to Maupin's bars. They were packed with a young crowd that included many rafting guides, and everybody seemed to know Joe. He sat drinking beers and watching two or more baseball games on the bar TVs while young guys came up to him, often asking for advice—"She's kissed me twice, Joe, and I mean, *she* kissed *me*. But I haven't even brought up anything about sex." Joe: "Hell, tee her up, man, and ask questions later!" At the end of the night a barmaid announced last call, and Joe told her, "I'll have another beer, and a cot."

• •

When Tiger Woods fished the Deschutes some years ago (with John Hazel, not with Joe), he did not pick up the spey cast right away, so I guess it's no surprise that I didn't, either. I simply couldn't get the message, and I told Joe I wanted to go back to the fly rod. Not possible, he said. He had no fly rod; and, at his insistence, I had not brought mine. He was a patient and remorseless coach, smoking and commenting on each attempt as I tried over and over. "You fucked up, Bud. Your rod tip was almost in the water on that last one. Keep the tip high." A failed spey cast is a shambles, like the collapse of a circus tent, with pole and line in chaos, and disgrace everywhere.

But he wouldn't give up. I worried that it might be painful for him to watch something he did so beautifully being done so wrong, but now I think his depression gave him a sort of immunity. The tedium of watching me may have been nothing compared with what he was feeling inside. And when occasionally I did get it, his enthusiasm was gigantic: "That's it! *Money!*" he would holler as the line sailed out.

• •

So I'm in my motel cabin the night before our three-day float trip, and I can't sleep. I keep practicing the motions of the cast—one, two, three, four—like the present-arms drill in a commercial for the Marine Corps on TV. I practice the cast when I'm pacing around the motel-cabin floor and when I'm lying on my back in the bed. Joe has told me that the first pool we will fish is the best pool on the entire lower river. If I don't catch a fish there, I figure, my chances for success will go way down. He has shown me how to cast from the right side of the river and from the left; you turn the motion around, like batting from opposite sides of the plate. He has said we will fish this first pool from the right side, so I practice that cast only. I keep remembering that I have never caught a steelhead. I do not sleep a wink.

He has told me to come to his house at 3:45 a.m. The early start is essential, he has assured me, because another guide is likely to be in the pool before us if we're late. At 3:15 I put on my gear and drive to his house. All his windows are dark. The moon is up, and I wait in the shadow of Joe's trailered drift boat. No sign of activity in the house. At the tick of 3:45, I step noisily onto the front porch in my studded wading shoes and rap on the door. Through the window I can see only darkness, and the corner of a white laundry basket in a patch of moonlight. I call Joe's name. A pause. Then, from somewhere inside: "Th' damn alarm didn't go off!"

He comes out, rumpled and sleepy, and puts on his waders, which were hanging on the porch rail. We get in the Tahoe and take off, stopping on the way to pick up some coffee and pastries from the free breakfast spread at a motel considerably more expensive than my own. Joe assures me this is okay; no one is around to disagree. We rattle for half an hour down a county road beside the river, leaving dust behind, and then pull into a location he asks me not to disclose. He backs the drift boat down to the river and launches it and we get in. At the second or third scrape of the oars against the boat's aluminum sides, headlamps light up at a place not far from the boat launch. Guys are camped there so as to get to this pool at first light, and we have beaten them to it, Joe says with satisfaction. We go a short distance downstream and stop under the branches of trees on the right-hand bank.

The moon is not high enough to reach into the canyon, so the water is completely dark. We wait, not talking. I unwrap and eat the Heartland Bakery cinnamon Danish from the more expensive motel's breakfast spread and crumple the wrapper and put it in the top of my waders and rinse my fingers in the river. The sky lightens and the water becomes a pewter color. Faintly, its ripples and current patterns can now be seen. Joe puts out his cigarette and applies ChapStick to his lips. We slide from the boat into the river.

My fear of wading has receded, thanks partly to my new wading staff. We go halfway across the pool. Joe tells me where to put the fly—a pattern called the Green Butt Skunk—and I begin to cast. Suddenly, I'm casting well and throwing line far across the river. Joe exclaims in astonishment and yells, "Money! Goddamn! You're throwing line as good as Abe Streep!" (He is referring to an editor of *Outside*, a fine athlete who fished with Joe the year before.) I am elated and try not to think about how I am managing to cast this well. I fish the fly across and downstream as the line swings in the current. I strip in the line, take a step downstream, and cast again.

Cast, step, cast again; I work my way down the pool, Joe next to me. We pause as a train goes by, hauling a collection of graffiti on the sides of its white boxcars. I notice a purple, bulbous scrawl that reminds me of something. Joe tells me to cast toward a pile of white driftwood on the bank. I send fifty or sixty feet of line straight at it, lay the fly beside it, swing the fly across. The light is now high enough that the ripples and the lanes of current are distinct. At the end of the swing, a swift, curved disturbance appears in the pewter surface of the river, and the line pulls powerfully tight.

••

Joe's father, William Randolph, was a navy pilot who flew many missions in Vietnam and could be gone for months at a time. Brenda, Joe's mother, stayed home with Joe (called Joey); his older sister, Kay; and his younger sister, Fran. The family spent much of the kids' childhood at Naval Air Station Lemoore, south of Fresno, California, where Joe often rode his bicycle down to the Kings River to fish. Sometimes he hunted for ducks with family friends. Later he even had a scabbard on his bicycle in which he could carry his shotgun. His friends had shotguns, too, and sometimes they would stand about a hundred yards apart in a field and shoot at each other with the lighter sizes of bird shot. The pellets did not penetrate but "stung like crazy" when they hit. Once, when Joe was speeding along on his bicycle without a helmet, he came out from behind a Dumpster, and a passing garbage truck ran into him and knocked him unconscious. There was not much male supervision on the base with the dads away at war.

Joe's mother had problems with depression, which the kids did not understand until they were in their twenties. Once or twice they went to stay with relatives while she was hospitalized. When Joe was in grade school, she and his father divorced. Joe's main emotional problem, as Kay remembers, was getting angry, often at himself for personal frustrations. As a boy, he played tennis and traveled to tournaments and earned a national junior-level ranking. Being tall, he had a big serve, but his inability to avoid blow-ups on the court ruled out tennis for him. Other sports he excelled in were basketball, baseball, track, and volleyball. He went to high school in Fresno but did not graduate, although he did get his GED. To acquire a useful trade, in the late 1980s, he attended a school in the Midwest where he learned to be a baker; then he decided that was not for him and returned to California. He was kicked off the basketball team at Monterey Peninsula College for skipping practice to fish. Various injuries—elbow, knee, a severe fracture of the left ankle—interfered with his promising college basketball career. He once watched a doctor chip a bone spur off his knee with a chisel and did not pass out.

In his thirties, in Monterey, he tried to qualify for the semipro beach-volleyball circuit and took steroids to improve his game. The drugs caused him to feel invincible and aggressive and righteously angry, and added a foot to his vertical leap, but he did not make the roster. While playing volleyball he met a woman named Tricia, and they married. The couple had two children—Hank, born in 1995, and Maddi, born in 1997. He and Tricia separated in about 2000 and later divorced.

••

Now the sun had risen over the canyon, and Joe was navigating us through the rapids whose splashes wet my notebook as I recorded the details of my first steelhead—a six-pound hatchery fish from far upstream, according to the identification made by Joe on the basis of the fish's clipped maxillary fin (a tiny fin by the mouth).

"The tug is the drug," steelheaders say, describing that first strike and the fight that follows. This was true, as I could now affirm. The afterglow was great, too. I looked up at the canyon walls rising like hallelujah arms, their brown grasses crossed by eagle shadows, and at the green patches where small springs came up, and the herd of bighorn sheep starting mini rockslides behind their back hooves, and the hatch of tiny crane flies like dust motes in the sunlight.

Happiness! The pressure was off, I had caught the fish, defeated the possible jinx, the article would now work out. In this mood, I could have drowned and not minded, or not minded much. The morning had become hot, and Joe asked if I wanted some water. He opened the cooler. Inside I saw a few bottles of spring water and a thirty-pack of Keystone beer in cans. Joe's assistant for the trip, a young man named J. T. Barnes, went by in a yellow raft loaded with gear, and Joe waved. He said J.T. would set up our evening camp downstream.

Every fishing trip reconstructs a cosmogony, a world of angling defeats and victories, heroes and fools. Joe told me about a guy he fished with once who hooked a bat, and the guy laughed as the bat flew here and there at the end of his line, and then it flew directly at the guy's head and wrapped the line around the guy's neck and was in his face flapping and hissing and the guy fell on the ground screaming for Joe to get the bat off him and Joe couldn't do a thing, he was laughing so hard.

"Do your clients ever hook you?" I asked.

"Oh, hell yes, all the time. Once I was standing on the bank and this guy was in the river fly-casting, and he wrapped his backcast around my neck, and I yelled at him, and what does the guy do but yank harder! Almost strangled me. I'll never forget that fucking guy. We laughed about it later in camp."

The next pool we fished happened to be on the left side. I had not practiced the left-side cast during my insomniac night. Now when I tried it I could not do it at all. The pool after that was on the right, but my flailing on the left had caused me to forget how to cast from the right. Again the circus-tent collapse, again chaos and disgrace. My euphoria wore off, to be replaced by symptoms of withdrawal.

• •

I liked that Joe always called me "Bud." It must have been his standard form of address for guys he was guiding. The word carried overtones of affection, familiarity, respect. He got a chance to use it a lot while trying to help me regain my cast, because I soon fell into a dire slump, flop sweat bursting on my forehead, all physical coordination gone. "Bud, you want to turn your entire upper body toward the opposite bank as you sweep that line . . . You're trying to do it all with your arms, Bud . . . Watch that line, Bud, you're coming forward with it just a half second too late." I was ready to flip out, lose my temper, hurl the rod into the trees. Joe was all calmness, gesturing with the cigarette between two fingers of his right hand. "Try it again, Bud, you almost had it that time."

By midafternoon Joe started in on the thirty-pack of Keystone, but he took his time with it and showed no effects. Our camp that night was at a wide, flat place that had been an airfield. J.T. served shrimp appetizers and steak. Joe and I sat in camp chairs while he drank Keystone and told more stories—about his Cajun grandfather who used to drink and pass out on fishing excursions, and Joe had to rouse him so he wouldn't trail his leg in the gator-infested waters; about a stripper he had a wild affair with, and how they happened to break up; about playing basketball at night on inner-city courts in Fresno where you put quarters in a meter to keep the playground lights on. At full dark, I went into my tent and looked through the mesh at the satellites going by. Joe stayed up and drank Keystone and watched sports on his iPhone.

I was back in the river and mangling my cast again the next morning while Joe and J.T. loaded the raft. Out of my hearing (as I learned afterward from J.T.), their conversation turned to J.T.'s father, who died when J.T. was fifteen. Joe asked J.T. a lot of questions about how the death had affected him.

• •

J.T. misunderstood Joe's instructions and set up our next camp at the wrong place, a narrow ledge at the foot of a sagebrush-covered slope. Joe was angry but didn't yell at him. During dinner that evening, J.T. told us the story of his recent skateboarding injury, when he dislocated his right elbow and snapped all the tendons so the bones of his forearm and hand were hanging only by the skin. Joe watched a football game and talked about Robert Griffin III, who was destined to be one of the greatest quarterbacks of all time, in Joe's opinion. As I went to bed I could still hear his iPhone's signifying noises.

At a very late hour, I awoke to total quiet and the sound of the river. The moon was pressing black shadows against the side of my tent. I got out of my sleeping bag and unzipped the tent flap and walked a distance away, for the usual middle-of-the-night purpose. When I turned to go back, I saw a figure standing in the moonlight by the camp. It was just standing there in the sagebrush and looking at me. At first I could not distinguish the face, but as I got closer, I saw that it was Joe. At least it ought to be, because he was the most likely possibility; but the figure just stood in silence, half shadowed by sagebrush bushes up to the

waist. I blinked to get the sleep out of my eyes. As I got
closer, I saw it had to be Joe, unquestionably. Still no sound,
no sign of recognition. I came closer still. Then Joe smiled
and said, "You, too, Bud?" in a companionable tone. I felt a
certain relief, even gratitude, at his ability to be wry about
this odd moonlight encounter between two older guys
getting up in the night. Now, looking back, I believe that
more was going on. I believe that what I saw was a ghost—
an actual person who also happened to be a ghost, or who
was contemplating being one.

• •

The poor guy. Here I was locked in petty torment over my
cast, struggling inwardly with every coach I'd ever disappointed, and Joe was . . . who knows where? No place good.
In fact, I knew very little about him. I didn't know that he
had started guiding for the Fly Fisher's Place in 2009, that
he'd done splendidly that year (the best in modern history
for steelhead in the Deschutes), that he had suffered a depression in the fall after the season ended, that he'd been
broke, that friends had found him work and loaned him
money. I didn't know that after his next guiding season, in
2010, he had gone into an even worse depression; that on
December 26, 2010, he had written a suicide note and swallowed pills and taped a plastic bag over his head in the back
offices of the Fly Fisher's Place; that he'd been interrupted
in this attempt and rushed to a hospital in Bend; that afterward he had spent time in the psychiatric ward of the hospital; that his friends in Sisters and his boss, Jeff Perin,
owner of the fly shop, had met with him regularly in the
months following to help him recover.

I didn't know that after the next season, in late 2011, he
had disappeared; that Perin, fearing a repetition, had called
the state police; and that they had searched for him along

the Deschutes Valley with a small plane and a boat and eventually found him unharmed and returning home. Joe later told Perin he had indeed thought about killing himself during this episode but had decided not to.

I didn't know that Perin had refrained from firing Joe on several occasions—for example, when Joe was guiding an older angler who happened to be a psychiatrist with the apt name of Dr. George Mecouch, along with one of Dr. Mecouch's friends, and a repo man showed up with police officers and a flatbed, and they repossessed Joe's truck (a previous one), leaving Joe and his elderly clients stranded by the side of the road in the middle of nowhere at eleven o'clock at night. Dr. Mecouch, evidently an equable and humorous fellow, had laughed about the experience, thereby perhaps saving Joe's job. I did not know that Perin had permanently ended his professional relationship with Joe when Joe refused to guide on a busy Saturday in July 2012 because he had received no tip from his clients of the day before.

• •

The spot where Joe killed himself is out in the woods about six miles from Sisters. You drive on a rutted Forest Service road for the last mile or two until you get to a clearing with a large gravel pit and a smaller one beside it. Local people come here for target practice. Splintery, shot-up pieces of plywood lie on the ground, and at the nearer end the spent shotgun-shell casings resemble strewn confetti. Their colors are light blue, dark blue, pink, yellow, forest green, red, black, and purple. Small pools of muddy water occupy the centers of the gravel pits, and the gray, rutted earth holds a litter of broken clay-pigeon targets, some in high-visibility orange. At the clearing's border, dark pine trees rise all around.

Probably to forestall the chance that he would be interrupted this time, Joe had told some friends that he was
going to Spokane to look for work, others that he would be
visiting his children in California. On November 4, 2012,
he spent the afternoon at Bronco Billy's, a restaurant-bar
in Sisters, watching a football game and drinking Maker's
Mark with beer chasers. At about six in the evening he left,
walking out on a bar tab of about $18. The bartender thought
he had gone outside to take a phone call. At some time
after that, he drove to the gravel pit, parked at its northwest
edge, and ran a garden hose from the exhaust pipe to the
right rear passenger-side window, sealing the gaps around
the pipe and in the window with towels and clothes. A man
who went to the gravel pit to shoot discovered the body on
November 14. In two weeks, Joe would have been forty-
nine years old.

He left no suicide note, but he did provide a couple of
visual commentaries at the scene for those who could de-
code them. The garden hose he used came from the Fly
Fisher's Place. Joe stole it for this purpose, one can sur-
mise, as a cry for help or gesture of anger directed at his
former boss, Jeff Perin. Over the summer, Joe's weeks of
illegal guiding had caught up with him when the state police presented him with a ticket for the violation. He would
be required to go to court, and in all likelihood his local
guiding career would be through, at least for a good while.
Joe thought Perin had turned him in to the authorities;
and, in fact, Perin and other guides had done exactly that.
Joe was often aggressive and contentious on the river, he
competed for clients, and his illegal status made people
even more irate. But, in the end, to say that Joe's legal difficulties were what undid him would be a stretch, given his
history.

Joe's friend Diane Daviscourt, when she visited the scene,

found an empty Marlboro pack stuck in a brittlebrush bush next to where Joe had parked. The pack rested upright among the branches, where it could only have been put deliberately. She took it as a sign of his having given up on everything, and as his way of saying, "Don't forget me."

··

John Hazel, the Deschutes River's senior guide, said Joe was a charismatic fellow who took fishing too seriously. "I used to tell him, 'It's only fishing, Joe.' He got really down on himself when he didn't catch fish. Most guides are arrogant—Joe possessed the opposite of that. Whoever he was guiding, he looked at the person and tried to figure out what that person wanted." Daviscourt, who had briefly been Joe's girlfriend, said he was her best friend, and had made a much better friend than boyfriend. "He fooled us all," she said. "I haven't picked up a fly-fishing rod since he died." She made a wooden cross for him and put it up next to where she found the Marlboro pack. The cross says JOE R. on it in black marker, and attached to it with pushpins is a laminated photo of Joe, completely happy, standing in the river with a steelhead in his hands and a spey rod by his feet. On the pine needles beside the cross is a bottle of Trumer Pils, the brand Joe drank when she was buying.

Just before Joe died, J. T. Barnes was calling him a lot, partly to say hi, and partly because Joe had never paid him for helping on the trip with me. (He did split the tip, however.) For someone now out $600, J.T. had only kind words for Joe. "He was like the ideal older brother. And he could be so up, so crazy enthusiastic, about ordinary stuff. One day we were packing his drift boat before a trip, drinking beer, and I told him that I play the banjo. Joe got this astonished, happy look on his face, and he said, 'You play the banjo? No way! That is so great—I sing!' That made me laugh, but he was totally being serious. I play the banjo, Joe sings!"

Joe had $6 in his wallet when he died. His sister Kay, who lives in Napa, thought Joe's chronic lack of money was why he lost touch with his family. "Joe was always making bad decisions financially. Maybe, because he had a lot of pride, that made him never want to see us. But he was doing what he loved, supporting himself as a famous fishing guide. He had no idea how proud his family was of him."

Alex Gonsiewski, a highly regarded young guide on the river, who works for John Hazel, said that Joe taught him most of what he knows. When Gonsiewski took his first try at running rapids that have drowned people, Joe was in the bow of the drift boat helping him through. "It's tough to be the kind of person who lives for extreme things, like Joe was," Gonsiewski said. "His eyes always looked sad. He loved this river more than anywhere. And better than anybody, he could dial you in on how to fish it. He showed me the river, and now every place on the river makes me think of him. He was an ordinary, everyday guy who was also amazing. I miss him every day."

• •

The paths along the river that have been made by anglers' feet are well worn and wide. Many who come to fish the Deschutes are driven by a deep, almost desperate need. So much of the world is bullshit. This river is not. Among the many natural glories of the Northwest that have been lost, this valley—still mostly undeveloped, except for the train tracks—and its beautiful, tough fish have survived.

Joe was the nakedest angler I've ever known. He came to the river from a world of bullshit, interior and otherwise, and found here a place and a sport to which his own particular sensors were perfectly attuned. Everything was okay when he was on the river . . . except that then everything had to stay that way continuously, or else horrible feelings of withdrawal would creep in. For me, the starkest sadness about Joe's death was that the river and the steelhead weren't enough.

At the end of my float trip with Joe, just before we reached the river's mouth, he stopped at a nondescript wide, shallow stretch with a turquoise-flowing groove. He said he called this spot Mariano, after Mariano Rivera, the Yankees' great relief pitcher, because of all the trips it had saved. I stood and cast to the groove just as told to, and a sudden river quake bent the spey rod double. The ten-pound steelhead I landed after a long fight writhed like a constrictor when I tried to hold it for a photograph.

The next evening, not long before I left for the airport, Joe and I floated the river above Maupin a last time. Now he wasn't my guide; he had me go first and fish a hundred yards or so ahead of him. Dusk deepened, and suddenly I was casting well again. I looked back at Joe, and he raised his fist in the air approvingly. At the end of his silhouetted arm, the glow of a cigarette could be seen. I rolled out one cast after the next. It's hard to teach a longtime angler anything, but Joe had taught me. He knocked the rust off my fishing life and gave me a skill that brought back the delight of learning, like the day I first learned to ride a bicycle. I remembered that morning when we were floating downstream among the crane flies in the sunlight. Just to know it's possible to be that happy is worth something, even if that feeling doesn't last. Hanging out with Joe uncovered long-overgrown paths back to childhood. Peace to his soul.

September 2013

Word

There is a word that can be talked about forever. The word was the center of a discussion in an elementary-school classroom on Staten Island on a recent Sunday afternoon, when a group of about sixty people, mostly from that borough, met for an event billed as "Race Issues in Mark Twain: A Community Dialogue on Language & Dialect in *Tom Sawyer* and *Huckleberry Finn*." The event was part of a two-month program called the Big Read, sponsored by the National Endowment for the Arts. The Big Read had chosen *Tom Sawyer* for Staten Island. Because the word occurs only eight times in that book, however, the discussion had been enlarged to include *Huckleberry Finn*, where it occurs more frequently.

What do young people think of the word? They are known to use it a lot in their music and in their socializing. Fortunately, Marianne Kent-Stoll, a teacher at Staten Island Academy, had brought some of the students from her sophomore English class. Without saying the word, and by means of a common term that refers to the word by its first letter, a question was put to the students. They replied that the word could sometimes have an affectionate meaning, if used in a form ending in an "a" in the singular and "az" in the plural. The students said they did not like the word or use it, even affectionately. A woman who identified herself as a retired teacher said, "I hate the word, and to this day I can't say it. I guess I want people to be able to say it, but I don't want to hear it, and I hear it too much. Recently, at a diner here on Staten Island, three men came in and sat in the booth next to me, and they were using the word constantly, and I wanted to say something to them, but I was afraid to, because they were obviously mobsters."

Kent-Stoll said that she lets her students say the word or skip over it, as they prefer, when they read Twain out loud. "We're never supposed to stop feeling uncomfortable about the word, and that's okay," she said. People then brought up words similar to the word—ones that in some cases, they said, had been applied to them. Such words could be reclaimed and used proudly against those who would use them pejoratively, a female participant suggested. It depended on who said the word, someone else added. Certain words could be said by some people but not by others. Various specific words referring to particular ethnicities, religious groups, sexual identities, or groups with disabilities were mentioned; some people in the room remarked that they had never heard one or two of those words before. During the entire two-hour conversation, almost nothing from either *Tom Sawyer* or *Huckleberry Finn* was discussed, except the word.

The organization that the NEA had chosen to host the Big Read on Staten Island is called Staten Island OutLOUD. According to its brochure, "Staten Island OutLOUD gathers neighbors for the fun of reading aloud and sharing ideas." It is staffed entirely by volunteers. Beth Gorrie, the executive director, said that other events in the two-plus months devoted to *Tom Sawyer* included readings, films, a photography exhibit, a discussion of masculinity in *Tom*

Sawyer as it related to westward expansion, a treasure hunt open to people of all ambulatory styles, and a display of kinetic sculpture in which the performance artist D. B. Lampman would represent the Mississippi River by wearing three hundred feet of sparkly garden hose.

During much of the discussion of the word, the only black person in the room was Virginia Allen, the secretary of Staten Island OutLOUD. She wore a leopard-print turban and slacks and a chunky necklace. Allen is eighty years old. From the age of sixteen to twenty-six, she worked as a nurse at the Sea View Tuberculosis Hospital, on Staten Island. Because of the dangers of infection and the Sea View nurses' devotion to their work, they were called the Black Angels. In 1995, Allen retired from her position as a surgical nurse at Staten Island University Hospital. After the meeting was over and people were putting on their coats, someone asked Allen what she had thought of the event. "I found it very interesting, and I was delighted we had such a good crowd," she said. "Such a lively discussion! I just sat back and took it in."

March 5, 2012

Desert Hideaway

Los Angeles is a desert (or almost), but sometimes you want even more desert. What you do then is get in the car and take the 10 to the 405 to the 5 to the 14, or the 55 to the 91 to the 15, or some other combination of highways heading roughly northeast from the city, and after an hour and a half or two hours the expanses of pavement have narrowed, the sky is a bright blue tinged with smog, and empty, unmistakable desert is all around. Brown hills dotted with small bushes as regularly spaced as beard stubble rise on the horizon; low brush beside the road holds shreds of fluttering trash. A canyon is filled with boulders heaped up like paperwork you'll never get to. Then comes a broad flat plain of nothing but gray sand and rocks, with a single anomalous object—an orange traffic cone or the hood from a barbecue grill—resting in the middle distance, as if to aid perspective.

If you stay on the 15 toward Las Vegas and night falls, the four lanes of headlights and taillights become a string dwindling far across the darkness. Suddenly, at the Nevada border, the lit-up casino town of Primm appears, as gaudy as a funhouse entrance. I don't go that way, though; for some reason, Las Vegas does not interest me. Instead I take the

14 north through the high-desert town of Mojave. Just past there a field of wind turbines hums in the wind, the long, propeller-like blades on towers eighty feet high throwing giant shadows as they turn, some clockwise, some counter-clockwise. Across the highway from them, to the west, an airfield full of used passenger jets bleaches in the sun. The map shows the Los Angeles Aqueduct as a blue line running nearby. In fact the aqueduct here is an imposing white pipe eight feet across that wanders the contours of the dirt-bike-furrowed hills like a garden hose. From 14 I cut across on a two-lane road to the old mining town of Randsburg, and from there continue to Trona, a lakeside town whose lake dried up twenty thousand years ago, leaving a bone-white salt flat that is said to contain half the natural elements known to man. IMC Chemicals, a sprawling enterprise, now mines the flat; Trona smells like sulfur and is windy, gritty, and hot. Past Trona, over some hills and across another vast and shimmering desert flat, is the western boundary of Death Valley National Park.

$$\cdot\cdot$$

Death Valley is the largest national park in the lower forty-eight states, and it includes more than three million acres of wilderness. At its center is the long, low desert valley from which the park takes its name. Toward the east side of the valley is a fancy inn, the Furnace Creek Inn, and an eighteen-hole golf course. The first time I went to Death Valley was to play golf. I had wondered what a golf course in the desert, 214 feet below sea level, would be like. When I got to the pro shop, a high wind was whipping the tama-risk trees that enclose the course, and dark storm clouds were pouring over the barren Panamint Range to the west like spilled paint. The guy in the pro shop said the storm was supposed to hit in an hour, but if I wanted to play, it was my money. The bad weather had emptied the course, a situation I like; I am such an indifferent golfer that I prefer there be no witnesses. Also, I am afraid of injuring somebody. I teed off, occasionally running down to a green to reset a flag knocked over by the wind. By the time I reached the fifth hole, the storm had turned to the north, the wind had dropped, and the sun emerging on the horizon lit the course like a klieg light. Mourning doves were eating the recently sown grass seed on the tees, and a pair of coyotes had emerged to stalk the ducks and Canada geese gabbling in the hazards. A coyote with eyes only for the waterfowl was sitting on his haunches on the fringe of the seventh green.

The village of Furnace Creek occupies a natural oasis and makes a green rectangle on the desert floor. Along with the inn and the golf course there are campgrounds, a motel, and the headquarters of the Park Service. Tour buses and little rental cars come and go, and tourists—many of them Germans, who seem to have a thing for deserts—line up at the cash registers in the gift shop. Just a step on the other side of the tamarisk-tree border, extreme desert begins. One afternoon I ducked through the trees at a corner of the golf course and walked across desert like gray piecrust to the village of the Timbisha Shoshone Indians, a half mile or so away. I had heard that the Timbisha had been high-handedly evicted from the oasis years ago. Among the irregularly spaced mobile homes of the Timbisha village I found the one belonging to the tribal chairman, Pauline Esteves, a dour, heavyset woman in her seventies. After many questions about who I was and what I wanted to know, she reluctantly agreed to talk to me. Sitting with her head in her hands at her dining-room table, she said that people who write about her almost always get everything wrong. To my

questions about Timbisha history she responded first by
staring back at me, irritatedly and long.

She said that the Timbisha people had lived here for
thousands of years; that they had been the first to use the
natural springs at Furnace Creek to cultivate the land; that
a mining company had dispossessed them and bulldozed
their houses in the 1920s; that the golf course was near where
her house used to be; that despite such incursions the
Timbisha had never left and didn't intend to leave. She added
that they found the name Death Valley insulting. I asked
about a local landmark, and what the Timbisha name for it
had been. She buried her face in her hands for a while in silence. Then she looked at me and said, "Impossible to trans-
late." She said that the tribe had been working for decades
to get their land back but that she doubted they ever would.
(A few weeks after I talked to her, I saw in the paper that the
federal government had agreed to return three hundred acres
of land at Furnace Creek oasis to the Timbisha, along with
about seventy-two hundred acres outside the park. Congress
has yet to approve the plan: I have a feeling that Pauline
Esteves will believe it when she sees it.)

In the evenings I sat in my motel room and listened to
the whirring of the lawn sprinklers on the golf course and
read a book called *Desert Shadows: A True Story of the Charles
Manson Family in Death Valley*, by Bob Murphy, which I had
bought in a little museum in a nearby town. The woman
minding the museum had said it was an interesting book,
and it is. When I got to the end of it, I went back to the beginning and read parts over again. Somehow I was in the mood
to think about Charles Manson. Manson was arrested—in
Death Valley, as it happened—in 1969. He and his followers roamed all over this desert back then, on foot and in
chopped Volkswagen dune buggies, and they used it for a
hideout. At the time of his arrest, Manson was wanted only

for auto theft and for torching an earthmover belonging to the Park Service; his involvement in the famous murders in L.A. came out afterward.

Desert Shadows says that Manson was captured at a cabin on the Barker ranch, his remote hideaway in an isolated part of Death Valley, up a canyon called Goler Wash. The book describes how difficult it is to drive or even hike up the canyon, and refers to it as "treacherous" Goler Wash. I considered: Would I like to see a place like that—the desert hideout of a deranged killer? I decided that, all in all, I would not. Then I thought about it some more and decided that I actually would.

••

I spent a day driving and asking around to locate Goler Wash, which is in the Panamint Range in the park's southwestern corner. Early one morning I drove to the ghost town of Ballarat, and then continued south about sixteen miles on a road of gravel and sand to the foot of Goler Wash. I left my car, took a day pack with sandwiches and sunblock and water, and started up the canyon.

You might miss the entrance if you didn't know it was there: from a distance the canyon looks like just another seam in the mountain front. But within fifty yards, high walls rise up to enclose a passage about the width of two cars, and the way winds between the walls like a narrow street in lower Manhattan. Grayish dawn light showed the canyon as I ascended; though the time was past sunrise, the sun would not get there for a while. This was the sort of place that needs the accompaniment of foreboding minor chords on a bass viol. But when I stopped and listened, I heard not a sound. As I went on, the stones clicking under my feet at a steep part seemed indiscreetly loud.

After about a mile the canyon opened out, and I could

see farther. The sun lit the top of one ridge and then slid
to the next. I passed greenery—mesquite trees, scrubby
willows—and thumb-shaped cacti poking from the canyon
walls. In the crook of a switchback was a spring, upwelling
and dark-tinted among creepers and weeds. After another
few miles the day became hot. The sun, now overhead, filled
the widened canyon with a fierce brightness unmarred by
any shade. The silence remained vast. A raven glided over a
ridge, and I thought of the Manson family members, some
of them young women with babies, hiking up this track
barefoot back in 1969. Then I began to think about 1969 in
general, and what an unhinged year it was, and how the
insane expression in Charles Manson's eyes in that photograph of him on the cover of *Life* magazine seemed a perfect
image for that time. I had begun to give myself the creeps
when I was distracted by the sound of an engine, and then
by the sight of a bright-red vehicle coming up the road. It
stopped beside me, and its window rolled down. In it were
Scott and Marv, businessmen from suburban Chicago, who
were tooling around the desert in Marv's high-tech, diesel-
powered, tank-like, very expensive Hummer while their
wives played blackjack in Vegas. They were looking for
Manson's hideout, too. They had read about it in a guidebook. They offered me a ride, and I hopped in.

Marv was dark and stocky, Scott blond and thinner.
Scott was driving. Each was smoking a big cigar. Scott said
he especially wanted to find Manson's bus, which their
guidebook also mentioned. In 1968 Manson drove the
family's green-and-white school bus up to the Barker ranch,
in what was perhaps the only noncriminal real achievement
of his life. According to the guidebook, the bus was still
there. As Scott negotiated the road's dicey parts, occasionally adjusting a control on the dash in order to add extra air
to the Hummer's tires and raise the vehicle's underside an

inch or two over the high spots, he kept saying, "I can't *believe* he got a school bus up here!" At a vista point with desert waste stretching beyond, Scott said, "Marv, when I look at scenery like this, I feel small." Marv puffed his cigar and said, "Drive, Scott. Just drive."

Marv told me about his glass-and-mirror company, and how it had installed the mirrors in the Chicago-area mansion of the basketball star Michael Jordan. As the throbbing Hummer motored upward, Scott kept saying, "The Hummer loves this, Marv. He loves this place."

The Barker ranch is on a tributary canyon that joins Goler Wash from the south. We took a couple of wrong canyons before we found it. Then we passed another spring, hung a right, squeezed through a narrow defile and under a low-hanging cottonwood, and there was the Barker cabin. The cabin where Charles Manson and his followers were captured is a trim one-story structure of local stone set against a low hillside and surrounded by willows, cottonwoods, and a pomegranate tree that was blooming crimson. An ingenious network of plastic pipes connected to a spring irrigates the grounds. It's the sort of place one comes across unexpectedly now and again in America—a homemade utopia, or (in this case) dystopia.

No one lives there. The cabin now belongs to the Park Service, which maintains it as a backcountry stopover for hikers and other off-road travelers. A notice on the door lists the rules for visitors, and another warns that the house and its contents are protected under the Archaeological Resources Protection Act of 1979 and the American Antiquities Act of 1906. Scott and Marv and I poked around—no sign of the historic school bus, disappointingly—and then we shook hands and they continued on their way, following a route that would take them over the mountains and into the valley from the western side. Three minutes after they left, the silence had returned. The sun now stood directly above; I had never before been anyplace so still at midday.

Gingerly, I went through the cabin a second time. Its dimensions—of windows and ceiling and doorways— seemed slightly miniaturized. The man who built it (I later learned), in the 1940s, was a former L.A. police detective with a small wife, and she liked the reduced scale of Pullman sleeping cars. Perhaps this smaller scale also appealed to the five-foot-two-inch Manson. The highway patrolman who arrested Manson found him hiding in a little cupboard in the bathroom, under the sink. The cupboard is now gone, and most of the fixtures are, too. Past visitors to the cabin have left behind playing cards, books, a bird's nest with feathers stuck in it on the mantelpiece, *Far Side* cartoons, animal vertebrae, candles, .45- and .22-caliber shell casings, a bottle of dishwashing soap, a pitching wedge, nonperishable foods, and an oil painting of the view from the front porch. In an outbuilding I found only a set of bedsprings and, on the wall, a map of the Orion Nebula.

The Park Service or someone has provided the cabin with a guest book. It was nearly full, with entries dating from several years to just a few days before. Being in the cabin made me jumpy, so I took the book outside and read it sitting on the edge of the porch, in the shade. Entries from polite Europeans with good handwriting complimenting us Americans on our magnificent scenery alternated with all-capital-letter scrawls from apparent fans of Manson: HELTER SKELTER DUDE! WELL HERE'S TO ANOTHER YEAR OF KILLIN'! There were ballpoint sketches of Manson, and mystifying symbols, and obscure references to the date of his arrest; a ranger at Park Service headquarters had told me that members of the Manson family come back to the cabin sometimes. As I was reading a comment signed by someone named Feral Jenny, suddenly I heard what sounded like a scream from the hillside above. I don't know what it could have been—a coyote or a wild burro, maybe. Unobtrusively, I stood up to see where the sound had come from. I looked all around, but I saw nothing besides a dilapidated fence at the edge of the property, some weeds along it, some tire tracks in the dirt dwindling away, the bare and hot hillsides, and over all a bright blue western sky of endless, careless possibility.

February 2000

Dearly Disconnected

Before I got married I was living by myself in an A-frame cabin in northwestern Montana. The cabin's interior was a single high-ceilinged room, and at the center of the room, mounted on the rough-hewn log that held up the ceiling beam, was a telephone. I knew no one in the area or indeed the whole state, so my entire social life came to me through that phone. The woman I would marry was living in Sarasota, Florida, and the distance between us suggests how well we were getting along at the time. We had not been in touch for several months; she had no phone. One day she decided to call me from a pay phone. We talked for a while, and after her coins ran out I jotted the number on the wood beside my phone and called her back. A day or two later, thinking about the call, I wanted to talk to her again. The only number I had for her was the pay phone number I'd written down.

The pay phone was on the street some blocks from the apartment where she stayed. As it happened, though, she had just stepped out to do some errands a few minutes before I called, and she was passing by on the sidewalk when the phone rang. She had no reason to think that a public phone ringing on a busy street would be for her. She stopped, listened to it ring again, and picked up the receiver. Love is pure luck; somehow I had known she would answer, and she had known it would be me. Long afterward, on a trip to Disney World in Orlando with our two kids, then ages six and two, we made a special detour to Sarasota to show them the pay phone. It didn't impress them much. It's just a nondescript Bell Atlantic pay phone on the concrete wall of a building, by the vestibule. But its ordinariness and even boringness only make me like it more; ordinary places where extraordinary events have occurred are my favorite kind. On my mental map of Florida that pay phone is a landmark looming above the city it occupies, and a notable, if private, historic site.

I'm interested in pay phones in general these days, especially when I get the feeling that they are all about to go away. Technology, in the form of the phones in our pockets, has swept on by them and made them begin to seem antique. My lifelong entanglement with pay phones dates me; when I was young they were just there, a given, often as stubborn and uncongenial as the curbstone underfoot. They were instruments of torture sometimes. You had to feed them fistfuls of change in those pre-phone-card days, and the operator was a real person who stood maddeningly between you and whomever you were trying to call. And when the call went wrong, as communication often does, the pay phone gave you a focus for your rage. Pay phones were always getting smashed up, the receivers shattered to bits against the booth, the coin slots jammed with chewing gum, the cords yanked out and unraveled to the floor.

You used to hear people standing at pay phones and cursing them. I remember the sound of my own frustrated shouting confined by the glass walls of a phone booth—the

kind you don't see much anymore, with a little yellow venti-
lating fan in the ceiling that turned on when you shut the
double-hinged glass door. The noise that fan made in the
silence of a phone booth was for a while the essence of romantic lonely-guy melancholy for me. Certain specific pay
phones I still resent for the unhappiness they caused me,
and others I will never forgive, though not for any fault of
their own. In the C concourse of the Salt Lake City airport
there's a row of pay phones set on the wall by the men's
room just past the concourse entry. While on a business
trip a few years ago, I called home from a phone in that row
and learned that a friend had collapsed in her apartment
and was in the hospital with brain cancer. I had liked those
pay phones before, and had used them often; now I can't
even look at them when I go by.

There was always a touch of seediness and sadness to pay
phones, and a sense of transience. Drug dealers made calls
from them, and shady types who did not want their where-
abouts known, and otherwise respectable people planning
assignations, and people too poor to have phones of their
own. In the movies, any character who used a pay phone
was either in trouble or contemplating a crime. Pay phones
came with their own special atmospherics and even accessories sometimes—the predictable bad smells and graffiti, of
course, as well as cigarette butts, soda cans, scattered pam-
phlets from the Jehovah's Witnesses, and single bottles of
beer (empty) still in their individual, street-legal paper bags.
Mostly, pay phones evoked the mundane: "Honey, I'm just
leaving, I'll be there soon." But you could tell that a lot of
undifferentiated humanity had flowed through these places,
and that in the muteness of each pay phone's little space,
wild emotion had howled.

Once, when I was living in Brooklyn, I read in the newspaper that a South American man suspected of dozens of

drug-related contract murders had been arrested at a pay phone in Queens. Police said that the man had been on the phone setting up a murder at the time of his arrest. The newspaper story gave the address of the pay phone, and out of curiosity one afternoon I took a long walk to Queens to have a look at it. It was on an undistinguished street in a middle-class neighborhood, by a florist's shop. By the time I saw it, however, the pay phone had been blown up and/or firebombed. I had never before seen a pay phone so damaged; explosives had blasted pieces of the phone itself wide open in metal shreds like frozen banana peels, and flames had blackened everything and melted the plastic parts and burned the insulation off the wires. Soon after, I read that police could not find enough evidence against the suspected murderer and so had let him go.

The cold phone outside a shopping center in Bigfork, Montana, from which I called a friend in the West Indies one winter when her brother was sick; the phone on the wall of the concession stand at Redwood Pool, where I used to stand dripping and call my mom to come pick me up; the sweaty phones used almost only by men in the hallway outside the maternity ward at Lenox Hill Hospital in New York; the phone by the driveway of the Red Cloud Indian School in South Dakota where I used to talk with my wife while priests in black slacks and white socks chatted on a bench nearby; the phone in the old wood-paneled phone booth with leaded glass windows in the drugstore in my Ohio hometown—each one is as specific as a birthmark, a point on earth unlike any other. Recently I went back to New York City after a long absence and tried to find a working pay phone. I picked up one receiver after the next without success. Meanwhile, as I scanned down the long block, I counted a dozen or more pedestrians talking on their cell phones.

••

It's the cell phone, of course, that's putting the pay phone out of business. The pay phone is to the cell phone as the troubled and difficult older sibling is to the cherished newborn. People even treat their cell phones like babies, cradling them in their palms and beaming down upon them lovingly as they dial. You sometimes hear people yelling on their cell phones, but almost never yelling at them. Cell phones are toylike, nearly magic, and we get a huge kick out of them, as often happens with technological advances until the new wears off. Somehow I don't believe people had a similar honeymoon period with pay phones back in their early days, and they certainly have no such enthusiasm for them now. When I see a cell-phone user gently tuck it inside his jacket beside his heart, I feel sorry for the beat-up pay phone standing in the rain.

People almost always talk on cell phones while in motion—driving, walking down the street, riding on a commuter train. The cell phone took the transience the pay phone implied and turned it into VIP-style mobility and speed. Even sitting in a restaurant, the person on a cell phone seems importantly busy and on the move. Cell-phone conversations seem to be unlimited by ordinary constraints of place and time, as if they represent an almost-perfect form of communication whose perfect state would be telepathy.

And yet no matter how we factor the world away, it remains. I think this is what drives me so nuts when a person sitting next to me on a bus makes a call from her cell phone. Yes, this busy and important caller is at no fixed point in space, but nevertheless I happen to be beside her. The job of providing physical context falls on me; I become her call's surroundings, as if I'm the phone booth wall. For me to lean over and comment on her cell-phone conversation would be as unseemly and unexpected as if I were in fact a wall, and yet I have no choice, as a sentient person, but to hear what my chatty fellow traveler has to say.

Some middle-aged guys like me go around complaining about this kind of thing. The more sensible approach is just to accept it and forget about it, because there's not much we can do. I don't think that pay phones will completely disappear. Probably they will survive for a long while as clumsy old technology is still of some use to those lagging behind, and as a backup if ever the superior systems should temporarily fail. Before pay phones became endangered I never thought of them as public spaces, which of course they are. They suggested a human average; they belonged to anybody who had a couple of coins. Now I see that, like public schools and public transportation, pay phones belong to a former commonality our culture is no longer quite so sure it needs.

I have a weakness for places—for old battlefields, car-crash sites, houses where famous authors lived. Bygone passions should always have an address, it seems to me. Ideally, the world would be covered with plaques and markers listing the notable events that occurred at each particular spot. A sign on every pay phone would describe how a woman broke up with her fiancé here, how a young ballplayer learned that he had made the team. Unfortunately, the world itself is fluid and changes out from under us; the rocky islands that the pilot Mark Twain was careful to avoid in the Mississippi are now stone outcroppings in a soybean field. Meanwhile, our passions proliferate into illegibility, and the places they occur can't hold them. Eventually pay phones will become relics of an almost vanished landscape, and of a time when there were fewer of us and our stories were on an earlier page. Romantics like me will have to reimagine our passions as they are—unmoored to Earth, like an infinitude of cell-phone calls flying through the atmosphere.

January/February 2000

Bus Ride

The most dangerous bus route in the city, the B46, crosses a large section of Brooklyn from north to south. It starts near the Marcy Avenue el stop for the J, M, and Z subway trains, in Williamsburg, and ends at the Kings Plaza mall, in Flatlands, about eight miles distant. Bushwick, Bedford-Stuyvesant, and East Flatbush are along its way. The B46 bus goes down Broadway under the el tracks, turns onto Malcolm X Boulevard, makes a quick jog right at Fulton Street, and then follows Utica Avenue for miles; a short stretch of Flatbush Avenue brings it to the Sears entrance of the mall, where it turns around. In the past year, forty-one incidents involving assaults on drivers or harassment of them have occurred on the B46—far more than on any other route, according to the MTA. On February 26, two police officers attempted to arrest a B46 fare beater, who then ran away and shot at them with a .45-caliber pistol as they pursued. Officer James Li, a rookie who joined the force last December, was hit in both legs but survived. The B46 was known as a dangerous bus long before that shooting. In 2008, a fare beater on a B46 stabbed a driver to death.

If you get on at the route's southern terminus, by the mall, you're almost at Jamaica Bay. Mill Basin, an arm of the bay, comes up to the mall's back entrance. Hurricane detritus straggles along the chain-link fence, a sea breeze blows, clouds drift above. To ride the B46 north on Utica Avenue is to feel the city accumulate and intensify on both sides. "Bus operators are protected by New York State law. Assaulting a bus operator is a felony," a recorded voice says. The B46 passes EZ Pawn Corp., Baby Genius Day Care Center, Miracle Temple Church of God, Cameo Auto Body, Victory Tabernacle of Praise, Tree Stump Barber Shop, Beulah Church of God Seventh Day, Inc., the Lingerie Zone, Sinister Ink Tattoo & Piercing, Brooklyn for Jesus 7th Day Adventist, Rag Top Lounge, Holy Order of Cherubim and Seraphim Movement Church, Grace Church of the Firstborn, Bobby's Dept. Store, Sneaker King, Saint Jude Religious Items, Tropical Breeze Car Wash, First United Church of Jesus Christ Apostolic, Inc., Yahya Hardware & Discount Store, Plain Truth Temple of Praise, Sunny Corner Restaurant, King Emmanuel Missionary Baptist Church, 3-Star Juice Lounge, Eglise de Dieu, Asian Yummy House, Byways and Hedges Youth for Christ Ministry, Pawn Rite, and New Hope Healing Series (Space Available for Worship).

On a recent morning's run, nothing bad happened on the B46 at all. The driver lowered the bus so that a lady with a cane could step down, and she said, "God bless you." Another lady dropped a dollar bill on the floor and profusely thanked the man who pointed it out to her. Most people focused on their phones. Nobody boarded without paying. When the bus reached the end of the route and sat idling, the last passenger to get out stopped to talk to the driver, Carolyn Daley, a young-looking woman with long wavy hair and delicate hands. "Yes, I know this is a dangerous route, depending on the time of day or night," Daley said. "Anytime after five or six o'clock can be bad. Today,

I hope I finish before three, when the kids get out of school. But every trip is different. Some trips, you're, like, 'Lord, help me!' All kinds of people think they should be able to ride for free—it's not just the kids. Adults, elderly people with walkers and wheelchairs. They say they don't have the fare—hey, everybody goes through times like that. But then you let them on and some of them will become nasty to you anyway!

"I've never been assaulted, but I was threatened not too long ago," Daley said. "I'm not going to lie to you, it shook me up. The man had his hand in his pocket, and I don't know what he had in there. But I took it as an isolated incident. I keep getting back in this seat. Many trips are enjoyable. The B46 can be more relaxing than the other route I drive, the B41, because the B41 goes on Flatbush Avenue most of the way, and Flatbush has more traffic. And I sympathize with the passengers more than they know. I live in East New York, and I take the B46 to work myself."

MTA policy is that drivers not get into confrontations with fare evaders. The drivers just push a button on the dash to record that a passenger did not pay. Edwin Thomas, the B46 driver who was killed, began to argue with the fare beater only when the man, as he was getting off, demanded a transfer.

April 14, 2014

Back to the Harbor

The other morning I went looking for seals. Although I live in New Jersey, I drove over to Staten Island, because I know many places to look there, and it's near my house. I brought a lunch, a notebook, and old binoculars that fit into my coat pocket. The dawning sky was clear, the temperature just above freezing. Crusted snow glittered in the headlights. Potholes, which rule the roads these days, opened before me suddenly in a wicked row on the ramp for the Outerbridge Crossing, popping my left front tire. I thought I had no spare, but when I pulled over and checked, I did. I changed the tire in a lot in Perth Amboy and got to Staten Island just after sunrise.

Hylan Boulevard, the only surface road that goes from one end of the island to the other, is a pothole festival now. I slalomed among some real craters to the boulevard's end, parked, and slid on the snow crust down to the beach along the Arthur Kill, where there's a little park with a pavilion. Something so hopeful and blithe occupies an empty beach on an early morning like this, when the sun is just up and the sky is blue and the waves are pocket-size and the flag flaps on the flagpole. All the park benches had blankets of snow pulled up over their knees. A plaque by the beach noted that horseshoe crabs like to spawn here, and that the blood of horseshoe crabs contains limulus amebocyte lysate (LAL), used by science for the detection of bacterial toxins. In the extraction of the blood, the crabs are not harmed, the plaque went on to say. A flock of brants on the water croaked their creaky calls, ring-billed gulls on the breeze teetered like skateboarders, two swans groomed themselves at the water's edge. Not a seal to be seen.

Back to the car. Another slalom run along Hylan, until I turned off at Joline Avenue. Last year, the *Staten Island Advance* ran a photograph of three seals sunning themselves on a Jet Ski dock just off the Joline Avenue beach. Then, two days after a storm, locals observed a young seal entangled beside a floating mooring here and called the police. A police helicopter landed on the beach and two NYPD frogmen emerged. In full scuba gear, they waded out to the seal and disentangled it from a web of monofilament snagged on the mooring. The seal swam away, apparently fine. The frogmen high-fived. It was the first time they had rescued a seal.

Now, glassing the waters from the foot of Joline Avenue, I saw no Jet Ski dock, no mooring, no seals. More brants, more gulls. A woman was walking a German shepherd along the sand. On a higher part of the beach, a single patio chair of molded white plastic commanded a wide view. Someone might have put it there to enjoy a beer in, or for winter sunbathing. Then again, it might have been flotsam. I have seen this identical type of plastic chair in photos of the Lagos, Nigeria, city dumps in the *Times*. A photo of a memorial gathering for a slain Al Qaeda leader in Jordan showed a row of these same chairs in a tent. I own six of these chairs myself. I believe this type of white molded-plastic chair belongs to the growing category of the world's ubiquitous objects.

Continuing in my car in a northeasterly direction, I stopped at Mount Loretto park, with its mile of unimproved shoreline, where seals sometimes come up on the rocks. The walk along the Mount Loretto cliffs offers a bracing seascape and many convenient observation points. People I've encountered here in the past have told me about seals they've seen, and shown me the good spots, but I found no seals this morning. However, on one of the nature signs along the path I read BAY SCALLOPS HAVE 32 BLUE EYES THAT CAN SEE SHADOWS BUT NOT IMAGES. I paused to contemplate this. Past the old Mount Loretto lighthouse, on the beach at Lemon Creek Park, a man walking his dog told me he had seen two seals on a little piece of rock about fifty feet away, year before last. The man wore a blue ski cap and many silver earrings, and he had an ogre tattooed on each side of his neck.

A few miles farther up Hylan is Lipsett Avenue. At the end of Lipsett, in the last house before Europe, a young woman named Millissa Myers could look out the kitchen window on certain mornings and see one or more seals on a rock in the nearby cove. For a resident of New York City to be able to watch a wild seal without leaving her house is a rare thing, and Millissa appreciated it. She checked for seals every morning when she woke up, November to April (the months when seals are around). She had the sweetest and happiest voice whenever she called to tell me the seals were back, as I asked her please to do. The last time she called my cell phone with this news, I happened to be in Columbus, Ohio. Recently, Millissa moved in with her boyfriend in Queens, and her father's girlfriend, Leah, took over the job of calling me. But I have never got to Lipsett Avenue in time to see a seal. On this morning, the seals' preferred rock was just going under a rising tide, seal-free.

To the east, open ocean; near the horizon a ship dieseled away from its trail of smoke.

Last year on the Internet I found a video of a dog barking at a seal on the Great Kills beach, but now when I went there—nothing. A huge tractor tire on its side with herring gulls standing on it, a row of white pines a recent storm had knocked down, deep snowdrifts, a man in a car in the parking lot doing a crossword puzzle. Waves rolled onto the shore with a rhythm like breathing. And at the northeastern tip of the island, under the Verrazano-Narrows Bridge, where I knew for sure that seals had been recently seen—similarly nothing. That part of Staten Island is a New World symphony, though, with the bridge humming above, and the tall towers holding up their roadway span like a great gate, and tanker ships anchored at different angles in the harbor, and the tidal currents colliding.

••

Just north of the bridge, in the parking lot of Von Briesen Park, I met Paul Sieswerda, the top expert on the city's seals. Anybody looking for seals in New York City stands a good chance of running across him. Paul Sieswerda is retired from the New York Aquarium, where he worked for twenty-one years, many of them as curator. He worked at the New England Aquarium before that. He is in his late sixties and has a strong Boston accent; moist, dark eyes; and a mouth that turns down at the corners. A conscientious observer would mention that he does look sort of like a seal. Sieswerda was born and grew up in Malden, near Boston. Watching Jacques Cousteau movies as a boy made him fascinated with the sea. His connections to seals go back to the early seventies, when he was just starting out on the staff at the New England Aquarium and brought an abandoned harbor-seal pup home to care for—an act that would not be possible today. Today, most aquariums do not accept sick or stranded animals, because of the trouble of caring for them and the risk of infection inside their tanks. Also, federal law now keeps humans away from wild seals.

Having the pup at their house changed the Sieswerdas permanently. Mrs. Sieswerda fed it a mixture of cottage cheese and cream supplied gratis by a local dairy. The seal ate five baby bottles full, five feedings a day. Paul Sieswerda did the disagreeable work of cleanup. (Seals are known for their carelessness about hygiene.) The pup spent much of its time in a kiddie pool in the Sieswerdas' backyard, where their two young children played with it. It had a starring role at one of their birthday parties. The children named it Cecil, and the family made up a rhyme that went, "Cecil, the seal, who came from the sea, / Lives at the Sieswerdas', just like me."

When fully recuperated, the seal was returned to the New England Aquarium, where it became part of the collection. In time, Cecil turned out to be Cecile and had offspring with a male harbor seal named Hoover, one of the aquarium's celebrities. Hoover had spent his youth in the aquarium's outdoor exhibition pool, available to people walking by on the Boston waterfront twenty-four hours a day. Some seals pick up language the way parrots do, and can develop a vocabulary. When Hoover reached adolescence, the age at which many animals begin to vocalize, he suddenly began to speak phrases that passersby apparently had repeated to him. In the local accent, he came out with "Hey, Hoovah, g'wan, get outta heah." Similar remarks followed, with the result that scientists began to study him. (The aquarium still has a recording of Hoover's speech on its Web site.) Hoover died in the eighties and Cecile in '92, but some of their descendants at the aquarium have received scientific attention as well; a male named Chacoda (Chuck), who can say a number of words, is under study today. Through Cecile, the Sieswerdas may be said to be part of a distinguished New England seal family.

Another famous seal at the New England Aquarium during Sieswerda's tenure was Andre, the long-distance traveler from Rockport, Maine. This seal, who had been rescued from a fishing net, spent winters at the aquarium and every spring swam 180 miles, from Marblehead, Massachusetts, back to Rockport. A movie was made about him, starring Keith Carradine as the man who rescued him. Andre was also a harbor seal. The harbor seal (*Phoca vitulina*) is one of the world's most common seals. Its range is the East and West Coasts of North America—Baja California to Alaska, and the Carolinas to Iceland—and along the western coast of Europe as far south as Portugal and the east coast of Asia as far south as Japan. In the grouping Pinnipedia, which also includes walruses, harbor seals belong to the family Phocidae, the "earless" seals, also called the "true" seals. Their heads are smooth, like an earless dog's.

Because a harbor seal's hind flippers are parallel to its body, it can only wriggle, wormlike, on ice or land. Many people, when they think of seals, think of the ones that can maneuver upright and clap their front flippers and honk bicycle horns. Those are actually sea lions. The hind flippers of sea lions can bend forward, giving them more mobility when out of the water. Sea lions are of the family Otariidae, the "eared" seals. Their heads have small earflaps. Following show-business tradition, the animal who played Andre in the movie about him was a sea lion. In fact, there are no sea lions in the Atlantic Ocean. Like many entertainers, they inhabit the other coast.

••

I left my car in the lot at Von Briesen Park and got in Paul Sieswerda's, and we went over the Verrazano, took the Belt Parkway through Brooklyn, and turned south on Flatbush Avenue. Out here the city is mostly sky, water, and reedy expanses crossed by airplane shadows. On the other side of the Gil Hodges Memorial Bridge, on that far-flung Queens peninsula called the Rockaways, we parked by the dock of a ninety-five-foot three-engine boat, the *American Princess*. In half an hour it would be leaving on a seal-watching cruise in the harbor, as it does every week during seal season, weather permitting. Sieswerda often goes along as its naturalist and expert on seals.

Twenty years ago, you almost never saw a seal in New York City waters. Now the number of seals here has increased to the point that a boat can charge passengers $24 apiece (children and large groups less) for a three-hour seal-watching cruise, and be reasonably sure of success. The week before, the cruise had counted more than forty seals. What brought about the change was this:

Seals used to be regarded the way rats or coyotes are—every man's hand was against them. Those not killed for their meat or hides or oil got a bullet on general principles, because they competed with humans for fish. This applied especially to harbor seals, who tended to be the closest seals around. A harbor-seal skeleton on display at the aquarium has a bullet in one of its vertebrae. Naturally, seal numbers began to decline. Some species were believed to be endangered, others threatened. In the mid-sixties, the direness of the situation jolted the public with books and movies about the killing of baby harp seals off the Atlantic coast of Canada. The harp-seal hunt had always taken place where few could see. Now movies showed baby harp seals screaming as they were clubbed, and skinned seals writhing in agony.

Such images entered the collective memory. It's hard to overstate their effect. Seals have large eyes that are adapted to adjust quickly between dim underwater light and bright light on the surface, and their irises, like all pinnipeds', are dark. For people to react emotionally to an animal, it can't have little piggy eyes, and seals don't. They are what environmentalists call "charismatic megafauna"; staring with big brown eyes into a camera lens proved to be a survival advantage for them. In 1972, Congress passed the Marine Mammal Protection Act, whose prohibitions included the killing or harassment of any wild seal. After this law, you couldn't even go within a hundred yards of one, and anyplace seals colonized became off-limits to humans—a provision that has led to the takeover of docks and piers in San Francisco by sea lions, and of a popular children's beach in San Diego by sea lions and harbor seals.

Add to this the movie *Jaws* (I'm speculating here), which inspired more anglers to fish for sharks, thus reducing the population of a major seal predator; the cleanup of American coastal waters following additional environmental legislation in the seventies; the growing numbers of herring, a favorite seal food; and maybe the effects of global warming on water temperatures. In the mid-1970s, people began to notice an increase in seals in Long Island Sound, where they had not been plentiful since the 1930s. In 1984, a biologist, observing the proliferation of seals on the coast of Massachusetts, predicted that they would continue to expand their range southward. Between 1975 and 1988, a marine-mammal stranding center on the Jersey Shore was seeing stranded seals in single-digit numbers every year. Soon there were many dozens.

An estimated four hundred seals wintered on Long Island in 1986. By '92 there were reports of seal pups being born on the North Shore. Along with harbor seals, several species of a more Arctic range—harp, ringed, hooded, and gray seals—began to turn up. The sound's seal population grew to more than a thousand. In 1993, Kevin Walsh, of the New York Aquarium, said there was a harbor seal living under the Williamsburg Bridge. In '97, Sieswerda reported that occasional seals could be spotted on out-of-the-way beaches in Brooklyn and Queens. In 2001, kayakers said that they saw about a dozen harbor seals living on Swinburne Island, in the Lower Harbor, two and a half miles from the Verrazano Bridge. This was the first report of a seal colony in city waters. Every year since then has brought an increase in the city's seals. In '04 a hooded seal "hauled out" and basked on the fuel dock at the World's Fair Marina, in Flushing Bay, by the Grand Central Parkway. In '06, Donald E. Moore III, the director of the Prospect Park Zoo, saw twenty-six seals off Orchard Beach, in the Bronx. A harbor seal slept for a day on the kayak dock at the Seventy-ninth Street Boat Basin in '08 and again in '09. A seal suffering a possible shark wound came ashore at Breezy Point, in the Rockaways, on January 18, 2010. And so on.

Meanwhile, in northern waters where the population expansion may have begun, a new abundance of seals attracted great white sharks. Last summer and the summer before, shark-chewed seals washed up on the shores of Cape Cod. The town of Chatham, Massachusetts, banned swimming within three hundred feet of seals. Spotters in an airplane reported a fifteen-foot great white shark chasing seals south of Nauset Beach, on the Cape, last July. Public beaches in the vicinity were later closed. Researchers put transmitters on some of the sharks, who left for waters off Florida in the fall.

∙∙

Sieswerda believes in "citizen science," he told the passengers, who were several families with children; a grant writer named Shari and her husband, Mitch, both bird-watchers; a well-dressed woman from Ukraine with her daughter; two dreadlocked guys and a young woman in patchy trousers; a hand-holding young couple; and a genial older guy in a corduroy baseball cap. Sieswerda was speaking into a feedback-prone microphone in the cabin while some parents figured out what the children would order at the snack bar. He explained that when the boat came upon seals today, he wanted each passenger to make an individual count and then tell it to him, and also to take as many photographs as possible. If the passengers were willing, they could later e-mail him the photos. Sieswerda collects seal information from boat captains, bird-watchers, fishermen, many kayakers, and people on seal cruises. Then he compiles it. Each year in March or early April he goes out with a group and does his own eyewitness census: the group counted nine seals in the harbor in 2006, twelve in '07, sixteen in '08, twenty in '09, and thirty-three last year.

The high-rise apartment buildings of Brighton Beach and the tall red T of the Parachute Jump ride at Coney Island passed in the starboard windows as Sieswerda ran through some of his seal photographs on the cabin's flat-screen TV. The one everybody wanted a closer look at showed a harbor seal with a shark bite. A friend of Sieswerda's took the picture last April at Swinburne Island. The seal is out of the water, reclining on its side on a rock, a large wound on its lower body turned to the sun as if for the healing rays. It appears to be in otherwise good health. Going in closer on the wound, Sieswerda pointed out that it had ragged tooth marks on its edges and conformed in shape and size to the jaw structure of a shark. He hoped that when the wound became a scar he could use it to identify this particular seal. Right now he has no way to tell one seal from another. He doesn't know if individual seals are returning every fall, or where they come from, or where they go in the spring.

After the lecture, people stepped out on deck, where it was bright and windy but not too cold. The boat's progress took it across the Ambrose Channel, the main shipping route into and out of the city. The captain sped up to avoid a huge inbound cargo ship, which went by in our wake with its containers piled high like a waiter balancing dishes. Its name was the CMA CGM *Florida*. Swinburne Island approached, and Sieswerda suggested that the captain make a wide circuit around it and then come up to its west side slowly, by imperceptible advances, the way he had seen Eskimos sneak up on seals in the Bering Sea. The captain liked the idea but said there wasn't time.

When islands are grim they can be grim indeed, and Swinburne is that. Nobody lives on it and visitors are forbidden by the National Park Service, which has authority, because the island is part of the Gateway National Recreation Area. Swinburne was dredged out of the water to house quarantined immigrants back in the late nineteenth century, as was its larger companion, Hoffman Island, three-quarters of a mile away. Staten Islanders who objected to having a quarantine hospital in their neighborhood had rioted and burned the hospital down, so these islands were created as isolated places for quarantine where no citizens would object. Hoffman held immigrants who had only been exposed to disease, while Swinburne was for the more seriously ill. A tall brick smokestack, said to have been the chimney of its crematorium, still stands as Swinburne's main landmark. Dark, buzzard-like cormorants roost in its stunted trees. The city is near enough so that you can see how traffic is moving on the Verrazano.

I have fished the shorelines of both Hoffman and Swinburne Islands with a guide out of Great Kills Harbor, casting up next to the rocks. At mean low water, the depth off Swinburne is just seven feet, but a few hundred yards to the south the bottom drops suddenly to twenty-four feet. Big fish wait in holes like that for bait tumbled by the tide; maybe the seals like to hunt there, too. In any case, the west side of Swinburne Island is their favorite place in the city. On that side the rocks are low enough for them to haul out on, and a few stumps of pilings can support them in an odd basking posture, curved like cocktail wieners on toothpicks. Last April, when I accompanied Sieswerda on his seal census, fifteen seals or more slid off the rocks and pilings as our boat eased around the western corner.

This time, our rather more abrupt appearance disclosed no basking seals. At the waterline the rocks were a dark greenish-black. Just above that, fresh seaweed made a band of bright green; above that was a stripe of plain gray rock with white splashes of droppings. Close scans of the rocks picked out only gulls standing on them or bobbing in the water alongside. Then among the pilings one seal head popped up, then another. The heads had their own smooth shininess, like wet rubber. Seals can't resist observing anybody observing them. Soon several more had come up to one side of the boat or the other. People were going to different places on the rail, pointing, lifting up children so they could see. A little girl in a hooded coat was fussing. "You have tissues in your pocket and you should use them," her father told her.

Sieswerda circulated from person to person, asking how many each had counted. The maximum number anybody seemed to have accumulated was ten, and eventually he decided that no more than ten were in attendance today. "The rest must be having lunch," he said. "They found a school of herring somewhere." The smell of the boat's new coat of white paint hung in the air, a helicopter thudded overhead, a gray coast guard boat went by. Seal-watchers standing in the bow all held their binoculars to their eyes with their right hands, and from the back they seemed to be saluting. Even such a small number of seals kept things lively, popping up in new places like a Whac-A-Mole. Sometimes when they ducked under they went headfirst and sometimes they leaned back with a sort of luxurious rearward yielding. A crew member kept announcing new seal locations loudly over the public address.

After a while, the boat moved on toward Hoffman Island, which has seals only on occasion, probably because its shoreline rocks are higher up off the water. During this interlude many people adjourned inside and bought hot eggplant sandwiches at the snack bar. Shari, the bird-watcher, stayed on deck with her binoculars and camera. She said that she and her husband had so far seen three kinds of gulls—herring, ring-billed, and great black-backed—along with brants, scoters, double-crested cormorants, long-tail ducks, and a loon. She said that in the past they had spotted other loons in New York City waters, and I asked if they'd ever heard a loon's cry here. They hadn't, and didn't know anyone who had. Do the loons make that glorious wild cry only in more remote settings, like the North Woods of Maine? Wouldn't it be something to hear it when you are, say, riding the Staten Island Ferry? Definitely the loons stop over here, but apparently they keep silent when they do—an ornithological peculiarity.

Past Hoffman the boat continued into the narrows until the bridge impended above. The captain cut the engines and let the tide pull us toward it, coasting a hundred yards offshore. With the engines quiet you could hear the trucks and cars. We came up almost to the place where I had looked

for seals on the rocks a couple of hours earlier. The crew-
man on the loudspeaker called out that there were seals to
the left. Someone said that a seal had just slid off a rock,
and I saw it a few seconds later. With typical seal curiosity
it gave us a good perusal—passing the length of the boat
and checking it out while doing a sidestroke—before it disappeared.

For security reasons, boats aren't allowed to sit under
bridges. Soon we turned around and headed back to have
another look at Swinburne Island. Sieswerda thought we
might find more seals this time, but when we got closer there
were fewer. The seal heads appeared farther from the boat
and over a wider expanse of water. Sieswerda made some
final totting up on his clipboard. He said all the seals seen
today had been harbor seals, as near as he could tell. The
winter sun was lower in the sky and lit the island differently, pouring through the row of narrow empty windows
of a one-story brick ruin. On a corner atop the chimney
stack a peregrine falcon had taken up a perch. The elegant
little predator came into focus against the sky framed by
the binoculars' circle, moving his head back and forth
surveillantly.

As usual when there are no clouds over the city, the
high, white streaks of jet trails stretched like chalk smears
across a blackboard. They combined with the landscape
lines funneling toward the bridge, the queue of ships getting smaller and smaller as they receded to the horizon, the
boat and helicopter traffic, the wheeling gulls. Everything
in the world seemed to be inrushing or outgoing. I thought
of the immigrants from all over who had ended up on these
Quarantine Islands, as they once were called; I imagined
the young Vito Corleone, fresh from escaping his mother's
murderers in Sicily, looking out the window of his room
on Swinburne Island with the chalk mark that designated

him as unhealthy still on his coat; and thought how he might even have seen this same sea view, had he been real.

That seals have recolonized New York Harbor, where they hadn't lived for at least a century, is a remarkable development made ordinary by the gradual way it occurred. Large carnivorous wild mammals now take up residence in the city's waters annually from November to April, and we know almost nothing about their greater life. Sieswerda would like to put a camera on Swinburne to observe its seals all day for whatever else he can learn, combining research with a live feed set up as an exhibit at the aquarium. But the red tape involved in doing that would be too much for him at his age, he says.

The only solid piece of evidence about where Swinburne's seals come from is a satellite tracking record provided by a transmitter on the back of a seal released in 2008 by the Riverhead Foundation for Marine Research and Preservation, on Long Island. This seal, a gray, had been rescued in a malnourished condition from a Montauk beach. A transmitter about the size of a cell phone was epoxied to his back when he was released, after some months of rehabilitation. (The transmitters, which cost about $4,500 each, send signals to a satellite when the animal is on the surface. The transmitter falls off when the animal molts.) The gray seal was put back in the ocean at Hampton Bays, and at first he headed east toward Montauk. After a few days he turned around and came down Long Island's ocean shore. Near the end of the island he suddenly veered left and swam out to the edge of the Continental Shelf, about 110 miles from land. After a while he came back in, and his transmitter began to send location readings consistent (accurate to a hundred yards) with those of Swinburne Island. Soon afterward, transmissions stopped.

Transmission records of other rehabbed seals released

by Riverhead staffers show a wide dispersal. Seals sometimes go from Long Island up to Maine, Canada, Green-
land. A ringed seal who came ashore at Smithtown, Long
Island, suffering from pneumonia was rescued, cured, and
fed until ready for release. He went back to the sea at the
Hampton Bays site in June 2006. His transmissions plotted
a route along the East Coast and into Davis Strait, above
Newfoundland. He then headed northwest along the shore
of Baffin Island. When transmissions stopped, in November, he was even farther north, near an Arctic fastness called
Devon Island, more than three thousand miles from his
starting point. Given this kind of data, it seems safe to say
that at least some of the seals who spend time in New York
City are widely traveled animals.

· ·

One of James Thurber's most famous cartoons is of a man
and woman lying in a bed, and the woman is saying to the
man, "All right, have it your way—you heard a seal bark!"
Meanwhile, behind the bed's headboard, and partly hidden
by it, a large seal looks off to the left. The animal is upright,
and thus must be a sea lion, not a seal, though mentioning
this discrepancy to Thurber probably would have irked him.
The drawing came about by chance. Originally, he was trying to draw a seal on a rock looking at two small figures in
the distance and saying to itself, "Hm, explorers." When
the rock Thurber produced looked more like a headboard,
he adjusted and kept going.

The famous cartoon is a moment of mad clarity, but the
one behind it is just as profound. Seals are really like the
one on the rock-headboard—curious, observant, sly, if not
always exactly thoughtful. They share a common ancestor
with canines and are among the animals that have evolved
from land back into the sea. Their sensitivity to humans

resembles that of dogs and gives them good coexistence skills. Helped by the protection of law, they are shaping up to be the type of adaptive animal—like starlings, buzzards, crows, raccoons, wild hogs, coyotes, wild turkeys, Canada geese, deer, Asian carp—that can fit in with the man-made world. In the future, they may become as common in the harbor as deer are in the suburbs. Seals have a self-promotional skill unknown to other wild animals and essential to the successful salesman: they find us interesting. Sole possessors of an excellent piece of real estate off-limits to humans but in the middle of it all, seals will probably be returning to the city every November from now on.

March 21, 2011

A Lonesome Death Remembered

Do you know the Bob Dylan song "The Lonesome Death of Hattie Carroll"? Put it on now and listen to it, if you happen to have it on a CD. If you don't, or you don't remember it, it's about a young society swell named William Zantzinger who, in 1963, killed a black serving-woman named Hattie Carroll at a ball at a Baltimore hotel by striking her with a cane. Dylan was just twenty-two when he wrote it, and the lyrics show him at his high-energy, internal-rhyme-spinning peak:

> William Zanzinger killed poor Hattie Carroll
> With a cane that he twirled around his diamond
>   ring finger . . .
> [She] Got killed by a blow, lay slain by a cane
> That sailed through the air and came down through
>   the room
> Doomed and determined to destroy all the gentle . . .

Zantzinger's motive, Dylan sings, was that he "just happened to be feelin' that way without warnin'." When Zantzinger came to trial, charged with first-degree murder, the judge "spoke through his cloak, most deep and distinguished," and then gave Zantzinger a six-month sentence. At this last injustice, the song ends,

> But you who philosophize disgrace and criticize
>   all fears
>   Bury the rag deep in your face
> For now's the time for your tears.

The song contains errors of fact. Dylan misspells the perpetrator's name, omitting the *t*—perhaps deliberately, out of contempt, or perhaps to emphasize the Snidely Whiplash hissing of the *z*'s. Zantzinger's actual arrest and trial were more complicated than the song lets on. Police arrested Zantzinger at the ball for disorderly conduct—he was wildly drunk—and for assaults on hotel employees not including Hattie Carroll, about whom they apparently knew nothing at the time. When Hattie Carroll died at Mercy Hospital the following morning, Zantzinger was also charged with homicide. The medical examiner reported that Hattie Carroll had hardened arteries, an enlarged heart, and high blood pressure; that the cane left no mark on her; and that she died of a brain hemorrhage brought on by stress caused by Zantzinger's verbal abuse, coupled with the assault. After the report, a tribunal of Maryland circuit court judges reduced the homicide charge to manslaughter. Zantzinger was found guilty of that, and of assault, but not of murder.

The judges probably thought they were being reasonable. They rejected defense claims that Hattie Carroll's precarious health made it impossible to say whether her death had been caused, or had simply occurred naturally. The judges considered Zantzinger an "immature" young man who got drunk and carried away, but they nevertheless held him responsible for her death, saying that neither her medical history nor his ignorance of it was an excuse. His cane, though merely a toy one he got at a farm fair, they considered a weapon capable of assault. They kept the sentence to only six months because (according to the *New York Herald Tribune*) a longer one would have required that he serve it in state prison, and they feared the enmity of the largely black prison population would mean death for him. Zantzinger served his six months in the comparative safety of the Washington County Jail. The judges also let him wait a couple of weeks before beginning his sentence, so he could bring in his tobacco crop. Such dispensations were not uncommon, apparently, for offenders who had farms.

·•

Nowadays I like to listen to Dylan's old protest songs. Something about them suits a current need, with commercial radio so jingly and dead and Dylan himself doing the music for Victoria's Secret lingerie ads. He must be proud of "The Lonesome Death of Hattie Carroll"; since the song came out in 1964 he has included it on a greatest-hits CD (*Biograph*) and on a live-concert CD. The song is also part of his touring repertoire, an exposure that has brought it many listeners in recent years. On the long and sad list of victims of racial violence, from Emmett Till to Amadou Diallo, many names are forgotten after the news moves on. Dylan's poetry has caused Hattie Carroll's name, and the sorrow and true lonesomeness of her death, to stick in people's minds.

Dylan describes Hattie Carroll as a fifty-one-year-old maid who waited on tables, took out garbage, emptied ashtrays, and "never sat once at the head of the table." He mentions that she had borne ten children. Of Zantzinger, he says,

William Zanzinger, who at twenty-four years
Owns a tobacco farm of six hundred acres

As I listened, I noticed the tense of that verb. "Hattie Carroll" was perhaps Dylan's most journalistic song, nearly contemporary with the events it chronicles. Hattie Carroll died on February 9, Zantzinger went to jail on September 15, and Dylan recorded the song in New York City on October 23, all in 1963. The immediacy of that "owns" got me wondering about the actual event, and about its consequences working themselves out through time.

For example, William Zantzinger: What happened to him? Does he own that farm today? Zantzinger is, it turns out, an amazing guy. In the semirural part of Maryland where he still lives, many people know his name. If you mention him to someone in real estate, the antiques business, the legal profession, or law enforcement, you get a reaction. People don't want to talk about him, or they do, or they want their names left out of it, or they shake their heads and laugh; they never have to be told who he is. Many say he's a wonderful person, always polite and smiling, a good friend. Because Dylan's song made him a "story," in the news sense, reporters come to Charles County, Maryland, every so often to see what Zantzinger is up to now. They are usually surprised, as I was, that he is hard to summarize.

When Zantzinger got out of jail in early 1964, he returned to his family and farm. He had a wife and two young boys. (His wife, Jane, had been charged with assaulting a policeman at the ball.) The farm is called West Hatton. Its main house, a three-story brick mansion, has pillars and a porch on the side facing the Wicomico River. A Revolutionary War veteran built the house in about 1790. Both of Zantzinger's parents also lived on the farm; his father could trace his ancestry from the earliest white settlers of Maryland,

and his mother, from a governor of Maryland. All along the river, lawns and fields lead up to mansions facing the shores, landmarks of the old tobacco-growing Maryland Tidewater. Neighbors of the Zantzingers owned enough land that you could ride to the hounds after foxes on it. Zantzinger loved foxhunting, and some of the 1963 news articles identified him as a "huntsman." Yet the Zantzingers were country gentry—he worked his farm alongside his employees, and he drank with the locals, black and white, in the nearby bars.

At some point, Zantzinger sold the farm and got into real estate. Notoriety did not pursue him, and his name stayed out of the paper until it began to appear regularly in the notices of Charles County property owners who were delinquent with their taxes. In 1986, because of the back taxes, the county took possession of some ramshackle rental houses he owned in a neighborhood called Patuxent Woods. What Zantzinger did next got his name back in the news. He knew that the county now owned the properties, but that the renters, all poor and black, did not know. Counting on a lack of attention all around, he simply went on collecting rents as before. Even more enterprising, when tenants fell behind on their rent, he filed complaints against them and took them to court for not paying him rent on property he no longer owned. The county court, in calm and bureaucratic ignorance, heard the cases. And to put the cap on it, he won.

Eventually, local authorities caught up with him. In 1991, a Charles County sheriff's deputy arrested Zantzinger at his real estate office on charges that included fraud and deceptive business practices. A number of newspapers, *The Washington Post* among them, did stories about this latest chapter in the Zantzinger saga. The houses he had been renting were such disasters—run-down shacks without plumbing or running water—that they embarrassed the county and gave traction to local fair-housing advocates, whose cause had been mostly frustrated until then. All the same, a few tenants came forward to speak up for Zant-zinger, saying that without him they'd be living on the street. When the judge sentenced him to eighteen months on work-release in the county jail, twenty-four hundred hours of community service, and about $62,000 in penalties and fines, there were people in the courtroom who cried.

The small building on Highway 301 in White Plains, Maryland, where Zantzinger's real estate office used to be, is now closed and empty, with a KEEP OUT sign on the door. The number listed for his real estate company in the Yellow Pages has been disconnected. A car dealership and a lumber-yard flank his former office, and across the highway is a tattoo parlor. Similar enterprises—featuring bagels, blinds, birdseed, braiding, bail bonds—not to mention the usual behemoth stores as common as traffic, spread along High-way 301 for miles and miles, interrupted only occasionally by patches of trees labeled with developers' signs. At this rate, what little remains of rural Maryland will probably be gone sometime next week, foxhunting fields, antebellum mansions, and all.

People say Zantzinger now lives on a farm in neighbor-ing St. Mary's County. They say he's had a few health prob-lems; he's a big man, six feet tall and heavy, and he's sixty-five. They say he still owns a lot of rental properties, some as run-down as Patuxent Woods. (He doesn't talk to report-ers, so I never found out for sure.) Candice Quinn Kelly, a former housing activist in La Plata, Maryland, told me, "I was on the other side from Zantzinger in the Patuxent Woods situation. In fact, it was our organization that uncov-ered his fraud to begin with. Maybe I've mellowed or sold out, but I don't see things as clear-cut as I did then. Billy

Zantzinger provides housing to marginal folks nobody's gonna give a lease to, because they don't have a job or a rent deposit or a bank account or whatever. I learned that you can offer people tons of help and they still can't get out of poverty. Billy rents to those people anyway. Since Patuxent Woods I've met him and talked to him a couple of times, and I feel strange saying this, but Billy Zantzinger is really a very nice man."

·

In Baltimore, seventy miles to the north, friends and acquaintances of Hattie Carroll don't agree. Carroll lived in Cherry Hill, a lower-middle-class black neighborhood, and attended Gillis Memorial Christian Community Church. At the time, the church was at the corner of Mulberry and Calhoun, downtown, but it has since moved to Park Hill on the city's northwest side. People at the church remember Hattie Carroll as a quiet, well-dressed woman, tall and poised, with good taste in hats. She sang in the church's over-forty-five choir and was a member of the Flower Guild, which does floral displays for the altar and other projects of church beautification. Away from work, at least, Hattie Carroll seems not to have fit the picture of the lowly person Dylan described. Few people I talked to at the church knew that her death had been the subject of a widely played protest song.

I stopped by the church on a Wednesday, just as the noon service ended. The minister, the Reverend Dr. Theodore C. Jackson, Jr., was making some final prayerful exhortations, boosted by an organ's repeated chords. In the parish hall, still glowing from his preaching, he told me that he had been a student away at seminary when Hattie Carroll died. Then he introduced me to two longtime parishioners, Dorothy Johnson and Mildred Jessup. The first wore a hat

of black mesh material in a broad-brimmed Stetson shape
and an ankle-length dress appliquéd with lighter patterns
like stylized leaves, and the second wore a white blouse and
tan slacks. Both are themselves preachers—the Reverend
Johnson for thirty years, and the Reverend Jessup for
twenty-eight. Both knew Hattie Carroll. They sat with me
for a while in the church's library and talked. "I remember
that Hattie went to work at the hotel that day, and later
word came back that she'd been struck with a cane," said
Reverend Johnson. "And right after that we heard that she
had died. Everybody in the church was very upset. It was
a terrible blow. She had a huge funeral, people filling the
church to the doors and hundreds more standing on the
street. A sad, sad day."

"I wonder what kind of respect did that man have for
people? What kind of respect did he have for ladies?" asked
Reverend Jessup. "He wasn't thinking about people at all.
He was acting under the slave mentality."

"Hattie's family suffered so, her children, after she died,"
said Reverend Johnson. "They don't go to this church anymore. Four of them, I think, became Muslims. One daughter
ended up in a mental institution. But whatever you cause by
word and by deed, it's all comin' back to you."

"If I was that man's nurse—I used to be a nurse at Johns
Hopkins—I would give him so much prayer to think
about that he'd be miserable," said Reverend Jessup.

I asked the reverends if they thought God would forgive
Zantzinger.

"You see, you are not your own," Reverend Johnson
said. "You belong to God. God gives you agape love—deep,
unconditional, fatherly love. And with God all things are
possible. Didn't he forgive Peter, who denied him three
times? Now, if the man who killed Hattie Carroll is willing
to repent, and if he is really godly sorry for what he did—and

God knows if you are truly godly sorry—I know God will forgive."

"How about you?" I asked. "Could you forgive him?"

"Yes, I believe I could," said Reverend Johnson. "I've forgiven people that did worse than he's done."

"For myself, I don't know about that," said Reverend Jessup. "Things may be possible for God that are not possible for me. But I will tell you one thing. Because of what happened to Hattie Carroll, I have a phobia about canes to this day. I don't like to even see 'em, and I can't stand when people be foolin' with 'em. Just don't be bringin' no canes around me."

According to press accounts of Zantzinger's trial, he and his wife arrived at the ball, a charity event called the Spinsters' Ball, at the Emerson Hotel on Friday evening, February 8, 1963. He was in top hat, white tie, and tails, attire with which a cane is optional. Unlike other guests, Zantzinger didn't check his cane at the door because, as he said, "I was having lots of fun with it, tapping everybody." Tapping turned to hitting; a bellboy named George Gessell said Zantzinger struck him on the arm, and a waitress named Ethel Hill said Zantzinger argued with her and struck her several times across the buttocks. At about 1:30 a.m., he ordered a drink from the bar from Hattie Carroll, one of the barmaids. When she didn't bring it immediately, he cursed at her. Carroll replied, "I'm hurrying as fast as I can." Zantzinger said, "I don't have to take that kind of shit off a nigger," and struck her on the shoulder with the cane. Soon after, Hattie Carroll said, "I feel deathly ill, that man has upset me so." She then collapsed and was taken to the hospital.

"What makes it hard to bear was that no one at the party challenged him, no one stopped him," Reverend Jessup said. "He was bold enough to behave like this in the presence of many people, and not one of them intervened. Maybe they had connections to him, maybe they came for business, or their hands were tied by who he was. But not one of those people stood up for her."

"Can you imagine waking up from a drunk to find out you'd done something like that?" asked Bobby Phelps, a friend of Zantzinger's since childhood. He and I were talking on the front porch of the post office in Mount Victoria, a hamlet just up the road from Zantzinger's old farm. "I'd've probably blown my brains out if it had been me," Phelps said. "And what I really can't understand is, when Billy started getting crazy at the party, why somebody didn't just kick his ass for him and throw him out on his ear.

"You think about it and you feel bad for everyone. Billy is somebody I would trust with my life. Billy didn't hate black people—he used to set with them here in my bar and drink with them. A colored woman that used to work for the Zantzingers told me that Mr. Zantzinger—Billy's father— was pacing the floor and saying, 'How could my boy have done such a thing?' His parents were just devastated. What a hell of a sad thing that was, that Hattie Carroll killing. You look back and wonder, 'How in hell did that all happen?' "

• •

Zantzinger was sentenced in the Hattie Carroll killing on August 28, 1963. As it happened, that was the day of the March on Washington, when Martin Luther King, Jr., delivered his "I Have a Dream" speech. *The New York Times*, *The Washington Post*, and *The Baltimore Sun* all ran stories about the sentencing; the *Times* gave it a short, single-column write-up on page 15; the stories in the *Post* and the *Sun* were not much longer. None mentioned that anybody objected to the lightness of the sentence.

All three papers devoted pages and pages to the march;

and it is striking, to a reader with the perspective of four decades, how blind (for want of a better word) the coverage in all three papers was. What comes through in the stories about the march is a vast relief—shared, presumably, by the reporters, the papers' management, and their readership—that the 200,000-plus assembled Negroes hadn't burned Washington to the ground. All three papers used the adjective "orderly" in their headlines; all reported prominently on President Kennedy's praise for the marchers' politeness and decorum. The *Post* and the *Sun* gave small notice to Dr. King, and less to what he said. Neither made much of the phrase "I have a dream." James Reston of the *Times* understood that he had witnessed a great work of oratory, but even his story veered into brow wiping at the good manners of the Negroes.

Listening to "The Lonesome Death of Hattie Carroll" today, you can hear Dylan shouting against exactly this blindness. The song he wrote took a one-column, under-the-rug story and played it as big as it deserved to be. Dylan's voice sounds so young, hopeful, unjaded, noncommercial—so far from the Victoria's Secret world of today. Even the song's title is well chosen: before I went to Hattie Carroll's church, I hadn't quite understood why her death was "lonesome." But as Reverend Jessup noted, "not one of those people stood up for her"; in a party full of elegant guests, Hattie Carroll was on her own.

If it weren't for TV and videotape, we would not know how powerful the March on Washington, or Dr. King's speech, really was. And if it weren't for Dylan, nothing more would have been said about Hattie Carroll.

September/October 2003

Form and Fungus

Gavin McIntyre, the co-inventor of a process that grows all-natural substitutes for plastic from the tissue of mushrooms, holds a pen or pencil in an unusual way. Gripping it between two fingers of his right hand, he moves his arm across the paper so that his wrist grazes the inscribed line; because of this, he uses pens with ink that doesn't smear. When he draws an explanatory diagram of the chitin molecule—chitin is the principal component of mycelium, the white, rootlike vegetative structure of fungi—he bends over his work, then looks up earnestly to see if his hearer has understood. The gesture makes him appear younger than his age, which is twenty-eight. He wears glasses and has straight black hair, dark eyes, and several piercings, with studs in his lip and ears.

The other co-inventor, Eben Bayer, won't be twenty-eight until June. Bayer is almost six foot five and often assumes the benign expression of a large and friendly older brother. His hair is brown, short, and spiky, his face is long, and his self-effacing manner hides the grand ambitions that people who come from small towns (Bayer grew up in South Royalton, in central Vermont) sometimes have. When he says, of the company that he and McIntyre founded, "We want to be the Dow or DuPont of this century," he is serious. He is their company's CEO, McIntyre its chief scientist. People with money and influence have bet that they will succeed.

Not long ago, McIntyre and Bayer and I sat and talked in the conference room of their thirty-two-thousand-square-foot factory, in Green Island, New York. They have been friends ever since they met in a design class at Rensselaer Polytechnic Institute, in nearby Troy, during the fall semester of their sophomore year, almost nine years ago. During our conversation, they leaned back and forth and sideways in the room's flexible ergonomic chairs, meanwhile tapping their iPhones to send and receive texts and e-mails to and from many people, including each other. McIntyre was wearing running shoes, jeans, a plaid shirt, and a forest-green pullover, and Bayer approximately the same. As they talked about their invention, they mentioned Burt Swersey, the teacher at RPI who became their mentor and adviser.

I said that when I had talked to Swersey a few days before, I had told him of an invention of my own—a device to remove plastic bags from trees, which my friend Tim McClelland and I patented in 1996. Swersey had reacted to my small boast with scorn, saying, in so many words, that it was ridiculous to focus on annoyances like plastic bags in trees when humanity had far worse problems. McIntyre and Bayer both laughed. "Burt was always telling me my inventions sucked!" Bayer said. "And when I came up with an invention he liked he would only ask how I was going to make it better. If I came in with a cure for cancer, Burt would've said, 'Okay, but what about HIV?'"

••

A real, serious problem that humanity has right now is Styrofoam. If the name is used accurately, it applies only to the foamed, extruded polystyrene product patented by Dow Chemical in 1944. Dow's Styrofoam is blue and serves mainly as a building insulation. More commonly, however, Styrofoam is the name people give to the white foamed polystyrene from which packing peanuts and coffee cups and fast-food clamshells are made. In widespread commercial use since the 1950s, Styrofoam is now everywhere. After Hurricane Sandy, its clumps and crumbs covered beaches along the Atlantic Coast like drifts of dirty snow.

Pieces of Styrofoam swirl in the trash gyres in the Pacific Ocean and litter the world's highways and accumulate in the digestive systems of animals and take up space in waste dumps; to reduce New York City's landfills, Mayor Bloomberg recently proposed a ban on the commercial use of Styrofoam containers. Foamed polystyrene breaks down extremely slowly, in time spans no one is sure of, and a major chemical it breaks down to is styrene, listed as a carcinogen in the 2011 toxicology report issued by the National Institutes of Health.

The Dow chemist who invented Styrofoam, O. Ray McIntire, made it by accident while looking for a substitute for rubber insulation. Many plastics were invented to imitate natural substances, like rubber, wood, bone, silk, hemp, or ivory.

Bayer and McIntyre's invention, in postmodern fashion, creates natural substances that imitate plastics. The packing material made by their factory takes a substrate of agricultural waste, like chopped-up cornstalks and husks; steam-pasteurizes it; adds trace nutrients and a small amount of water; injects the mixture with pellets of mycelium; puts it in a mold shaped like a piece of packing that protects a product during shipping; and sets the mold on a rack in the dark. Four days later, the mycelium has grown throughout the substrate into the shape of the mold, producing a material almost indistinguishable from Styrofoam in form, function, and cost. An application of heat kills the mycelium and stops the growth. When broken up and thrown into a compost pile, the packing material biodegrades in about a month.

The name of the company is Ecovative Design, LLC. "Ecovative" is pronounced with the accent on the first syllable, like "innovative," and the first *e* is long. I found it hard to get the hang of pronouncing the name, and for a while I thought that Bayer and McIntyre should look for a simpler one. But after talking a lot about the company with its principals and employees, almost all of whom are under thirty, I got to like "Ecovative" because of the way they said it. The people who work for the company are devotees of it, and of larger causes. Some employees took vacation days to participate in Occupy Wall Street; two of them were arrested there.

Founded six years ago, the company has doubled in size every year and now employs about sixty people at the Green Island factory. Last June, Ecovative licensed its process for making mycelium-based packing material to Sealed Air, a $7.6 billion international packaging company best known for Bubble Wrap. Sealed Air is building a factory to manufacture Ecovative packaging products in the Midwest. The products can be made almost anywhere, with local agricultural wastes and minimal use of energy. Ecovative's eventual goal is to displace plastics all over the world.

••

Kathleen and Gary "Mac" McIntyre, Gavin's parents, have spent most of their careers working for Brookhaven National Laboratory, on Long Island. Mac is a mechanical engineer who designs and sometimes also makes parts for

Brookhaven's heavy-ion collider and other experimental apparatus. Kathleen, whose degrees are in radiation science and biology, has held a variety of jobs at the laboratory. She is now the operations manager for its Radiological Assistance Program. Gavin was a good student and an Eagle Scout, and he picked up a wide knowledge of science and engineering from his parents. Starting in high school, he did intern jobs at Brookhaven. By the time he was twenty, he was working on accelerator optics, helping to design programs for the focusing and steering of particle beams.

Gavin went to Longwood High School, near Yaphank, Long Island, which has almost three thousand students and seven hundred or more in a graduating class. Eben, in rural Vermont, attended school in a one-story building where the kindergarten was at one end and the high school classrooms at the other. Eben's mother, Robin Dutcher, is a writer and publicist. From 1997 to 2003, she was the editor of Steerforth Press, a publishing house in South Royalton. His father, Todd Bayer, was a maple-sugar farmer with a 145-acre sugar bush. After Eben's parents divorced, when he was ten, he divided his time between the maple-sugar farm and his mother's apartment in town.

Todd Bayer is now seventy-eight, with the upright frame of a young man and a full white mustache and head of hair. He still lives on the farm, though he no longer makes syrup commercially. Eben was a strong kid who could do heavy farmwork with his dad—haying, logging, splitting firewood, and constructing a sugarhouse out of salvaged parts and recycled metal. To boil the sap, Todd enlisted his help in assembling a complicated wood-chip gasification burner that attained temperatures of two thousand degrees and required care so that the smokestack wouldn't set the roof on fire.

Ranks of maple trees rise on the rocky hillsides above

the farm. In early spring, Todd and Eben would tap several thousand of the best trees and connect them to a vat in the sugarhouse by PVC tubes in a far-flung network along the steep ground. "It's quite a job to get over the sugar bush on snowshoes twice a day, checking for leaks," Todd told me when I visited. "No one was faster or better at that than Eben." Another of Eben's chores was to move the wood chips to the burner from an open bunker made of telephone-pole sections and chicken wire. Though covered with a tarp, the pile of chips sometimes got wet and sprouted mushrooms. Eben noticed how the fine white fabric of their mycelium sometimes grew through the pile so tenaciously that big bunches of chips stuck together in a single clump when he lifted them with a pitchfork.

••

Burt Swersey's grandfather Loeb Rosen died in the Triangle Shirtwaist Fire, in lower Manhattan, on March 25, 1911. The story of that disaster remained current in the family. After getting a degree in mechanical engineering from Cornell, in 1959, Swersey invented a superaccurate scale to monitor the progress of burn victims. He made other inventions in the medical field, created and sold several medical-equipment companies, and in his fifties moved on to other enterprises (farming, running a plant nursery). He is seventy-six years old and has been teaching at RPI for twenty-three years. Swersey's face is particularly well adapted to register eureka moments: his dark eyebrows shoot up, his eyelids widen in delight, and the many worry lines around his eyes smooth out.

One of the classes that Swersey teaches is called Inventor's Studio. In it he leads students toward making inventions and, eventually, building companies with them. When Eben and Gavin took the class in the fall term of their senior year, neither came up with anything very workable at first. Gavin's idea for a car-exhaust attachment that would burn off emissions with charged plasma was ingenious but probably unsafe. ("Basically, you'd be driving around with a lightning bolt in your tailpipe," Gavin says.) Eben's idea for a no-moving-parts turbine that could generate electricity in high winds by means of sound did not impress Swersey at all. "He was coming up with cockamamie wind generators that would only work in hurricanes, different ways of saving energy with window sealant—just nonsense," Swersey said.

Toward the end of the semester, Eben thought of a previous RPI class, in which he had been given the problem of making insulation panels out of a mineral called perlite. The difficulty with perlite is that it's loose, like handfuls of popped popcorn, and tends to settle. Remembering what the mycelium had done in the wood-chip pile, Eben had ordered a grow-it-yourself mushroom kit while he was home during a break. He took the mushroom spores the kit contained, combined them with water and nutrients in a glass jar, added some perlite, and put the jar in the basement. When he checked a few days later, the jar held a solid white disk of perlite knit together by mycelium strands.

With not much else to show for the semester of Inventor's Studio, Eben brought the perlite disk to class. "He takes this thing out of his pocket," Swersey recalled, "and it's white, this amazing piece of insulation that had been *grown*, without hydrocarbons, with almost no energy used. The stuff could be made with almost any waste materials—rice husks, cotton wastes, stuff farmers throw away, stuff they have no market for—and it wouldn't take away from anybody's food supply, and it could be made anywhere from local materials, so you could cut down on transportation costs. And it would be completely biodegradable! What more could you want?"

Swersey knew that Eben and Gavin had been talking about starting a company. He told them to take his course again the following semester. They wouldn't have to come to class, just work on this invention and on starting a business around it. He would oversee, and put them in touch with a patent attorney. At the end of that school year, during a reception for the new graduates of the School of Engineering, Swersey gathered Eben and Gavin and their parents and hugged them all together and said, "We have to support these kids."

••

In the Ecovative conference room, Eben was leaning in one direction in his flexible ergonomic chair and Gavin in another, each meanwhile looking at his iPhone out of the corner of his eye. I asked what they had done after graduation.

Eben said, "I went home to Vermont. But Burt kept calling me, saying I had to come back and work on our invention, because it couldn't wait. He said we had to jump with both feet. I forget how many times he called. One time, I was out in the yard with my girlfriend and I wanted to throw the phone."

Gavin: "We were thinking we would start the jobs we'd been offered and work on the invention in our spare time. But Burt said that wouldn't be enough."

(Swersey: "I told them I would take money out of my IRA and invest it with them if they would come back to Troy and use the start-up facilities at RPI and devote themselves to their invention and their business full-time. Also, that summer they won a fifteen-thousand-dollar grant from the National Collegiate Inventors and Innovators Alliance, which I'm a member of. Now they couldn't refuse.")

Eben: "So Burt persuaded us. I had a defense-industry

job, at Applied Research Associates, in Vermont, and I went in on my first day and said I wasn't going to be taking it, and Gavin turned down his job at Brookhaven. We moved back and got an apartment in Troy. We figured we had about three months of money."

Gavin: "RPI gave us free space on the ground floor of a building they called the Incubator, which was for students and recent graduates starting businesses. At first, we had no idea what we were doing."

Eben: "We were experimenting with all kinds of materials to use for the substrates. We set stuff on fire—"

Gavin: "I wanted to sterilize a fifty-five-gallon steel drum so we could keep some materials in it. I poured some isopropyl alcohol all around on the surface of the inside and tossed in a match, and nothing happened, so I looked in, and—*poof!* The flame took off my eyebrows and scorched the front part of my hair to ash. I thought I might have a burn, but I sat for a while with a bag of frozen peas on my forehead and I was okay."

Eben: "We tried all kinds of substrates—lint from a clothes dryer, Jell-O, lobster shells (those smelled so disgusting our interns made us promise never to do it again), even hair that we got from Sam Harrington, the first RPI graduate we hired. He had long hair then. If it worked, we were going to call the product Hairsulate."

Gavin: "It was an iterative process, very Edisonian."

Eben: "We used a drying oven with aluminum flashing and it caught fire all the time and set off the fire alarms."

Gavin: "The first time or two, we said, 'Sorry, we were microwaving some popcorn.' But there were some awful smells. People caught on."

Eben: "The Fire Department was coming about twice a month. Everybody in the building would have to troop down to the parking lot, and we became kind of unpopular. But, you know, a lot of the other businesses in the Incubator were Internet start-ups."

I pointed out that he seemed to say "Internet start-ups" with disdain.

"All you need to be an Internet start-up is a desk, an Internet connection, a couple of beanbag chairs, and some cases of Red Bull," Gavin said.

"Internet start-ups are great," Eben said. "But they're not, you know, *making* anything."

••

Herbert Henry Dow, the founder of the Dow Chemical Company, went to the Case School of Applied Science (now part of Case Western Reserve University), in Cleveland, Ohio, and started his first chemical company in 1889, when he was twenty-three. Dow was fascinated with brine, and with the vast sea of it that underlies Ohio and Michigan. His first patent was for a means of extracting bromine from brine. Dow Chemical, which he founded in 1897, at first sold mainly bromine, bleach, and other chemical substances derived from brine.

According to *Growth Company: Dow Chemical's First Century*, by E. N. Brandt, the company got into plastics in the 1930s. Willard Dow, who took over when his father died, wanted his chemists to come up with new uses for ethylene, a gas with many applications, which Dow was producing in abundance at a new factory. Robert R. Dreisbach, "one of the most eccentric persons who ever worked for Dow," proposed combining ethylene with benzene, a liquid obtained from coal tar, to make ethylbenzene. That chemical could then be put through another process to produce a monomer called styrene, from which many plastics could be made. The idea proved feasible, but Willard Dow decided against pursuing it.

The dedication of Robert Dreisbach and other Dow employees who believed in styrene kept that project alive, more or less secretly, despite the company's determination to cancel it. At a Dow facility in Michigan, there were hundreds of steel drums of styrene sitting in a field and threatening to explode in the sun; they had to be hosed down regularly, and nobody knew what to do with them. Then the Second World War began. The Japanese invaded Southeast Asia, and America lost its main source of natural rubber. The most practical way to make artificial rubber involved combining styrene with butadiene; the need for artificial rubber lifted styrene to the status of a vital war material. Dow was the only American company making it. Production of both chemicals increased gigantically, Dow built styrene plants all over the country and in Canada, and Dreisbach and the other original supporters of styrene at the company were heroes.

Styrene is called a monomer because its molecule is a basic building block from which more complex molecules—polymers—can be made. Polystyrene, a polymer of styrene, is one of the main plastics of the world. Like almost all plastics, polystyrene is a hydrocarbon derived mainly from oil or natural gas. Through reactions induced by combining chemicals under differing conditions of temperature, pressure, and catalysis (high school chemistry, don't fail me now), hydrocarbon molecules can be transformed into a great variety of substances that did not exist before. As Ecovative's boosters point out, plastics manufacturing takes hydrocarbons that the earth required sixty-five million years or more to create, transforms them in an instant or two of chemical reaction, and produces materials that may still be around sixty-five million years from now.

People did not give much thought to that during the war. The war weaponized plastics, in a sense; many of their first

uses were military. When O. Ray McIntire foamed polystyrene with a gas under pressure and created a solid—
Styrofoam—that was 95 percent air, he gave the navy and
the coast guard a new flotation material that quickly saw
use in boats and life rafts. Other inventors adapted his process to make containers and packaging.

The word "polymer" has its origins in chemistry. It
comes from two Greek words, "many" and "part." A polymer is a compound or a combination of compounds con-
sisting of structural units (molecules of styrene, for example)
that repeat. The endless variability of plastic polymers has
been a wizard's wand. They are like infinitely manipulable
Legos that can be put together to make almost anything—
but then are difficult or impossible to take apart. Herbert
Henry Dow based his company and his future on an insight he had as a young man, when he guessed that the
bitter taste of brine from an Ohio well indicated bromine.
Eben Bayer's inspiration of the wood-chip pile, the source
of future inventions and industry, saw the engineering
possibilities of a living polymer, fungal mycelium.

• •

Instead of hunting for venture capital, Eben and Gavin
financed their company at first by winning grants and com-
petitions. They were calling the company Greensulate then,
because they were concentrating on a promising insulation
panel that the National Institute of Standards and Technology, in Gaithersburg, Maryland, had let them test in its labs.
Greensulate had performed better than Styrofoam as a fire
retardant and only 15 percent less efficiently as an insulator.
(To compensate, they made the Greensulate panel 15 percent
thicker.) In November 2007, they won a $5,000 engineer-
ing competition in Seattle, and in December they came in
first in an international competition for environmental

entrepreneurship hosted by the business school of Oxford University.

They were still in their ground-floor offices in the Incubator, still proceeding by Edisonian hit-or-miss. The Oxford competition, with a $20,500 first prize, got the attention of the Albany *Times Union*. Other papers in the region had also noticed them. Sue Van Hook, a senior teaching associate in biology and natural sciences at Skidmore College, in Saratoga Springs, saw one of the articles and called them on the phone.

Van Hook is a tall, slim woman in her fifties, with straight blond hair and eyes as blue as Sinatra's. She taught at Skidmore for eighteen years. When studying for her degree in botany at Humboldt State University, in California, she took a course in mycology—the study of mushrooms—and was smitten. She wrote her graduate thesis on macrofungi and has been studying mushrooms in the field and under microscopes ever since. "That first phone call, Eben and I talked for two hours," she told me recently. "I asked if he or Gavin knew anything about fungi, and he said, 'Not that much.' I told him that I felt the universe had been directing me to change my life. Skidmore had cut fungi out of the curriculum, and at a Dreaming with the Dead workshop in '05 I had received a message: 'Life is mushrooming.' I was testing him to see how he would react. I told him what had happened the night before—I had seen a milk snake doing a dance of death beside a road near my house, and when I checked again the snake was curled in the shape of a heart. This was a sign that I should do what I loved. Eben listened, and totally got what I was saying. That's when I knew I could work with him. I asked him, 'Can we get married?'"

Soon after this conversation, Van Hook started as an unpaid mycological consultant with the company. She led mushroom-collecting hikes in nearby forests, giving Gavin and Eben and others an idea of the fungal intelligence running through nature, so the company would be grounded in Earth energy and not just in superfungi that could be used for the product. The Incubator offices were a chaos of airborne spores and dust particles; she taught aseptic techniques to prevent contamination of test samples. In closeup detail, she took everybody through fungal biology. Fungi are plantlike organisms that also resemble animals—they don't make their own food by photosynthesis, as plants do, but live by digesting organic matter. The mycelium, the basis for all of Ecovative's manufacturing processes, is the part that does the digesting.

Mycelium consists of threadlike cells called hyphae. These link to one another in various configurations, and the tips of the hyphae liberate enzymes that digest the food sources in the host, which can be dead or living matter. (Certain fungi feed differently, establishing symbiotic relationships with roots of other plants, usually trees.) Mycelium is considered a polymer because of the hyphae, which repeat in the mycelium's structure just as styrene molecules repeat in polystyrene. Hyphae can be of three kinds—structural, binding, or generative. Ecovative is most interested in the first two. Although hyphae grow from spores, strands of hyphae may be taken from live mycelium, like plant cuttings, and will continue to grow in a new place under proper conditions. Thus Ecovative's manufacturing processes can occur without the involvement of spores, which is important, because people don't want to buy products that might contain spores.

Certain mushrooms are better than others for Ecovative's purposes, and a very few are ideal. Van Hook went on wide-ranging mushroom hunts collecting new species for the company's archives. At Skidmore's bio labs, she and her students spent hours cataloging the finds and recording their characteristics. (Skidmore was as enthusiastic about Eben and Gavin's invention as RPI had been.) A useful kind of mycelium came from a group of fungi called polypores, which grow mostly on wood. The mycelium of polypores has extrastrong hyphae, as demonstrated by how difficult it is to pull a hard polypore like chicken of the woods off the trunk of a tree. These hyphae can knit a molded piece of substrate solidly together; in general, a single cubic inch of substrate contains eight miles of mycelium.

On her best searches Van Hook began by opening herself to messages she was receiving from her surroundings and letting them lead her, and on one outstanding afternoon in the woods she went from revelation to revelation until she saw before her the polypore that became one of the company's first workhorses. When she found it, she knelt down and thanked the universe for leading her to it. This polypore is a local conk—a thick, tough kind of polypore—but its name is proprietary information.

At fifty-five, she was able to retire from Skidmore, and she began to work for Ecovative full-time as its chief mycologist (a salaried position). She sometimes gives lectures about the company; I went to one last February at Cooper Union, in Manhattan. The lecture room was packed. Students and older people, many of them amateur mycologists, filled all the rows and sat in the aisles and stood by the door, where they couldn't see. On a screen she projected the molecular structures of chlorophyll, starch, glucose, cellulose, lignin, and chitin. She said, "I always tell students of engineering and design that they must understand these molecules. These are the materials that nature builds with. For us to have a sustainable planet, we must design and build with these."

• •

The world's biggest competition for CO_2-reducing business plans, the Postcode Lottery Green Challenge, takes place each year in Holland. People outside the environmental field may not have heard of it, but the first prize—€500,000, or about $700,000 dollars—stays in the mind. Finalists make their presentations to an international jury during the PICNIC Festival, a cross-disciplinary conference held in Amsterdam in September. In 2008, after being in business for only about a year, Ecovative sent an entry to the competition, and it made the cut. Eben went to Amsterdam for the presentation, which was to include a speech and PowerPoint display onstage before a thousand attendees. In previous competitions, he and Gavin had always appeared together, but the rules here limited them to a single presenter. Eben had more stage experience, having performed in many plays in high school. He prepared a speech of about ten minutes.

Today, Ecovative often refers those with inquiries about the company to the online video of this speech, along with videos of speeches that both Eben and Gavin have made at TED techno conferences. The speeches serve as founding documents, introductions to the company. Eben's PICNIC presentation came off with an air of easy authority and persuaded the jury. When Burt Swersey received the phone call telling him that Ecovative had won the €500,000, he was teaching a design class. He let out a tremendous yell.

Instead of being sought, venture capital now began to seek Ecovative. Eben and Gavin accepted some investors— the 3M Company, and their alma mater, RPI, among them— and rejected others. More grants and prizes arrived; the annual World Economic Forum at Davos invited Eben to attend. From the offices at the Incubator, Ecovative moved to an eight-thousand-square-foot space at the Green Island industrial park. In the PICNIC speech, Eben had talked only about their insulating material, Greensulate, but after production of those large panels had to be delayed, they decided to shift emphasis temporarily to their packaging product, because its pieces are smaller and easier to make. Steelcase, Inc., an office-furniture company in Grand Rapids, Michigan, came to them for V-shaped blocks to protect the corners of tables in shipment, and for other buffers and inserts. Dell Computers, Crate & Barrel, and Puma athletic gear made similar requests.

Ecovative still uses its original eight thousand square feet at Green Island, but in 2011 it took over a much larger space, just across the parking lot. The new factory is about the size of a big-box store like a Lowe's or a Costco. Steel shelves holding sixty thousand in-progress molds filled with substrate and mycelium ascend to the thirty-five-foot-high ceiling. On some days, there is a smell like cream-of-mushroom soup. In a corner of the building, a sealed-off space called the Dirty Room receives the agricultural wastes and other substrate materials when they come in. Big white nylon bags stand there in rows, filled with chopped-up cornstalks and husks, crushed remains of cotton plants after the cotton has been removed, barley hulls, peanut hulls, buckwheat hulls, milo hulls, hemp pith, rice husks, wheat straw, and ground-up old blue denim. The smell of that room leans you back against a hayrick on an autumn afternoon.

Before the substrate materials leave the Dirty Room, they go through the steam pasteurizer, which eliminates contaminants and spores. Presumably, that piece of machinery makes noise. Otherwise, the factory is quiet. Industrial lights hang overhead, casting a purplish tinge. Young people in sweat clothes go here and there, pushing wheeled racks and carrying clipboards.

••

In the conference room, the messages on Gavin's and Eben's iPhones were becoming importunate, sometimes efflorescing into ringtones. The conference table held a wide assortment of products that Ecovative makes, or plans to. The flexible ergonomic chairs pointed their arms here and there as the young inventors showed me stout packaging blocks, pieces of insulation with velvet-soft surfaces, tough flip-flop sandals, and boards as hard as plywood, all grown from mycelium and agricultural waste. "We think we've found a pretty good polymer," Eben said, glancing at his phone.

My father, who was a chemical engineer at a research lab, used to bring home samples of substances never seen before on the planet—strange milky plastics as brittle as ice or as slick and pulpy as squid. Gavin leaned his flexible chair to show me a wonder that reminded me of those. It was a block about the size of half a stick of butter, lighter than balsa but as hard as pine: a piece of solid mycelium, pure chitin that had been grown from nutrients and without any substrate. He said it had possible applications for aeronautics. I rolled it in my fingers, trying to get a handle on its complete unfamiliarity. He added that chitin is also an excellent insulator and began to explain how he and his colleagues are growing electric circuits on fungal tissue made of the mycelium of household mold.

In the presence of toxic metals, he said, certain molds get around the toxicity by sequestering the metals onto their cell walls. Therefore, you can put tissue taken from the mold into a copper solution, for example, and impregnate the tissue with varying amounts of copper by changing the concentration. In other words, you can make a fungal resistor that can be part of the circuitry in a computer or a cell phone. Then, instead of sending old computers and phones to be taken apart hazardously in the Third World, you can recycle them, with the chitin providing nutrients for new tissue and the metals going back into a solution to be reused.

But now Eben and Gavin's next meeting had arrived—a delegation of Chinese executives and engineers who wanted to license the process for making mushroom packaging. They were waiting in an observant group near the conference-room door. I shook hands with Eben and Gavin and went out, and the Chinese delegation came in.

••

Green Island occupies a fortunate place in the landscape. Ever since the channel on its western side was filled in, it's an island only during extreme high water. On its eastern side, the Hudson River runs just fifty feet behind the high school. The river is tidal all the way from its mouth to here; an incline at Green Island with a cumulative drop of fourteen feet stops the tidal motion from extending farther upstream. When Henry Hudson sailed up the river in 1609, searching for the Northwest Passage, one look at the rapids here told him that this waterway would not be it. A dam has spanned the river from Green Island to Troy since the mid-1800s. In 1922, Henry Ford took advantage of the drop by building a generating station to provide power for a car-parts factory on Green Island. The factory is gone, but the power station is still operating.

The Mohawk River joins the Hudson in numerous branches above the dam, making the Hudson so wide that different parts of it reflect different parts of the sky. Most of the river flows over the dam in a white falls, but about six thousand cubic feet of it go through the turbines every second. The whole generator building hums, and the flat, whorled water slides out the downstream side like a moving sidewalk. Ecovative likes to say that it gets its electricity only from renewable hydropower. The way power flies around the national grid, that might not always be true; in any case, a lot of Ecovative's electricity comes from the turbines at Green Island. Most electric power is generated and consumed almost simultaneously. The river with its wide-screen reflection of sky and clouds is keeping Ecovative's lights on in the moment that it flows past.

Whenever I visit the company, I like to stop first at an abandoned railroad bridge at the north end of Green Island. The branch of the Mohawk that the bridge spans has carved low bluffs from the island's four-hundred-million-year-old shale. The bluffs resemble stacks of very thin reddish-black crêpes. All river confluences are glorious. Canoes full of Iroquois Indians traveled past here, and fur traders, and soldiers, and surveyors for the Erie Canal. The canal turned left near this point, followed the Mohawk's shale valley westward, tapped into the Great Lakes, and made the fortune of New York City. Here, as at all confluences, wildlife congregates. In the early morning, it's an amphitheater of birdsong, while Canada geese add their familiar commotion. So many crows show up in the evenings that they plague the town of Green Island, and the mayor has to scare them away with a blank pistol.

One Wednesday after a meditation here, I crossed the Hudson to Troy and stopped by Burt Swersey's Inventor's Studio class. Rensselaer, the oldest technological research university in the country, overlooks the Hudson from the east. The view from Swersey's classroom windows, however, was of a roof with some crookneck ventilator ducts that rotated back and forth. On the corkboard were pictures of Eben and Gavin, and news stories about them. They are heroes at RPI. The university's president, Dr. Shirley Ann Jackson, often mentions Eben and Gavin in her speeches. She says that they exemplify the best of RPI and the goal that she champions: "Expedite Serendipity."

Swersey began the class by having the students tell what they were working on. A young ROTC cadet who was dressed in camo described his idea for a uniform with built-in tourniquets that would deploy automatically when a soldier was wounded. Other students' ideas had to do with helping the homeless, asthma sufferers, or people with Alzheimer's disease. A student from Kuwait suggested a public-area surveillance device that would detect people with incapacitating depression; then professionals could intervene and stop suicides. Swersey listened, offered a mixture of encouragement and skepticism, and told the students to talk to ordinary citizens to get feedback. "Getting out there and talking to people is absolutely critical," he said. "If you don't get out and talk to people, your grade is going to suffer."

Afterward, when most of the students had left, he was franker with the few who hung around to talk. "You're still not really getting it," he said. "You're thinking in terms of ideas. I don't care about ideas. Find a *problem*, not an idea. Then solve the problem. Somebody had an idea to help stores in India so the food touched by untouchables didn't have to be thrown away. No, leapfrog that problem! Find the real problem! Forget about the thrown-away food— make it possible for the untouchables to be *touchable*! It's all about empathy! Right now you're attempting small things. I want something fantastic. Not something good, not even something great—something fantastic. Find a problem so outrageous in its scope that it's probably impossible. Start on it right away—next class. You have only seven more weeks in the semester."

A young woman named Paula, whose project involved thermoengineering with plots of solar-heated sand, had been arguing with Swersey, but at this she gave in. "Okay, Burt," she said. "Before the next class, I will come up with something impossible."

May 20, 2013

Burt Swersey died in March 2015.

The Unsettling Legacy
of General Shrapnel

Before shrapnel was shrapnel, it was a man. The murderously efficient exploding projectile of that name entered history in 1804 with its first letter capitalized, a reference to its inventor, British artillery officer Henry Shrapnel. Like Colt, Luger, and Kalashnikov, the name Shrapnel came to mean the weapon rather than the man, and people used the word (and the weapon) with no thought for the man. But unlike those others, Shrapnel lost his capital letter and, as lowercase "shrapnel," scattered across the earth with the deadly fragments the word was used to describe, taking on meanings more generic, and perhaps even scarier, than Henry Shrapnel could have foreseen.

I first came across mention of Henry Shrapnel in a windy spot above the city of St. John's, Newfoundland. St. John's has a perfect harbor, which the colonial powers often fought over in past centuries; in the 1760s the British built a fort (now mostly gone) on a high and steep hill at the harbor's mouth. I was walking around the fort site, looking at the historic markers, when I saw one commemorating Lieutenant (later General) Shrapnel, stationed with the Royal Artillery at the fort from 1780 to 1784. The marker included a portrait. The cold North Atlantic stretching away behind it, dotted with an iceberg or two, suggested how far-flung and transitory had been the empire Shrapnel served.

Shrapnel's unremarkable, slightly plump face in its white wig gave no outward sign of the passion that possessed him and that drives so much of modern civilization—I mean the passion for blowing stuff up. He appears to have been an ordinary and proper middle-class person in every way. His father was a clothier, like many Shrapnels before him in the southwestern English county of Wiltshire. Henry was born in 1761, and although the family's youngest son, he inherited the bulk of the estate, due to his brothers' deaths or childlessness. He later said that he went through all his fortune in pursuit of his military experiments. He received his commission in the Royal Artillery at eighteen and spent all his career in the service, some at the artillery school at Woolwich and some at posts including Barbados, Grenada, and Antigua.

According to one account, Shrapnel got the idea for his invention while with British forces under siege by the Spaniards at Gibraltar. He noticed that heavy cannon fire aimed at Spanish troops did not kill many of them, while bursting mortar shells killed more. He reasoned that if he could make a cannonball burst like a mortar shell and do it at a cannon's greater range, he could achieve the effect of massed small-arms fire on troops a cannon shot away. He invented a hollow cannonball stuffed with musket balls and loaded with a powder charge just strong enough to break the cannonball open. Set to a timed fuse, the charge, as he envisioned it, would explode and disperse the musket balls in a cone-shaped spray fifty or seventy-five yards from the target, to which they would continue with killing force derived from the original momentum of the projectile.

Getting the fuse to go off at the right instant was tricky, and there were other problems to be solved as well. For years Shrapnel devoted his free time to perfecting his invention, and eventually he got it to work dependably. In 1802 he demonstrated it before the king and army officers at a firing ground in London. The following year the army's board of ordnance recommended the shell for general use. In 1804 it had a great success in a battle with the Dutch in Suriname, in South America. So awed were the Dutch by the shell's power, the British artillery commander said, they surrendered after the second shot. British artillerists all over soon were reporting favorably on the combat effectiveness of "Shrapnel's shell."

Shrapnel had his most notable triumph in the war against Napoleon. During the fighting in Spain, the French could not understand how they were being hit by British musket balls when British lines were over a mile away. After the Battle of Waterloo, the Duke of Wellington told Shrapnel how important his shell had been to the victory, while Sir George Wood, Wellington's artillery commander, said that without the shell the British probably could not have retaken a key strategic point and "hence on this simple circumstance hinged entirely the turn of the battle." Napoleon had ordered that any unexploded shell found on the battlefield be examined so the French could discover the secret. But during the course of the war they never figured out how the shell worked.

Wellington ordered that news of the shell be kept from the public, to preserve military advantage. Because of this, Shrapnel did not receive recognition he might have gotten otherwise. Later he asked the board of ordnance to reward him for the Shrapnel shell and his other military inventions, saying that he had been working on them independently for twenty-eight years. The board said it was unable to give such rewards, but eventually gave him a small pension. When Shrapnel was almost fifty, he married a woman nineteen years younger than he, and they had two daughters and two sons. He continued to hope for a reward or a title that he could pass on to his descendants. Long after his retirement from active duty, he met King William IV and received the king's praise for his services, along with the king's agreement that Shrapnel would be awarded an honor. The king was ready to make Shrapnel a baronet, but unfortunately the king then died, and the notion was forgotten. Shrapnel got no public commemoration, and almost no notice in history. He died in Southampton in 1842 at the age of eighty, a disappointed man.

The numbers Shrapnel's invention killed during his lifetime were nothing compared to the millions it killed after. At the start of the First World War, the cannons of all the armies fired shells that were refinements on Shrapnel's original design. British field guns used Shrapnel ammunition only. Shrapnel shells caused the majority of artillery-inflicted wounds in that war. With military technology advancing, as it always does, high explosives of more sophisticated chemical composition began to replace gunpowder. Military science discovered that high-explosive projectiles did not need to be stuffed with bullets, because the shattered pieces of metal shell casing that flew through the air when the projectiles exploded did as much damage and more. By the Second World War, all artillery shells were made with high explosives, and shells based on Shrapnel's design had become obsolete.

The word "shrapnel," as a noun, originally meant the shell; then it meant more commonly the bullets dispersed by the shell. This second use was widespread in the First World War. As technology moved on, "shrapnel" came to mean any metal fragment of a bomb, projectile, or mine sent flying by its explosion. In this more general meaning, a not-quite-accurate borrowing from the original, the word

seems destined to last forever. Shrapnel is the nails and
pieces of shaved metal in the bomb of a suicide bomber, and
the deadly cube-shaped metal fragments a tenth of an inch
on a side that advanced metallurgy has designed modern
bomb casings to shatter into. In recent years, U.S. scientists
have built a new high-tech weapon that shoots 20mm air-
burst "smart shells" equipped with laser guidance systems
to steer them around obstacles and kill enemies hiding
behind; the particles the bomblets kill with are called
shrapnel. When combat moves into space, as is expected,
satellite-killing missiles will knock out targets by exploding
near them and hitting them with shrapnel. Human destruc-
tiveness long ago surpassed Shrapnel's nineteenth-century
tinkerer's ingenuity, but apparently it will never get over its
infatuation with his name.

The reason, of course, is poetry. Had the inventor of a
shell like Shrapnel's been Jones or Williams, the language
would not remember. With "shrapnel," it found a miracle
of onomatopoeia: the incoming whistle of the "sh-," the explosion of the "rap-," the death knell of the "-nel." In the
mouth, the word is a minidramatization of what it describes.
It's so satisfactory to say, that it has become a part of many
foreign languages in more or less its English pronunciation;
someday it will be one of those universal words ("e-mail,"
"okay") that are the same all over the world. If you believe in
the devil, the complete poetical aptness of the word "shrapnel" is evidence that he/she has a literary turn of mind.

And if you believe in the soul, what of Shrapnel's? He
was only trying to help. He did his duty, and he went way
beyond it, adding a hard-won invention to the store of
human knowledge in the best traditions of selflessness and
enterprise. Also, he contributed to Napoleon's defeat,
undeniably a good outcome for mankind. Why, then, do
I fear he rests unquietly? I see him in an arid underworld

conversation pit with Molotov (of the cocktail) and Gatling and Uzi and the rest, all of them agitated, all pacing back and forth, ears pricking at the sound of their names echoing from above. Among them Shrapnel is especially jumpy, because he hears his name over and over in contexts of horrible death and suffering. Imagine it sounds something like this: "The children died from the concussion of the blast, and from wounds caused by pieces of [your last name here]."

When British ships attacked Fort McHenry near Baltimore in the War of 1812, they probably used Shrapnel's shells. They also used rockets, another new invention, which they had learned about in India and China. The bombs bursting and rockets glaring that Francis Scott Key wrote about were the latest in weapons technology of the time— appropriately, for a poem that became the anthem of a nation as in love with up-to-date weaponry as ours is. But while our war technology continues to leave all other nations' far behind, the example of Henry Shrapnel might be a cautionary one. Monuments are built to people who eradicate polio or invent the airplane; for achievements like Shrapnel's, no matter how singular, we feel no real gratitude. Success like his, in a larger sense, participates only in human failure. The oblivion into which Shrapnel's countrymen let him fall speaks not just of their negligence but also of their fear and distaste.

September/October 2003

Hogs Wild

Of all the domesticated animals, none become feral more readily, or survive better in the wild, than the hog. Of all the larger animals, none reproduce as quickly and abundantly as the hog. The combination of the first fact with the second means that the number of wild hogs in the United States—maybe four and a half million, maybe five—is unlikely to go down. The wild hog is an infestation machine. The Great Smoky Mountains National Park, in western North Carolina and eastern Tennessee, has today a population of about five hundred wild hogs. Since 1977, when the park began a policy of trying to reduce the number of its hogs, its hog-control officers have removed about ten thousand hogs. When hunted, wild hogs often become nocturnal. They are as smart as, or smarter than, dogs. A study done in South Carolina found that catching wild hogs in traps required about twenty-nine man-hours per hog. Past a certain point, removing hogs is too expensive and hard on the environment to be worthwhile. Like other places (not including some islands) that have wild hogs, the Great Smoky Mountains National Park has no expectation that it will ever get rid of its hogs.

A maker of fences in the nineteenth century advertised

a new kind of fence as being "bull-strong, horse-high, and pig-tight." In fact, as regards pigs, few fences ever are. Pigs root under, wriggle through. They have been getting away since people first domesticated the species *Sus scrofa* in Asia and the Middle East nine thousand to ten thousand years ago. When archaeologists find an ancient pig skull, they try to tell by certain measurements of the upper second molar whether the pig was tame or wild. The original *Sus scrofa*, the Eurasian wild boar, has a longer snout than domestic swine and thus a different spacing of teeth in the jaw. (The wild boar is also taller, narrower, and rangier, with bristly hairs standing up along its spine, and a straight rather than a curly tail.) Often, though, the ancient pig skull has indeterminate, gray-area molar measurements, and it's impossible to tell which side of the fence the pig was on.

In the United States, the wild hogs with the longest pedigree are descended from ones that escaped from Polynesian Islanders who first brought pigs to the Hawaiian Islands in about A.D. 750. This strain eventually reinvigorated itself by crossbreeding with escapees from later Hawaiian settlers; many places in the islands have a vexing wild-pig problem today. The first feral pigs in continental North America deserted from the expedition of Hernando de Soto, the Spanish explorer who crossed the Southeast to beyond the Mississippi River in 1539–42. Wild pigs that got away from Spanish colonists in Florida survived in the woods and swamps so successfully that today some of their descendants represent the only modern examples of old Spanish breeds that long ago disappeared in domestication.

In frontier times, farmers let their hogs run loose, then collected them with the help of dogs on butchering day. Many hogs chose to skip this event, naturally. After America became rich, circa 1890, sportsmen with money imported Eurasian wild boars to stock hunting preserves. When these

animals escaped and crossbred with feral swine, they created a tougher and even better-adapted (some say) feral hog.
The fact that wild swine have been living in America for
centuries does not dissuade wildlife biologists from referring to them as a "nonnative" species. Feral hogs of the
species *Sus scrofa* live on every continent but Antarctica,
and also on many islands and archipelagoes. Except in the
original range of the Eurasian wild boar, feral hogs are nonnative everywhere.

Tame or wild, hogs can eat anything humans can eat,
and plenty more. They find many different environments
congenial. It is perhaps lucky for the planet that hogs have
sebaceous glands that do not produce sweat; consequently,
hogs need someplace cool and wet to wallow when the
weather is hot. This means that very arid regions seem to
be safe from hogs for the time being. The current American style of real estate development—expanding horizon-
tally, taking over rural areas, mallifying farmland, leaving
only the soggy places and creek beds and river margins more
or less the same, and then passing ordinances prohibiting
the discharge of firearms in the new municipalities—suits
the hogs just fine. Plus, once in a while enterprising people
who love to hunt hogs go to a swamp down south, live-trap
a party of hogs, and transport them illegally north to a
woods more convenient to the hog hunters' homes. The
recent arrival of wild-hog populations in previously hog-
free counties in Illinois and Indiana (among other places)
probably came about in just this way, wildlife scientists
believe.

In 1982, eighteen states in the United States had wild
hogs. By 1999, nine more states had reported populations
of them. By 2004, wild hogs could be found in twenty-eight
states; three more have acquired wild hogs since then. States
where there had been hogs all along also saw a sudden

growth in wild-hog numbers beginning in the early 1990s. People who think about wild hogs wonder how far they will expand their range. "The number of states with wild hogs is going to continue to grow," says John J. Mayer, a wild-hog expert and the coauthor of *Wild Pigs in the United States: Their History, Comparative Morphology, and Current Status*, the definitive text. "We're going to wind up with populations in all fifty states eventually."

Well and good, or (more likely) not; but what you really want to know is, "What about Hogzilla?" I understand your concern. The question comes up whenever one mentions the subject of feral hogs. People don't pronounce the name neutrally, either. There's always a pause, a kind of awed emphasis: "But what about this . . . Hog-*zilla*?!" It's a deeply resonant latter-day American name: HOGZILLA. I am going to deal with the Hogzilla question now, so it won't be hanging over us.

Hogzilla is a phenomenon of the Internet, although he would have had a lively career in folklore even if he had existed long before. Hogzilla was a giant hog, said to be a wild hog from the swamps, who was shot and killed in June 2004 on a fish farm/game ranch in south Georgia by an employee of the property named Chris Griffin. Griffin said that he was doing maintenance chores when he saw the beast emerge from the swamp onto the road, and he killed it with a single shot. An Internet photograph of Griffin next to the dead and upside-down-hanging Hogzilla was what caused all the commotion. It was huge. And tusked. And ugly. But the picture looked a little strange, also—possibly faked, though you couldn't be sure—like real hair that happens also to resemble a hairpiece, but, then again, maybe actually *is* a hairpiece . . . Griffin and Ken Holyoak, the property owner, explained in the accompanying story that the hog's meat proved to be unusable, so they buried the

carcass soon after taking the photograph. Later news stories reported that they had put a white cross on the grave.

The subsequent excitement and Internet back-and-forth
can be imagined. Griffin and Holyoak's claim that the hog
had been a thousand pounds and more than twelve feet
long aroused incredulity. In terms of size, hogs are more or
less comparable with humans; a three-hundred-pound hog
is a really big hog. And the fact that the pair had buried it
rubbed people wrong. Wherever I went on my wild-hog
explorations, someone would take me aside and confide,
"If only they hadn't *buried* it. Something about that don't
seem right."

The Hogzilla story, plus photo, happened to hit one of
those deep veins whose existence isn't suspected until it
appears. A minor Hogzilla craze ensued, with invitations
to Griffin to be a guest on the *Tonight Show* with Jay Leno
and on other TV and radio shows, and national news
coverage, and a Hogzilla festival in the fall in the town of
Alapaha, Georgia, near where Hogzilla died. The National
Geographic Channel sent a documentary crew down to
look into the tale. Hogzilla's grave was located, and guys in
biohazard suits unearthed his remains and scientists examined them. They found that the hog had been seven and a
half feet long, not twelve, and eight hundred instead of a
thousand pounds—a big hog, if not quite a Hogzilla.

John J. Mayer, the wild-hog expert, who was also called
in, concluded that the hog had been pen-raised. The hog's
long tusks (in the wild, boars break their tusks fighting
over sows), its weight (that much food simply isn't available
in the wild), and its hooves (their wear indicated a lot of
time spent standing on concrete) contributed to Mayer's
verdict. National Geographic played the story for thrills all
the same, beginning the documentary, "Monsters—they
haunt the dark places of our planet . . . Now a new monster

has emerged from the swamps of Georgia, in the southern U.S." When the documentary aired, last April, it drew the second-largest number of viewers of any program in the channel's history.

After Hogzilla came the predictable imitators. There was Hog Zelda, a huge sow; and the Big Hog, also allegedly feral, in central Florida, which apparently did weigh eleven hundred pounds. It is also sometimes called Hog Kong. A man said he shot it after he found it swimming in one of his stock ponds. John J. Mayer believes that this hog was also pen-raised.

••

Next question: What do wild hogs do that's so bad?

Oh, not much. They just eat the eggs of the sea turtle, an endangered species, on barrier islands off the East Coast, and root up rare and diverse species of plants all over, and contribute to the replacement of those plants by weedy, invasive species, and promote erosion, and undermine road-beds and bridges with their rooting, and push expensive horses away from food stations in pastures in Georgia, and inflict tusk marks on the legs of these horses, and eat eggs of game birds like quail and grouse, and run off game species like deer and wild turkeys, and eat food plots planted specially for those animals, and root up the hurricane levee in Bayou Sauvage, Louisiana, that kept Lake Pontchartrain from flooding the eastern part of New Orleans, and chase a woman in Itasca, Texas, and root up lawns of condominiums in Silicon Valley, and kill lambs and calves, and eat them so thoroughly that no evidence of the attack can be found.

And eat red-cheeked salamanders and short-tailed shrews and red-back voles and other dwellers in the leaf litter in the Great Smoky Mountains, and destroy a yard that had previously won two "Yard of the Month" awards on Robins Air Force Base, in central Georgia, and knock over glass patio tables in suburban Houston, and muddy pristine brook-trout streams by wallowing in them, and play hell with native flora and fauna in Hawaii, and contribute to the near extinction of the island fox on Santa Cruz Island off the coast of California, and root up American Indian historic sites and burial grounds, and root up a replanting of native vegetation along the banks of the Sacramento River, and root up peanut fields in Georgia, and root up sweet potato fields in Texas, and dig big holes by rooting in wheat fields irrigated by motorized central-pivot irrigation pipes, and, as the nine-hundred-foot-long pipe advances automatically on its wheeled supports, one set of wheels hangs up in a hog-rooted hole, and meanwhile the rest of the pipe keeps on going and begins to pivot around the stuck wheels, and it continues and continues on its hog-altered course until the whole $75,000 system is hopelessly pretzeled and ruined.

Oh, them hogs. Noses with bodies and legs appendaged, bristled vacuum-cleaner bags attached to snouts, is what they are. The hogs' noses actually have a special bone in them called the nasal sesamoid bone, which is connected to the skull only by cartilage and which provides extra rooting support for the rhinarial disk—the pig's nose, the business end, with its two hypersentient, staring nostril holes. Wild pigs' noses soon become callused from rooting, and are generally muddy. Sometimes a pig will stop in the middle of rooting and raise its head and blow dirt out its nose. Pigs have a powerful and highly nuanced sense of smell. They can detect scent coming from as far away as seven miles cross-country and from twenty-five feet underground.

To reach islands, wild hogs have been known to cross

tracts of open ocean as much as two miles wide. They are very good at swimming, a skill their environment often requires. Floods seldom inconvenience them seriously. In Bayou Sauvage, the New Orleans wildlife refuge, wild hogs swam to high ground after the hurricane and came through fine. Shelley Stiaes, operations specialist at the refuge, says law-enforcement people who patrolled there after the hurricane dispatched a lot of hogs. "We've still got plenty of them, though," she says. "They could've shot a hundred without making a dent in how many hogs we've got here."

And the diseases! The parasites! A study done in 1982 found that wild hogs in the Southeast hosted thirty-two parasite species, from scabies to hog lice and various ticks, plus liver flukes, kidney worms, lungworms, tapeworms, and more. An official guide to wildlife diseases notes that many of these parasites are little threat to humans, though they do surprise hunters sometimes when they clean and dress the hogs and see what's inside. Among the most common wild-hog diseases are the pseudorabies virus, which causes abortions in adult sows and fever and death in piglets, and swine brucellosis, which also causes abortions, and also infertility and other reproductive symptoms. Oddly, the diseases wild swine carry don't seem to slow them down much but would be catastrophic if passed on to domestic swine.

In the interests of science, civilization, and good order, an elite team of veterinarians in Athens, Georgia, keeps tabs on the hogs. These veterinarians work for the Southeastern Cooperative Wildlife Disease Study—commonly known by its acronym, SCWDS, pronounced "*skwid*-is"—part of the University of Georgia College of Veterinary Medicine. Sixteen states, most of them in the Southeast, fund the cooperative, but it studies diseases of wildlife all over the United States, paying special attention to diseases that also affect domestic animals, and to ones like West Nile virus and avian influenza that could be passed on to humans. SCWDS is like the Centers for Disease Control, only for wildlife. Its vets are unusually cool people. Many are PhDs who research and write scientific papers at the top of their fields, yet are also able to spend weeks at a time in disagreeable near-wilderness swamps trapping and taking nasal swabs, blood, and tissue samples from hogs.

One day, I went to Athens and met Joe Corn, a senior wildlife biologist for SCWDS, who has trapped and studied thousands of wild hogs. Joe Corn is tall and lean, in his late forties, with curly dark hair and blue eyes that sometimes betray an unscientific amusement at the hogginess of wild hogs. For example, he was describing a type of wire pen used in trapping hogs, and he said that the pen had no ceiling and was of a height that one could lean over and look down at the hogs; but, he added, one should never do that. I asked why, and he said, "Because they'll jump up and bite your face." And that look—amusement combined with a sort of admiration—lit his eyes.

As disease vectors, wild hogs pose a greater danger if you don't know where they are. To counter this, SCWDS periodically does surveys of wild-hog populations nationwide and publishes maps with the results. Joe Corn unrolled two of these maps on his desk. Both were of the continental United States, with insets for Alaska, Hawaii, and territorial islands. The first map, dated 1982, showed the feral-hog population centered in the Southeast and Texas, with a modest population in California and a few smaller groupings elsewhere. The latest map, current to 2004, portrayed a dramatically expanded situation. Now the lower South was wild-hog-positive from the Rio Grande in West Texas to the coast of the Carolinas, with only a few small blank areas indicating counties still hog-free. Above that, in the next tier of states northward, wild-hog counties were not as tightly massed, though still plentiful. Even farther north, in mostly hog-free states, counties shaded to show the presence of wild hogs appeared scattered but spreading, like burnings downwind of a forest fire. Joe Corn said that the SCWDS maps would be vital in the event of a disease outbreak carried or amplified by wild hogs.

As I leaned over the map and studied it with Joe Corn, suddenly my attention shifted. This map, with its intricate little counties and occasional whole states shaded green to highlight the potential disease-vector threat of wild hogs, reminded me of the red state–blue state map of America. At first glance, the states that voted for George Bush in 2004 and the states marked on this map as having feral hogs seemed to be one and the same. I mentioned this oddity to Joe Corn, who, scientist-like, declined to comment beyond the area of his expertise.

Afterward, I could not get this strange correspondence out of my mind. I compiled '04 red state–blue state data and matched it with SCWDS hog-population information on the map of that year. I found my first impression to be essentially correct. The presence of feral hogs in a state is a strong indicator of its support for Bush in '04. Twenty-three of the twenty-eight states with feral hogs voted for Bush. That's more than four-fifths; states that went for Kerry, by contrast, were feral-hog states less than a fifth of the time.

The solidly feral-hog South was, of course, solidly for Bush. The small islands there without wild hogs—Little Rock, Raleigh–Durham—voted for Kerry. Democrats who predicted a Kerry win in Florida in '04 might have been less confident had they known that all of Florida's sixty-seven counties, even its urban ones, have feral hogs. Texas, a gimme for Bush, is the state in the union with the most feral hogs. Estimates of the feral-hog population in Texas are more than a million and a half, though nobody knows for sure. To go along with its high feral-hog numbers, Texas produced more than four and a half million votes for Bush in '04, the second-largest total of any state. All the north-eastern states voted for Kerry. None of the northeastern states have feral hogs—with one exception. That is New Hampshire, where Eurasian wild boars escaped from a game preserve years ago and now are on the loose in the mountains of Sullivan County, between Newport and Lebanon. Is it merely coincidence that New Hampshire (Kerry 50 percent, Bush 49 percent) is the northeastern state Bush came closest to winning?

Ohio, Indiana, and Illinois are among the states that have acquired feral-hog populations since 1982. Of the twenty counties (all rural) that have feral hogs in those states, seventeen voted for Bush in '04. Ohio and Indiana both have more feral-hog counties than Illinois; Bush won Ohio and Indiana, lost Illinois.

A prominent feature of the red state–blue state map is the sweep of red coming up from Texas and the South through the center of the country. Experts say that feral hogs are starting to do the same. They have increased their numbers in Oklahoma and appeared in counties in Kansas and Nebraska, where they weren't previously. An AP news story from last year described packs of wild pigs tearing up yards and destroying crops in Sumner County, in south-central Kansas. People there speculated that the pigs were formerly domestic animals that had been turned loose when hog prices crashed some years before. Sumner County pre-ferred Bush to Kerry in '04 by a margin of 68 percent to 31 percent.

California, an important blue state, seems to go against the pattern, because fifty-seven of its fifty-eight counties have feral hogs. However, one must look below the surface to see the deeper significance of this state. Kerry did indeed win the popular vote in California, and the state's key electoral-vote total of fifty-five. But in this state, widely infested with feral hogs, 5,509,826 people voted for George Bush—the most of any state, more even than Texas—contributing vitally to the popular-vote win seen by Bush as mandate bestowing.

It is tempting to say that the more feral hogs in a place, the greater the support for Bush. But, even for experts, accurate feral-hog numbers in specific counties are hard to come by. One *can* say, however, that in the deepest areas of feral hogdom support for Bush is extrastrong. East Texas counties with chronic feral-hog problems went for Bush at two-thirds margins and above. Berrien County, Georgia, the county of the storied (but probably not wild) Hogzilla, preferred Bush by 70 to 29 percent. Wild hogs seem to be everywhere that the red-state red can't get any redder and starts to turn into a Confederate flag.

In northern New Jersey, where I live, the closest feral hogs are a state or two away. They're beyond the far end of Pennsylvania, in West Virginia, or they're the renegade Eurasian wild boars up in New Hampshire. Near my house, in the commuting town of Montclair, I see the usual suburban deer, raccoons, opossum, squirrels, etc., but I have encountered neither feral hogs nor rumors of feral hogs. True to the red-state feral-hog corollary, Montclair voted for Kerry by 79 to 20 percent. This near unanimity of local opinion is okay with me. I don't like arguing. At dinner parties, my neighbors and I agree with each other, and when we go home we agree with ourselves. Every so often, though, I feel a vague curiosity about the other side of the mirror. Recently when that happened I set out to find some feral hogs.

••

The South is something you fall back into, like falling backward off a diving board. I was driving around aimlessly in Georgia. After all I'd read about feral hogs, I figured I'd just go down and look out the window and there they'd be. In fact, as is well known, most places visible from a car in this country look exactly the same. Georgia could be Teaneck or anywhere. The only difference is, in Georgia you can get boiled peanuts at the 7-Eleven. Today, would anyone write a romantic ballad to a Southern place like "Sweet Home Alabama" or "Georgia on My Mind"? ("Sweet Home Pizza Hut"? "Meinecke Muffler on My Mind"?)

Out behind the superstore, though, or past the edge of pavement, the previous South is still there. Georgia pines still stand, red dirt roads run among them. The unpavable, overly swampy, too hilly parts of the South remain almost as moss-hung and haunted and dark and beautiful as ever. A few minutes' drive from generic suburban Atlanta highway sprawl, the little battlefield of Resaca, Georgia, looks about as it did when my great-great-grandfather's infantry regiment fought there in the Civil War. The Fifty-fifth Ohio Volunteer Infantry was part of a Union force under General Joseph Hooker trying to push the Confederate Army back to Atlanta. The Confederates had entrenched themselves well on a hill near a bend in the Oostanaula River. Colonel Charles Gambee, the Fifty-fifth's commander, turned pale and trembled in the saddle when given the order to storm the entrenchments. In the first assault, he was shot through the heart. Hooker later outflanked the Resaca position, rendering the attack unnecessary. Today, the battlefield is kind of a hole in the corner, its iron fences rusting, its monuments crumbling. Get in your car, and you're back in the traffic stream.

As I drove, I looked for stores that might have hog-hunting books or magazines. Near the South Carolina border I stopped at a little gun shop with only one car out front. In the shop I found the owner, who had just finished test-firing a pistol down a steel pipe set in the floor. He had no copies of *Boar Hunter* magazine, but told me instead a long story about the mounted wild-hog head above the workbench. The story involved a guy, the guy's wife, and the head falling unexpectedly off the wall. The owner then waxed philosophical on the subject of wild hogs. "We gave Europe turkey, and they gave us pigs," he said. "Far as I'm concerned, bacon beats turkey any day. We sure got the best of that deal."

In megasupermarkets bigger than New Jersey's, the books-and-magazines aisle extended well out of sight. Usually it included a large and fully stocked section for religious literature. In a Gainesville, Georgia, megamart I bought a paperback of *The Gnostic Gospels*, by Elaine Pagels, a book I'd long been meaning to read. I will go out on a limb and say that not one supermarket in New Jersey has that book for sale. In general I was surprised in the South by how many religious reminders I came across. Every other radio station seemed to be preaching evangelism, and the country-and-western songs kept mentioning God or angels or heaven. And the churches, which I'd heard were big, were bigger than I'd imagined, stretching beside the highway for blocks, with palace-like chandeliers in the main entrance, and day-care centers and schools and employment offices and out-buildings housing all-year rummage sales. To drive through the South is to overhear a nonstop Christian conversation rising from the many sayings on churchfront signboards. Some messages are friendly, like WE SPECIALIZE IN FAITH LIFTS; some are theological: FAITH IS NOT BELIEF WITHOUT PROOF, BUT TRUST WITHOUT RESERVATION. Deeper in the pinewoods, signboards at little white clapboard Baptist churches take a more severe tone: HOW WILL YOU SPEND

ETERNITY? SMOKING OR NON-SMOKING? Another, at a Free Will Baptist church on a winding little road, cautioned:

STOP, DROP, AND ROLL
WON'T WORK IN HELL.

I was on my way, meanderingly, to talk to John J. Mayer. I had asked him some questions on the phone, and he said that if I came down we could talk some more and he would try to show me actual feral hogs. John J. Mayer (called Jack) lives in Aiken, South Carolina, where he is a wildlife biologist at the Department of Energy's Savannah River Site. The facility used to make radioactive components for nuclear bombs; it is enclosed in 310 square miles of woods and swamp. Like many current or former government installations in the South, it has plenty of feral hogs.

Mayer catches and studies them sometimes. He is a rangy, bespectacled, enthusiastic man of fifty-four who can throw a 250-pound wild hog to the ground unaided. (Among hog hunters, I found, taking on a big hog alone with only the help of dogs is the apogee of hog hunting.) Mayer says he is not the leading wild-hog expert in America, but I think he is. Other scientists specialize in parts of the wild-hog picture, but Mayer follows the entire national and international wild-hog scene. He speaks with a certain relish of a fenced game preserve near Fairbanks, Alaska, that has wild boars, and of the inevitability of those boars' escape: "The coastal brown bears will just *love* that protein resource!" He is up on wild-hog doings in Canada and Finland, where the hogs have been seen far north of their previously assumed range, and in southern Sweden, where they are a pest, and near Kent, in southeast England, where ditto. Wild swine have recently made a comeback in England after being extinct in that country since the 1600s. Mayer also gave me the important news that there are now about twenty-three million wild hogs in Australia; according to census figures, Australia has only about twenty million human beings. (Disappointingly, from the point of view of theory, George Bush is not at all popular in Australia. The red state–feral hog corollary evidently does not apply overseas.)

After many wild-hog stories during breakfast at a Shoney's restaurant in Aiken, Mayer and I got in the car and began to scout. As often in the South, country roads were about seven minutes away. On a suburban/farmland road called Tennis Ranch Lane, Mayer suddenly stopped us, and we got out and walked into a field. Hog rooting had left it resembling a choppy sea under irregular winds. Mayer got down on his haunches and sifted the dust. "A lot of time, we'll find rooting like this and have no idea what they were looking for," he said. "Sometimes they'll just keep rooting down until the hole is three or four feet deep. A timber cruiser was walking through the woods near here marking trees awhile ago and fell in one of those holes and broke his foot. What food could be down that deep? Tubers? Grubs? Both are pretty unlikely. So we just don't know."

Farther on, the dirt road led past pine plantations, their loblolly and slash pines growing in rows; Mayer told me how wild hogs can rip up many acres of newly planted pine seedlings in a night, eating only the cambium-rich taproot and leaving the rest. The road then descended to swamp, with water oaks draped in Spanish moss, and switch cane, and spreading palmettos, and avenues of ocher muck receding around the buttresses of cypress trees. "This is pig country," he said. We stopped and walked around but saw only a pig track or two. Beyond the swamp the road crossed a soybean field bordered by a long line of telephone poles. Mayer pointed to the bottoms of the poles, which were covered with mud to a height of about three feet. I said the mud must be splashes from passing cars. Mayer said it was put there by hogs.

We got out for a closer look. The poles were indeed rubbed with mud, not splashed; from the wood splinters hog bristles stuck out, and tusk marks scored the surface like thumbnail scrapes. "All telephone poles are soaked in creosote to preserve them," Mayer explained. "After the poles have been standing awhile, the creosote begins to drain downward and leach out at the base. That's why the bottoms of telephone poles are black. Well, wild hogs just love this creosote. When they're muddy from a wallow, they'll come up to the poles, as they've done here, and rub against them until they've coated themselves with creosote. Any time you see phone poles that are muddy like this, look for wild hogs. The creosote is a good chemical protection against hog lice and other ectoparasites. But how would the hogs know that?" For a moment the look of amused wonder on his face was just like Joe Corn's.

The wild hogs around Aiken proved not obliging about being found. I spent a day searching with Jack Mayer, and on another afternoon I walked in a swamp by the Savannah River to no purpose on my own. I saw aspects of the hog, from tracks to wallows to bristles to (on shelves in Mayer's study) tusks and skulls—but no hogs themselves.

• •

A few months later, I took another trip to the South to try again. This time, I went with a young wildlife expert named Robbie Edalgo, who has done a lot of trapping for Joe Corn and SCWDS. Robbie and his friends hunt hogs near the south Georgia town of Cordele, where he grew up. He said we could stay in his house in Cordele with his dad and stepmom. As it happened, the town of Abbeville, twenty-five

miles away, would be having its Ocmulgee Wild Hog Festival while we were there. The Ocmulgee Wild Hog Festival
features arena contests between specially trained dogs to
see which are best at chasing, baying, and catching wild
hogs. It is held every year on the day before Mother's Day,
giving folks an interesting choice about how to spend the
weekend.

Robbie Edalgo was studying for a master's degree in
sociology at West Virginia University at Morgantown, so
first I drove there from New Jersey and picked him up.
Then we drove straight for fifteen hours down to Cordele,
and talked all the way. Robbie's last name comes from his
great-great-grandfather Francisco Hidalgo, who was an or-
phan in Mexico when he met a soldier from Georgia named
Henry Holliday, who adopted him and brought him back
to the United States. His adoptive father changed the spelling of his last name. Henry Holliday is best known as the
father of Dr. John Holliday, the famous Western gunfighter
usually called Doc. Francisco was older than John; family
lore says that Francisco was the person who taught Doc
Holliday to shoot. Francisco later served in the Confederate
Army in Georgia under the command of Joe Johnston. That
was the same army my great-great-grandfather was fighting
against in the battles in and around Atlanta.

The greenery along the road became lusher the farther
south we drove. Sometimes thickets of kudzu vine covered
everything, like a bulky green tarp. Robbie rolled down the
window so we could smell the honeysuckle and magnolia.
He said that Georgia smelled better than other places to
him, and he loved to breathe it in, especially at evening when
he crossed the state line on his way home. Along an exurban
stretch of freeway, suddenly traffic slowed, and we saw up
ahead a car with its doors open on the side of the road. Its
passengers had evidently run into the nearby underbrush,

to judge by the expressions of the highway patrolmen standing by the car and peering in the same direction. Also readable on their faces, I believe, was a reluctance to go after fugitives in that kudzu jungle with night coming on.

Arrival at Robbie's dad and stepmom's house, around midnight; sleep; big Southern breakfast; then Robbie and I were in his dad's truck headed for some possibly hog-filled swampland owned by a friend along Alapaha Creek. The morning was halcyon. Mist still hung in the pines, their needles reddish in the early sun. Peanut hulls crunched under the tires as we rolled carefully along a sandy trail at the edge of a plowed-up field. Lines of wild-hog tracks made penman-style flourishes across the field, with intervals of rooting in between. Some of the animals had been piglets. Their tracks were like two almonds side by side. Robbie said wild piglets are watermelon-striped. Many tracks went into the swamp at the line of brush beside the field, and we went in after.

Robbie was carrying a .50-caliber Hawken black-powder musket—unloaded, for the time being. Both he and I had on snake boots, laced up to the knee and thickly padded, because of the water moccasins and cottonmouths that inhabit the swamp. Notebook and pen were my only other accessories. We started out stepping from grass hummock to grass hummock across expanses of gray-pudding mud, which when I sank into it was a richer black farther down. Braided cross-vines ascended into the swamp's upper story like scenery cables into the flies. The trees were a mixture of cypress, swamp tupelo, tulip poplar, various oaks, and chinaberry. Beneath the chinaberries their little purple blossoms lay on the gray mud like a pattern on an old dress, sometimes with hog tracks squished in between.

In the brushier places, wisteria vines in full flower were dragging little trees to the ground, while blackberry and wild rose and unnamed vines entangled so thickly as to make a wall. Sometimes this obstacle could be breached by crawling beneath on our bellies; at others the best move was a kind of Rockette high kick to get above the vines and bushes and stamp them down. Unlike Robbie, I am not thirty, as the experience reminded me. At one point, tripping on cypress knees the shape of little fire hydrants, plunging into vines, compacting cubic yards of berry bushes to crush through them, we actually could not go forward anymore. We sagged into the brush as if it were an uncomfortable hammock, then turned and plunged back the way we'd come.

When the sun was high overhead and the swamp had become hot and buggy, we gave up. For just a second we saw something moving a long way off through the trees. But when at last we scratchily emerged onto the peanut field, we had the result that was becoming customary: no hog. I cursed, but Robbie Edalgo did not. I never once heard him use a curse word. I spent many hours with him, and I don't believe he'd curse regardless of the provocation.

At evening we went out again. Now we were on unfenced private land owned by a hunting club along a bigger creek called Turkey Creek. The land is managed for wild turkey and white-tailed deer. Robbie's friend Phillip, who runs the place, told us to shoot all the hogs we saw. Phillip is trying, unsuccessfully, to get rid of them; he traps and shoots them by the dozen and gives them to local people to eat, but the hogs keep coming. Though the hogs are his enemies, when he talked about them he could not suppress a half smile that sometimes became a laugh: "We had this one hog in a trap, and he kept charging the side of it again and again until he'd bent it out about this far, and the hog busted up his nose doin' it, he's all bloody and beat up and enraged, and we put some shelled corn in there for him to eat, and right away he goes to eatin' without a care in the world. Wild hog's the only animal that'll always eat, no matter how freaked-out he is."

Robbie loaded his Hawken musket with eighty-five grains of black powder, poured yellow oil on a squat, snug-fitting bullet, and tamped it down the barrel with the ram-rod. We left his dad's truck at the forest edge uphill from the creek and ducked into the gloom. Here trails had been cut conveniently through the undergrowth. We went along them quietly, twitching from mosquito attacks all the while. Anytime we stopped to listen, the mosquitoes really found our range, causing both of us a near-constant swat-ting, hopping, and flicking. I was wearing a netted hat like a beekeeper's and Robbie had wrapped a piece of camo bug netting around his head, babushka style. For all its insect life, the place also seemed extremely hoggy, with tracks and rooting and occasional distant branch-cracking sounds. The sun went down.

We were walking along a grassy track with a young pine-woods on our right and a park-like setting of tall trees and open ground on our left. Beyond lay wheat fields, which we thought the hogs might return to for a night's rooting. About two hundred paces ahead, two deer came out of the pines and crossed the trail. They turned and began walking directly at us. Robbie whispered that we should just hold still and see what they did. As they approached, excessively slowly, shrieking mosquitoes swarmed on me. I resisted the urge, but finally I had to swat.

The deer's ears flew up, and they spooked back into the pines. We continued on. After we'd gone about a hundred steps beyond the spot where the deer had emerged, Robbie turned back to look again. Immediately, he went to one knee and gestured to me to get down. I crouched, and saw what he'd seen. A hog, in dark silhouette, came out of the pines exactly where the deer had been. The spring green of the long grass behind him made his swamp-mud-black color stand out. Robbie brought the gun to his shoulder. A second ahead of him, the hog reversed ends balletically, his feet seeming not to touch the ground, and disappeared back into the pines.

We crept to the spot where we'd seen him. Robbie said that there had been another pig behind him, and that they had been extra wary because they had heard the deer we'd spooked. We looked, we waited. Robbie went back into the thick cover. No sign of any hogs.

I was ecstatic to have seen my first wild hog not dead or in a trap or along a highway but in its home territory. Robbie then led us to a brushy place of ambuscade beside a field, where we sat until full dark while a swampful of mosquitoes gathered around. There we didn't see a thing. Robbie had wanted to bring a hog home to his family for a barbecue—wild hog is delicious, and his dad is a prize-winning barbecuer—so he was disappointed. I felt relieved that my search had succeeded without including the death of a hog.

..

To understand the Ocmulgee Wild Hog Festival, you have to understand the dog guys. Before I went to the festival, I had never met any dog guys, though I had heard them referred to. When I asked wildlife-management people or scientists questions they didn't know the answer to, often they replied, "You need to ask the dog guys," their tone suggesting that the dog guys' universe was a different one, in which ordinary science did not necessarily rule. Jack Mayer told me stories of drag-out, hand-to-hoof battles between dog guys and wild hogs in which dogs got flipped in the air and came down tusk-stabbed and bleeding, while the dog guy almost bled to death from tusk wounds to the artery in his thigh. By reputation, the dog guys sounded mythic, Paul Bunyanesque, and themselves probably part dog, or hog.

Dog guys chase and capture hogs using packs made up of three categories of dog. The first, trail dogs, have good noses to find and follow the hog. The second, bay dogs, cause the hog to "bay up"—to take a defensive position, often at the base of a cliff or a tree—and then they hold him there by barking and making quick countermoves when the hog tries to dodge away. The loud baying of these dogs also helps the hunters, who are running along behind, to locate the fight. The third, catch dogs, attack the hog while he's bayed up, bite him on the nose or ear, and hang on. While the hog is thus preoccupied, the hunters (several, usually) arrive, go behind the hog, grab his hind legs, and throw him on his side. Wild hogs are flat-sided animals and, once tipped over, with a hunter atop them, cannot easily escape. The hunters then tie the hog's legs, or shoot it, or stick it with a knife.

Hunting hogs with dogs has disadvantages. Some people think it is horrible, and raise a complaint if they hear of it occurring on public lands. This limits the ability of state and federal wildlife officials to control hog numbers with dogs. Another problem is that running dogs through the countryside disturbs animals other than hogs: not all of the dogs can be counted on to chase hogs only. And, aside from the consequences for the hog, the battle between wild pig and dog can result in dead or badly injured dogs. Dog guys get to be self-taught field veterinarians, patching their wounded on-site with surgical stapling guns, suture kits, and blood-stop powder. Usually they take the extra precaution of dressing their most valuable dogs in puncture-proof vests of ballistic-strength fiber and in stout "cut collars" that come up almost to the ears.

Despite all this, hunting with dogs is by far the best way

to catch wild hogs. It works better than shooting or trapping, and may be resorted to when those methods fail. What the experts mean by their tone—"You need to ask the dog guys"—is that, in the end, nobody gets down to the hogs' reality better than the dog guys.

If I ever had any doubts about the fairness of the red state–feral hog corollary, I lost them when I saw the dog guys. As evidence of the connection between politics and feral hogs, they could be Exhibit A. The characteristic insignia of their sport is the Confederate flag. It's on their hats, their belt buckles, their bandannas, their insulated drink holders. Evidently, their views have not been represented adequately by any party since the Civil War. A favorite T-shirt they wear shows a pit bull's snarling head, with saliva strands connecting the top and bottom fangs, superimposed on a Confederate flag. On top, the shirt says DIXIE TRADITIONS and, below, SINCE 1861. Some T-shirts feature the Confederate flag with the words IF THIS SHIRT OFFENDS YOU, IT MAKES MY DAY, or IF THIS SHIRT OFFENDS YOU, YOU NEED A HISTORY LESSON. The puncture-proof vests worn by many of their dogs display the Confederate flag on the dog's chest. There are probably dog guys who disagree with these sentiments; I note only the general impression the insignias leave.

As for the history lesson, the town of Abbeville, site of the wild-hog festival, offers several right nearby. On the lawn by the elegant sandstone courthouse, at the town's main intersection, a historical marker indicates that Hernando de Soto discovered the Ocmulgee River near this spot in April 1540; it does not add that he was the man who introduced hogs to the continent. Another marker commemorates the capture of the fleeing Jefferson Davis, president of the Confederacy, by Union troops twenty-six miles southwest of Abbeville on May 10, 1865, "his hopes for a new nation, in which each state would exercise without interference its cherished 'Constitutional rights,' forever dead." Prisoners (all black, when I walked by) at the county jail just up the street stand talking through the fence to their visitors (all black). The prisoners wear jail clothes striped black and white, as in old movies.

The festival was at the fairgrounds, west of town. It had booths and kiddie rides and prize drawings, like any town fair. At the fairground's edge, where the woods began, the hog-baying arena had been set up among the trees. The shaded surroundings gave the place an air of semisecrecy. Chain-link fence about six feet high and reinforced at the bottom with coarse-woven black nylon fabric enclosed a circular area about eighty steps across. Within it, oaks and loblolly pines grew well apart from one another on ground that was bare dirt, pine needles, and leaves. Loudspeakers had been taped to the trees with silver duct tape. Outside the fence stood an irregular encirclement of bleachers, about seven rows high. The arrangement might have been a theater-in-the-round for a highly realistic production of *A Midsummer Night's Dream*. One side of the arena opened to an entry chute blocked with a piece of plywood. Behind it were the pens holding about thirty recently trapped wild hogs.

I went over and looked at them. They were all exactly the color of swamp mud, their bristles clumped in points like the hair of a person who hasn't showered for a while. Soupy gray mud had been provided for some of them to wallow in. The hogs in the wallow were all crowded into the farthest corner of it, as remote as they could get from the door they would eventually have to run through. One or two hogs lifted their snouts to the wind, rhinarial disks dipping and twitching prehensilely on the incoming scents from the fair. In an adjoining pen, the hogs had only a metal floor to lie on, and waited peacefully in a big heap of hogs, maybe four deep. There is nothing like the expression in a wild hog's eyes. I studied it for a while and the words I found were: "unromantic," "undeceived." The hog at the very bottom of the pile had his face a bit flattened out by the weight of the hogs above him. His mouth was a long straight line parallel to the floor. His eyes, not discontentedly, followed the passersby.

The dog guys, in their parking area behind the arena, sat on folding chairs beside their pickups. Many had dogs for sale. In the truck beds, kennel boxes with wire-mesh doors were stacked three and four high. One man had a cardboard box of pit-bull puppies, $50 each, straining upward with wrinkly, reptilian smiles. Bumper stickers advertised, I CATCH MORE HOGS WITH KEMMER CURS, or I CATCH MORE HOGS WITH CATAHOULA CURS, or similar slogans. The word "cur" is a higher-sounding synonym for "mutt." Any dog can be used to hunt hogs, but mutts are said to do better than purebreds. Leashed and panting at their owners' sides, the dogs seemed happy, but the dog guys themselves were oddly quiet, especially compared with the defiant inscriptions many of them wore. Later, a festival organizer told me that, on a hog hunt the night before, a widely known hunter up by Macon, Georgia, had gone into the Ocmulgee River to rescue one of his dogs and had disappeared in the water. Police divers were searching for his body now.

At the judging stand, Robbie introduced me to Bob Addison, the "godfather of hog hunting" (Robbie said) and the founder of the festival. Bob Addison owns a wild-hog-hunting camp in Abbeville. He is slope-shouldered, long-armed, powerful-looking, and more than six feet tall; he wore faded camo gear and a brown baseball cap with his hunting lodge's name. In his late fifties, he appears stronger for being that age, and his droopy, pale eyes are somehow made more intimidating, not less, by the thin-framed spectacles he wears. He told me the rules and procedures of the hog-baying contest and the details of the judging.

He said that good performance dogs like the ones here today are usually not the same as good hog-hunting dogs, who tend to be shy around crowds but much fiercer in the woods. We started talking about hunting. I asked him if he had ever had any dog killed while hunting hogs. He winced, as if I had stepped on his toe. "Yes, I have," he said. "I have had two dogs killed."

Then he said, "C'mon, let's go—I'll show you." He told a contest official he'd be back soon, led us to his immense red pickup, drove out the lane from the parking lot, turned east on the highway, crossed the Ocmulgee River, took another main road, maneuvered down a narrow gravel road, stopped in front of his hunting lodge, and led us inside. The walls of the lodge were covered with mounted heads of hogs and deer; hog skulls lined the mantelpiece. He took down a skull that had been sawed off just behind the snout. Its tusks were chisel-pointed, several inches long.

"This hog here killed both my dogs," he said, turning the skull back and forth in his hand. "This was a big old boar, lived up around Bonaire, Georgia, forty-five, fifty mile from here. In his life this hog killed fifteen dogs, including my two. He was about the biggest thing around there and didn't fear nothing. He charged a man's truck one time and flattened one of its tires. People called this hog Bear. Well, I went up on an afternoon to see some land I own in the area. It's three hundred acres, and sometimes I have field exercises there with my dogs. I let the dogs out of the truck and right away they th'owed up their heads and started baying. Then they went off running through the brush. I could tell by the sound they'd found a terrible big hog. I was by myself. I run in after 'em and caught up with 'em. They had this huge boar partially bayed and partially caught. I got around behind and took a hind foot and a front foot, and I picked him up to th'ow him—and the hog stood up with me! Never before or since have I found a hog I couldn't take by myself, but this one I couldn't. I stood there holding him, and he stood there on his hind legs with me, for maybe fifteen or twenty seconds, but it seemed a whole, whole lot longer, and I could see the dogs in front of him still barking, and finally I had to let him go, and as quick as that he went and—"

Bob Addison stopped, his eyes bleak and his lips tight. After a while, he continued.

"And he cut my bulldog's throat. Then he turned around and killed one of my bay dogs. I couldn't see no tree to get up, so I backed off. He looked at me and I looked at him, and I said, 'Bear, we'll be back.' And I swear the way he looked at me, he was saying, 'I'll be back, too.'

"I went to the closest pay phone and called Wayne, my trooper buddy, and I said, 'Bring ever' dog you have, come right now.' I also called David, who's big enough to hold three mules. We went back in after that hog, and the dogs struck his trail, and had him bayed minutes later, and we showed up and caught him and th'owed him down, and I put the handcuffs on him—"

("Handcuffs?"

Bob Addison: "Sure, a lot of hog hunters use handcuffs. They're the best and fastest way to immobilize a hog."

"You mean like those plastic handcuffs they use at protest marches?"

"Shoot, no! You need steel cuffs to hold a hog! I'm a retired state trooper. I use the same kind of cuffs I used on the job.")

"—and, once we had him cuffed, we lifted him into the back of the truck. And by the time we got home that hog was dead. Most likely he went into shock and died. That's what happens sometimes to old boars that have never been captured before. In his very last fight, he cut up (but didn't kill) three bulldogs. He was a most terrible hog."

· ·

At the arena, the bleachers were filling up. People toted drinks, paper plates of food, babies. Robbie brought me some excellent barbecue his dad had made. I ate it fast, then used the paper it came in to wipe the sauce off my face. I asked Robbie if I'd got it all, and he answered, "Uh, pretty much." Small groups of black people had found good vantage points from which to watch; some were right above the entry chute. They talked among themselves at volumes impossible to overhear. Almost everybody else was white. Some boys sported a souvenir I had never seen before—a green inflatable space alien with long, bendable arms and legs that could be wrapped around a person as if the alien were holding on.

In just a minute, the two-dog baying competition would begin. In pairs, bay dogs would chase a hog, run him down, get on either side of him, herd and worry him, and try to hold him in one spot. The pair that held the hog best for the space of two minutes, in the judges' opinion, would win a tall trophy and a couple thousand dollars. The hogs would run, snort, squeal, clack their teeth threateningly, charge the dogs, kick up dust, cause the handlers to dodge around trees. The hogs sometimes would be bitten, torn, grabbed, thrown, sat on, and finally shoved back into their pen. Many in the crowd would watch with an almost out-of-body concentration.

A man carrying his daughter on his shoulders came and stood near us. The girl was four or five years old. She had a blocky head, medium-length brown curls, and intent dark eyes. She wore flower-print sneakers, and her dad held her by them. I imagined her growing to adulthood as one of those strong-character Southern women who speak their minds and make people uncomfortable—a fearless old aunt, maybe, or a no-nonsense columnist. Before her dad brought her today (I'm guessing), he had told her she would be seeing dogs and pigs. She had pictured (I'm guessing) dogs like their dog at home and pigs like the ones in the storybooks.

The first pair of bay dogs entered the arena at the far side of it, a quarter circle around the fence from the hogs' gate. The dogs' holders bent down and took the clips at the ends of the leashes.

Skinny boys climbing on the hog pen banged it to get a hog to move into the chute. Somebody lifted the plywood door. A boy leaned forward and jabbed the hog through the fence bars. The hog came out into the arena and began to trot along the fence's perimeter. The dogs, suddenly released, went streaking toward him. In their many straps and bucklings, they looked like a SWAT team, striving faces pointed eagerly at the hog. From her high view the little girl looked at the dogs, at the hog. Her mind took a second to understand what was going on. Then, in a tone of the greatest emergency, with an authority that cut through every noise and rang above the assembly, the little girl cried, "Run, pig! *Run!*"

Some people laughed, the way a crowd does when a child makes a remark that everybody hears. Some people said "Aww . . . ," in sympathy. The little girl, seeing that the pig had nowhere to run to, began to cry, and her father lifted her down and comforted her. She cried louder when the pig squealed. A woman standing nearby took up the girl's cause, saying, "She's right! What are they doing!" and so on, until her neighbors shushed her. For a moment we all hesitated, uneasy and off-balance; then we turned back to the business at hand.

December 5, 2005

On Impact

People get excited when strange objects fall from the sky. We seek portents and meanings, we venerate the object, and we horripilate at the uncanny scent of our beginnings, or end. Even wised up by science as we are, we tend to freak. Here in the state of New Jersey, there hadn't been much call for that kind of excitement since 1829, when a meteorite fell on the town of Deal, in Monmouth County. At about twelve thirty in the morning on August 15, a fireball was seen over the town and multiple booms were heard. Several meteorite fragments may have been present, but only one was ever found—a stone meteorite about three inches long. In later years, the Deal Meteorite could be seen on display in Philadelphia at the Academy of Natural Sciences, which sold it with other museum specimens to a consortium of mineral dealers last fall; it is possibly in Colorado now.

A hundred and seventy-seven years and some months after the Deal Meteorite, an object descending at a steep angle and a high rate of speed shot through the roof of a house in Freehold Township—coincidentally also in Monmouth County. On January 2, 2007, at about four thirty in the afternoon, Mrs. Sundari Nageswaran was standing by the back door of her son's Canterbury-model house, in a development of many similar houses, when she heard a loud bang. Thinking it only a straggling firecracker from the holiday celebrations of the day before, she did not mention it to her husband; her seven-year-old grandson, just home from school; or her son, Srinivasan Nageswaran, who was at work in his office in the basement. Srinivasan, called Srini, is an information-technology consultant who does business both at clients' sites and from home.

Soon afterward, Srini's wife arrived from work, and the whole family had dinner. In the evening, while getting ready for bed, Srini went into the second-floor bathroom off the master bedroom to wash up. When he opened the door, he saw shreds of insulation, fragments of Sheetrock, and pulverized plaster dust all over the counter and the floor. In the bathroom ceiling above the sink was a hole about four inches long. The hole was clean and vaguely deltoid in shape on the side closer to the roof, and more ragged on the bathroom side, with a few pieces of Sheetrock held by liner paper dangling down. Climbing onto the counter and examining the hole more closely, he saw that it also seemed to go through the roof, just a foot or so above.

Srini called his wife, who observed the damage and then got a broom and began to sweep up the mess. When she lifted the green shag bathmat on the floor, she saw that a square of the porcelain tile beneath it had been shattered into many small pieces held in place by the mat. The broken tile lined up with the hole in the ceiling at an angle of about eighty degrees. In the bathroom wall, a foot or so above the broken tile, was a dent. While sweeping behind the toilet, Srini's wife noticed an object about three and a half inches long. It was a dull brownish-silver in color and shaped sort of like a small croissant. She picked it up and gave it to Srini, and said, "Look, this is what caused it." The object was about the same shape as the hole. Srini

looked at the hole in the ceiling again and pushed a broom-
stick through to the outside. Whatever the object was, it
apparently had struck with such force as to penetrate the
shingle, three-quarter-inch plywood, eight inches of fiber-
glass insulation, and half-inch Sheetrock, with enough energy left over to shatter the tile and dent the wall. Anybody
standing at the sink when it hit, he reflected, would probably have been killed.

At first, Srini and his wife thought the object might be a
part from a satellite or an airplane. It had a lot of weight for
its size, though, and somehow did not look like anything
from this world. Srini's parents joined the discussion. The
family held the object in their palms and passed it around.
Srini's father was the first to suggest that it might be a
meteorite.

In the morning, the Nageswarans called the Freehold
Township police. At about nine thirty, two officers came,
looked at the hole in the ceiling and in the roof, wrote up a
report on the damage, and took the mysterious object with
them for identification. When the officers returned to the
station, they left the object in the vehicle; Lieutenant
Robert A. Brightman, a coordinator of the police investigation, wanted to keep the risk of spreading any radiation
contamination to a minimum, should the object turn out to
be radioactive. After a check with a Geiger counter proved
that not to be the case, the object was brought into the station and put into a clear plastic cylinder used to hold pieces
of evidence.

Two investigators from the office of the Federal Aviation
Administration in Saddle River arrived at about noon. The
FAA gives out very little information. Jim Peters, a spokes-
man at the FAA office in Queens, told me that FAA investigators are not available to talk to the press, because they
don't understand the complexities of dealing with the

media. In any event, the investigators examined the object and photographed it at the police station for several hours. Then they told Lieutenant Brightman that the object showed no sign of having been manufactured or machined and was not a part of an aircraft. Arlene Murray, a higher-up at the FAA, informed the press of this finding later in the day.

Meanwhile, people who are paid to listen to police scanners for interesting developments heard that the Freeport Township police were investigating an object of unknown origin that had fallen from the sky. Those people told other people, with predictable results. By late afternoon, so many reporters and camera crews had shown up at the station that Lieutenant Brightman held a press conference to answer the questions in an organized way. He did not have much news to offer, besides the FAA's verdict and his assurance that the investigation would go on.

Scientists came to examine the object the following day. Wanting more than one opinion, Lieutenant Brightman asked the help of Peter Elliott, a metallurgist from Colts Neck, and Jeremy S. Delaney, a researcher in the Department of Geological Sciences at Rutgers University. Peter Elliott is an expert on distressed and corroded metals who has studied iron meteorites and has a PhD from the University of Manchester, in England. Jeremy Delaney has worked on meteorites for thirty years and has published many articles about the subject in scientific journals. He brought along Gail Ashley, a sedimentologist at Rutgers who also happens to be his wife, and Claire Condie, a student.

The scientists measured the object (9.6 centimeters, or about 3¾ inches long), weighed it (377 grams, or about 13 ounces), and looked at it through a hand lens. The Nageswarans had requested that no tests be done that would alter the object physically. Most meteorites have a fusion crust of oxidized or melted material on the outside as a result of coming through Earth's atmosphere; this object seemed to lack that, though it did have smooth areas on one side where molten material might have flowed and cooled. The scientists also brought up pictures of meteorites on their laptops and compared the object with them.

Judging by its density, magnetism, surface textures, appearance, and provenance, the scientists concluded that the object was probably an iron meteorite. To know for certain that an object is a meteorite you have to cut into it. Only by looking at a cross section under a microscope can you tell, first, if an object is a meteorite and, second, what kind of meteorite it is. The scientists emphasized that a cross-section test should be done. Short of that, Jeremy Delaney said he was as sure the Nageswarans' object was a meteorite as he could be.

For Lieutenant Brightman, this wrapped up the police investigation. The scientists' opinion combined with the verdict of the FAA persuaded him that the property damage at the Nageswarans' had not been caused by any person. He phoned the family, told them what the scientists had said, and told them they could come down and pick up their evidence. To satisfy the curiosity of reporters, science centers, planetariums, etc., that had been calling all day, he sent out an updated press release. Privately, he did not let himself get excited about having examined and handled an object from outer space. "I made no value decision of any kind," he told me, "especially in light of the technology for creating objects that exists today."

•••

A meteorite is a meteoroid that falls to earth. Most meteoroids don't, but burn out in the atmosphere as meteors, or shooting stars. Given Earth's surface composition, meteorites have a 71 percent chance of landing in water. Those odds, plus the atmospheric filter, keep the number of known meteorites down. Meteorites are given names based on the place of their discovery. Cambridge University publishes a catalog that lists 22,507 meteorites, a number that includes the nearly 20,000, most of them small, that have been found in the cold desert of Antarctica and the hot deserts of Africa. Visibility is, of course, a factor; in some states and countries, no meteorite has ever been found.

Most meteorites come from the asteroid belt, about a hundred million miles away. The asteroid belt is made up of fragments left over from the formation of the solar system; these fragments, some of them hundreds of kilometers in length and some with their own moons, occupy a solar orbit between Mars and Jupiter. The big fragments are called asteroids. Scientists sometimes refer to the asteroid belt as the junkyard of the solar system, and, as in any junkyard, things rattle around. Collision, the process by which the planets were assembled, has slowed in the intervening billions of years, but it is still going on. Objects crash into one another, collisions lead to other collisions; as fragments fly into new orbits, those orbits approach Earth's, coincidences happen, and gravity pulls the fragments in.

Meteorites are of three kinds: stones, irons, and stony irons. Each corresponds to a different part of planet formation. The stones resemble pieces of planetary crust and mantle; the irons, the planet cores; and the stony irons, the transitional area between core and mantle. In some stony irons, translucent crystalline structures interpenetrate with opaque mantle rock. Collectors sometimes cut stony irons into thin slices and illuminate them from one side for a gorgeous stained-glass effect. Only one percent of all meteorites are stony irons. Five percent are irons, and the remaining 94 percent are stones.

There are also meteorites from Mars. In the 1970s and

'80s, several of them were found in Antarctica. Comparison with information about Mars rocks sent back by the *Viking* spacecraft in 1975 confirmed these meteorites' origin. Evidently, cratering impacts on Mars a hundred million to three hundred million years ago knocked pieces clear of that planet's gravity, and they later ended up on Earth after the pattern of asteroid-belt meteorites. In the 1990s, astrogeologists examining the Mars meteorites found what seemed to be traces of primitive bacterial forms of life. This made news because of the speculation that life on Earth could have begun with life-forms arriving aboard a meteorite. Since then, further investigation has shown that the intriguing traces are probably not related to any kind of life.

Similarly, a number of meteorites have been identified as having come from the moon. Chemical matchups with lunar rocks brought back by the Apollo astronauts provided the proof. Among collectors, lunar and Martian meteorites are the most highly prized by far. Asteroid-belt meteorites sell by the gram; lunar and Martian meteorites sell by the milligram.

The fact that fragments of Mars have wound up on Earth does not imply, in all likelihood, that the reverse is true. Probably there are no Earth meteorites on Mars. The reason for this is that the general gravitational flow of the solar system is toward the sun; for pieces of Earth to reach Mars, they would have to travel upstream, gravitationally. Chances are greater that Earth meteorites have reached Venus and Mercury, because those planets are between the sun and us. Of course, we can be sure that certain objects of earthly origin are now on Mars, because we shot them there—including the aforementioned *Viking*, the Mars *Pathfinder* in 1997, and in 2006 the Mars rovers *Spirit* and *Opportunity*. On the moon, our manned and unmanned missions have left all kinds of relics of ourselves—cameras, nuclear-fuel casks, discarded plastic rock-sample bags, golf balls, a color photograph of the astronaut Charles Duke and his wife and their two children, and many astronaut footprints, preserved forever in the moon's absence of atmosphere.

More prosaically, the bulk of what we launch into space does not disappear permanently into the vastness but, instead, orbits Earth for some unspecified period of time and then comes back down. The proliferation of old satellites and other space junk in Earth orbit is a subject of recurring concern. The National Aeronautics and Space Administration knows of approximately eleven thousand pieces of orbital debris larger than four inches long. Over the past forty years, pieces of debris have fallen back to Earth at an average of one piece a day.

• •

Late in January, the Nageswarans decided to let the public see their meteorite—as the newspapers were now calling it—in a one-day-only display, on a Saturday, at the Rutgers University Geology Museum. I live not far from New Brunswick, so I drove down. From across the Rutgers campus I could locate the museum by triangulating the paths of the many people heading for the building; museum directors will tell you that, among science displays, meteorites are close in popularity to dinosaurs. On the museum's second floor, just beyond the door, a murmuring crowd concentrated around a small glassed-in case beside the wall.

There were rock hounds in blue jeans and hiking boots, cardboard boxes of rocks they'd brought in for identification at their feet; geologists with loose-leaf folders; teenage couples on dates; Rutgers personnel; and many parents carrying young children or holding their hands. The crowd's dominant color scheme, repeated in flashes on hats and sweatshirts and tote bags, was Rutgers red, a proud reminder of the school's football victory over Kansas State in the Texas Bowl the previous December. In about eight weeks, the Rutgers women's basketball team would make the school even prouder by playing in the NCAA championship game, an event with consequences, though none related to meteorites.

The line waiting to see the Nageswarans' exhibit up close stretched along the display cases. A few feet from the viewers leaning in next to the glass, a short, cheerfully emphatic man with a balding head and dark-rimmed glasses was providing commentary: "That little piece of iron (and probably cobalt and nickel) right there might be four point five billion years old! *Four point five billion!* Earth's a dynamic planet, always recycling itself, and we've never identified a rock on Earth older than about three point eight! And some meteorites have granules embedded in them that are from other star systems, older even than our sun! Meteorites are what we're made of! We're made of star stuff! That right there might be the very debris of which everything is made!"

During a pause, I introduced myself, and the commentator told me that he was Louis Detofsky, called Doc Rock by his geology students at Rowan University, in Glassboro, New Jersey. He then told me about a meteorite-hunting trip he had taken to Livingston Island, off Antarctica, and about the amazing wealth of meteorites there. He described photographs of some he had found in situ—little pieces of black scattered on the unlimited expanse of white.

By the door, Jeremy Delaney, the Rutgers geologist who had taken part in the identification and had helped arrange the exhibit, was trying to get away for lunch as people with questions kept stopping him. Jeremy Delaney is a tall, broad-faced man with a sheaf of white hair sitting aslant on his head like a beret. He talks with an Irish lilt, frequently widening his eyes and laughing at the amazingness of meteorites. Someone asked him the basic question: How much would this meteorite be worth? "If it's proved to be genuine, I imagine it will be very valuable, though I don't know a dollar figure exactly," he replied. "But if you remember the meteorite that hit Peekskill, New York, back in October of 1992—it came down about eight on a Friday evening, and there are some wonderful videos of it streaking across the sky of eastern Pennsylvania and upstate New York, because many people were outdoors at high school football games that evening and they had their cameras along. Well, the meteorite hit in a residential neighborhood of Peekskill on a family's driveway, and there was a Chevy Malibu parked there, and the meteorite went right through the trunk of the Chevy and out the bottom and landed on the pavement, and because of all the interest among collectors waiting to purchase that car it became maybe the most valuable Chevy Malibu in history, and I believe the family made enough money selling it that they were able to put a daughter through college."

At least half the visitors (by my count) viewing the display took pictures of it with their phones. Many also described it by telephone as they looked at it, or had others transmit pictures of them looking at it.

"How'd you like it if that fell through our bedroom wall?"

"Look at the photograph of the bathroom tile it smashed!"

"It happened January second. This year!"

"I didn't realize that."

"Get a picture of just Timmy with it."

"Tell Grandma you're looking at it right now."

"Chelsea, pay attention. This is probably the only chance of your life to see a real meteorite from outer space."

Gary Weinstein, the owner of Gary's Gem Garden, in Cherry Hill, remained unconvinced. After looking closely, his head held this way and that, he said, "I don't know. It looks like it's been polished with a wire wheel. And I don't see any real fusion crust there."

"You're just jealous because it didn't crash through *your* roof," the woman with him said.

"Hey, that's the excitement of it," Louis Detofsky put in. "Debate adds a freshness to it. Science is pursuit of truth, and if you're proved wrong you're happy to be proved wrong. You think that's a meteorite—okay, prove it!" He grinned challengingly.

When my turn came at the display case, I peered at the smooth, aerodynamic, silvery object sketched with razor-fine, crystalline-straight lines. I'd never seen anything like it. Though in shape and size it sort of resembled a Christmas cookie, it possessed no domestic qualities at all. It had the burnishings of Elsewhere, as if it had been Elsewhere forever; it seemed almost to hum inaudibly with the inhuman chill of space. I moved on. When I turned around I saw the people behind me, four preteenage boys, solemnly holding their cell-phone cameras at the object like small priests holding crosses at Dracula.

••

The scene now shifts to Arizona. Heated by an onset of meteorite fever, I remembered that some years ago, when I was flying east from Los Angeles, I had seen a huge crater in the desert. The crater turned out to be Meteor Crater, marked as a Point of Interest six miles off Interstate 40 between Flagstaff and Winslow on the Rand McNally map of Arizona. Now I decided I must see Meteor Crater up close and from the ground.

The flight from Newark to Phoenix took about five hours. The Phoenix I recall from childhood trips with my family, back in the 1950s, seemed barely a city. I remember standing on a street and seeing desert at both ends. Phoenix today is a replicating sprawl that flows around bare mountains in the hope of linking with the sprawl sprawling sprawlingly out of Las Vegas, which is also longing for union. Once the two megasprawls do join up, they'll head outward toward all points of the compass. Meteor Crater, 115 miles from Phoenix, is still in empty rangeland but may not be for long.

Two hours of crowded freeway driving, and I was almost there. Seen from miles away on the interstate, the crater suggests a giant bullet hole in the surrounding flatness, with rock lifted and folded back around its edges like curled metal around a puncture in a shot-through stop sign. And the minute you leave the highway you enter a much earlier moment in the automobile age: Route 66, the fabled Chicago-to-California road, used to run by here. In between sections of dirt lane and hardpan desert, some pieces of 66's original pavement survive. Meteor Crater was formerly one of a long list of Route 66 tourist attractions, and in the landscape of red sandstone, yellow grass, black cattle, and blue sky its weathered highway signs—SEE METEOR CRATER . . . PROTOTYPE FOR THE STUDY OF ALL IMPACT CRATERS IN OUR GALAXY—breathe pure 1959.

The Meteor Crater Visitor Center, with museum, movie theater, and gift shop, sits along the crater's north rim. Horizontal and vertical lines of the building comport harmoniously with the neighboring rock; the structure's previous incarnation was designed by Philip Johnson, an architect not often represented in tourist attractions along Route 66. I drove the winding asphalt up to the crater and got out in the parking lot. The place was crowded, causing me to suspect a meteorite awakening nationwide. I paid my $15 and walked to the top vantage point of the crater rim. A couple and their daughter were there, the father and little girl standing around while the mother finished a phone call: "I can make it Friday, I guess . . . Did you put a towel down on the living room? . . . Okay, I guess that wouldn't be a problem . . . We're at the big meteor crater . . . The *meteor crater* . . . No, she's going to have to learn to make her own appointments . . ."

Finally, the mother hung up, and she and the father persuaded the little girl to pose for one photo with the crater in the background. "Well, that's the most we can hope for, I guess," the father said as the family went back down the trail.

Alone for the moment, I looked out across the empty air. No question about it, this was one big hole. Meteor Crater is the best-preserved meteorite-impact crater on Earth. Slow rates of erosion in this dry environment and the relative recentness of the impact in geologic time have kept the crater largely unchanged. What happened was, about fifty thousand years ago an iron-and-nickel meteorite about 150 feet across came through the atmosphere from the northeast at an angle of about 80 degrees. (The steeper a meteorite's angle of arrival, the less atmosphere there is to slow it down, and the more damage it can do.) The meteorite probably weighed several hundred thousand tons. An object that size is not hard to imagine—it would fit into any supermarket parking lot, with plenty of spaces to spare—but it was also going perhaps twenty-six thousand miles an hour, and it struck the ground with an explosive force equal to more than twenty million tons of TNT.

Physical descriptions of the meteorite have to be speculative, because most of it vaporized or melted on impact. Scientists say that a light brighter than the sun as the meteorite descended, a cataclysmic noise, a deadly shock wave radiating for miles on impact, and a dense, rising cloud of molten metal droplets and pulverized or molten rock can all be assumed.

Beyond debate is what was left behind: a roughly circular bowl-shaped crater three-quarters of a mile across and 700 feet deep. Debris that fell back in and sedimentation over the millennia have reduced the depth to 550 feet, still enough (as the site's literature points out) to contain twenty football fields and two million spectators sitting on the crater's sides. The force of the collision blasted underground layers of sandstone and limestone up and out in chunks, some the size of houses, that landed in inverted order on the crater's rim, raising that part 150 feet above the surrounding plain.

More could be said about Meteor Crater, and about impact craters in general—about the Chicxulub crater, for example, a 110-mile-wide "impact feature" in the ocean off the Yucatán Peninsula, where scientists believe an asteroid the size of Mount Everest collided with Earth sixty-five million years ago and changed the global climate and possibly caused or contributed to the extinction of the dinosaurs and splashed up heat-fused silicates, called tektites, with such authority that they came down in places as far away as New Jersey, where some of them reside today beside labels in the Rutgers University Geology Museum—but instead I will limit myself to just one story.

The first geologists to see Meteor Crater, back in the late 1800s, when it was still known as Coon Butte, did not believe that it had been made by a meteorite. The site's uniqueness worked against it; the geologists had seen plenty of features caused by volcanoes, but none caused by a meteorite, so they attributed the crater to volcanic action or an explosion of underground steam. Daniel Barringer, a rich Philadelphian who was attracted by the many meteorite fragments found in the vicinity, filed a mining claim on the crater in the hope of locating the parent object buried below. He thought that object might be an iron meteorite weighing millions of tons. Iron was selling for $80 a ton at the time.

Barringer looked and looked for the meteorite but still had not found it when he died, in 1929. Because of what happened to the meteorite on impact, there was no massive object to find. In the 1950s, a graduate student in geology from Princeton named Eugene Shoemaker began to study Meteor Crater. By comparing it with craters left by nuclear testing at Yucca Flat, in Nevada, and particularly by examining a rare mineral created by extremely high pressures that he had discovered at both sites, Shoemaker proved that only the intense forces of a meteorite impact could have formed Meteor Crater.

Shoemaker went on to become one of the founders of the science of astrogeology. Largely because of him, scientists began looking at collisions as an important force in the development of the solar system. They also accepted that the craters visible on other planets and on the moon were of impact origin, and not volcanic, as had been thought previously. Shoemaker's contributions to the understanding of the moon's geology were of great use to the Apollo program. Astronauts bound for the moon came to Meteor Crater to train under his instruction for conditions they would find there. Shoemaker hoped to go on a lunar voyage himself; the dream of his life was to be the first geologist on the moon. He said he wanted to go up there and whack on the moon with his hammer.

By astronomical observation and by viewing telescope images through a stereoscopic microscope, Shoemaker and his wife, Carolyn, and an amateur astronomer named David Levy discovered the comet later known as Comet

Shoemaker-Levy 9. This is the achievement for which all three are best known. Soon after their discovery, pieces of Comet Shoemaker-Levy 9 crashed sequentially into Jupiter, leaving scars the size of Earth. Photos of that impact were among the most spectacular of the images sent back by the Hubble Space Telescope in 1994. Shoemaker's studies of meteorites and astrogeology changed the way people did planetary science and helped open the path for big-event theories of biological change, most notably the theory of species extinction associated with the Chicxulub crater.

Shoemaker never did go on an Apollo flight to the moon. In his thirties, he was diagnosed with Addison's disease, a condition of the adrenal glands, which disqualified him. In 1997, at the age of sixty-nine, he died in a car crash near Alice Springs, Australia. In 1998, a polycarbonate capsule containing an ounce of his ashes was put aboard NASA's *Lunar Prospector* spacecraft before its launch into lunar orbit. The *Lunar Prospector* circled the moon for eighteen months and performed various scientific operations. On July 31, 1999, having finished its tasks, the *Lunar Prospector* was sent to crash into the moon. A number of people have had their ashes shot into space; Eugene Shoemaker is the only inhabitant of Earth whose remains have ended up on another celestial body.

··

Had the object that struck the Nageswarans' house in Freehold Township come down instead in India, Denmark, or Switzerland, it would have been the property of the government. In America, however, a meteorite belongs to the person or entity on whose property it is found. A case more than a hundred years ago involving a meteorite that fell in an Iowa pasture established the legal precedent, and in several cases since then it has been upheld. The principle seems to make sense, and is congenial with the capitalist system, but possibilities for injustice remain; this was revealed by the Sylacauga Meteorite, the most famous American meteorite of the 1950s.

The Sylacauga Meteorite crashed through the roof of a house in Sylacauga, Alabama, at about one o'clock in the afternoon on November 30, 1954. Mrs. E. Hewlett Hodges, thirty-four, the wife of a tree surgeon, was lying on a couch in her living room when the eight-pound stone came through the ceiling, damaged a wood console Philco radio, ricocheted across the room, and struck Mrs. Hodges on her left wrist and side. Never before in history had there been a documented instance of a meteorite striking a human being. Mrs. Hodges was hospitalized soon afterward—not so much because of her injuries, which weren't serious, as because of the enormous public response to news of the event, which brought traffic-jam throngs of curious people to the Hodgeses' house. The U.S. Air Force showed up, too, and spirited the meteorite away for study; this was the era of the Red Scare and the rumors of a wrecked spaceship in New Mexico. Mrs. Hodges, a shy, overweight woman known as Ann, soon suffered a minor collapse from all the to-do.

Mr. and Mrs. Hodges hoped at least to get some financial reward for their trouble. Unfortunately, they were only renters of the house they lived in. Mrs. Birdie Guy, the house's owner, who was up on the law, announced to the press, correctly, that the meteorite was legally hers. After the air force returned the meteorite without finding in it any evidence of Russians or space aliens, Mrs. Guy sued the Hodgeses for possession. The parties eventually settled out of court, when the Hodgeses bought the meteorite from Mrs. Guy for $500. The big-spender meteorite collectors whom the Hodgeses had been counting on never materialized, and finally the couple donated the meteorite to the natural-history museum of the University of Alabama, where today it is the main exhibit that visitors come from out of state to see.

The Hodgeses later divorced. Ann's life did not turn out happily, and the only human ever known to be hit by a meteorite died, after a series of illnesses, at the age of fifty-two. Possibly, the unfairness of having to pay her landlady for the meteorite that hit her had upset her view of life. As the law is now, if you are hit and killed by a meteorite and you happen to be on property not your own, your heirs have no legal claim to the object that ended your life. Even with the world's expanding population, the chances of this happening remain small.

In any event, Srini Nageswaran took his responsibilities of ownership seriously. After the first press releases about the object, when his phone began ringing constantly with calls from reporters and meteorite collectors and interested institutions and friends, he chose a careful approach, allowing just one camera crew to film inside his house, and letting the stories disseminate from that coverage only. He didn't want too much turmoil to overwhelm his seven-year-old son, whom he sometimes refers to as "the little one."

A few weeks after the media interest died down, I gave Srini a call, and he kindly invited me to stop by. Srini is a quiet, self-possessed man of forty-six with a depth of expression in his dark-brown eyes and a gently precise manner. He wore a sweater of a subdued shade, blue jeans without fading or wrinkles, and no shoes, just socks. He asked me to take my shoes off in the foyer, and we sat in a living room that was so carefully furnished and well kept that it could have been the living room in the development's model home. Srini grew up in the city of Chennai, in southern India, and his family came to the United States in 1997. He has family in Chennai still, and relatives in Hong Kong and the U.K. and California, and friends in Kuwait and Japan. Many of them had got in touch with him after his name was in the news. He said that, all in all, being hit by a meteorite had been a nice experience so far.

Naturally, I wanted to see the famous bathroom. Srini led me up the stairs and through a bedroom with a large double bed and portrait photographs of family members on the walls. The bathroom door opened off the bedroom's back left-hand corner. We stepped into it tentatively, as if entering a shrine. In the ceiling the hole gaped, black and raw looking. I had seen photos of the damage, but what they hadn't made clear, or I hadn't noticed, was the skylight in the bathroom ceiling just a few inches to the left of the hole. There was nothing in the view through the skylight except the blue beyond, but I stared into it intently. I imagined a dotted line extending from the shattered tile on the floor and through the hole, out the roof, across the blank blue vista in the skylight, and onward and outward, incalculably far.

We stood for a while in the charged astronomical presence, then went back downstairs. I asked Srini what his plans for the object were now. He said he hoped eventually to sell it to a museum that would display it to the public, especially schoolchildren. "It didn't travel so many millions of miles for nothing, just to sit here and rest," he said. He said he had decided to have it tested soon, to remove all doubt. The idea of cutting it made him uncomfortable because of the danger of damaging the object's integrity and decreasing its value. Still, he thought that was the way to go.

As it happened, in a couple of months a new test became available that didn't require cutting at all. The American Museum of Natural History had just acquired a sophisticated device called a variable pressure scanning electron microscope, the latest improvement in that technology. Electron microscopes can determine the chemical composition of a substance by beaming electrons at it. The electrons excite electrons in the chemical elements in the substance, causing them to emit X-rays that the microscope then reads. Every element gives its own distinct X-ray signature. Variable pressure scanning electron microscopes have a sample chamber large enough to hold the Nageswarans' object. When Jeremy Delaney described this microscope to Srini, its noninvasiveness appealed to him.

On April 27, Srini retrieved his object from the safe-deposit box where he'd been keeping it and drove to the museum, accompanied by his son. Denton Ebel, the curator of the meteorite collection, met them when they arrived, showed them around, and explained the microscope and what it was going to do. He introduced them to Joe Boesenberg, a senior scientific assistant at the museum, who was about to get his PhD at Rutgers, and other museum staff. Then Ebel, Boesenberg, and colleagues took the object and studied it in the microscope for half an hour or forty-five minutes.

As soon as they finished, they told Srini and his son their findings. The object, Joe Boesenberg said, contained no nickel. It did contain a small percentage of chromium and manganese, because it was in fact an alloy, high-chromium steel, which is a type of stainless steel. High-chromium stainless steel is produced not in space but in factories. The absence of nickel would be decisive in itself; all iron meteorites contain nickel. In short, the Nageswarans' object was not a meteorite.

"I got a call from Joe Boesenberg," Jeremy Delaney told me afterward. "He said, 'Jerry—no nickel.' I said, 'Ooh, boy.' It sure looked like a meteorite, and it sure fooled me, that sneaky little devil. Well, if you keep on studying these objects, over time you'll see far fewer meteorites than meteor wrongs."

Remembering the doubter, Gary Weinstein, from the one-day display at Rutgers, I reached him at Gary's Gem Garden and asked if he'd heard the latest. "Yeah, how 'bout that?" he said. "That thing just didn't look normal to me. It had those straight, like, hash marks on the surface going every direction. I'd never seen that in any meteorite before. And there was the absence of fusion crust, and especially the very atypical regmaglypts—those are the thumb-shaped indentations that meteorites get when they come through the atmosphere.

"Plus," he said, "there were those objects that came down out west just two days after this object hit. Over Denver at about six forty-five in the morning on January fourth, all these amazing streaks were seen in the sky. A traffic copter took some good videos of it. Turned out it was a Russian rocket that had launched a French satellite back in December. Nobody knows where the wreckage landed—maybe in the New Mexican desert, maybe it kept going all the way to the ocean—but it was definitely Russian space junk, confirmed by tracking. That just seemed like too much of a coincidence to me."

After I hung up, I called Jeremy Delaney back and asked what he thought of the Russian-space-junk theory. "I suppose it's plausible," he said. "In the American space program, we generally use titanium, not steel, for parts that have to be really strong. Titanium is hard to work with, though, so maybe other countries' space programs consider chromium steel an acceptable substitute. I *am* inclined to think that the object is an orbital fragment of some kind, and not something that fell off an airplane. We've done calculations based on the damage at the Nageswarans', and I believe only an object falling from orbit would have the likely velocities.

But the object itself is a very common type of steel, of a composition so nondescript that its origin would be difficult to pursue, and I don't know if Srini would have the time or money or inclination to pursue it. In the end, we'll probably never know exactly where the object came from.

"When I tell people about this event, or series of events, I always put in a plug for science," he continued. "Scientists admit mistakes—no other profession or calling does that anymore, it seems. Scientists not only can be wrong but can be shown to be wrong very publicly. You examine evidence, you put together a hypothesis that seems the most likely, or least wrong. Then the tests come back and say, 'Sorry, guys.' This time I got to be the one who says, 'Oops, I was wrong.' "

When I caught up with Srini a few weeks after the test at the museum, he sounded down. "We're not sure what the object is, but it is not a meteorite, no," he said quietly. "We have to accept this and move on. The experience has been educational. My son was very excited to meet the scientists, and soon after the meteorite—I mean, the object—hit our house, my son and I went to a rocks and minerals show, and he began a rock collection. And he enjoyed going to the museum and seeing the microscope. So this has been absolutely good for him."

"Maybe because of this your son will grow up to be a scientist," I said. For the first time in the conversation, Srini laughed. "Yes, definitely—that would be a very good outcome," he said. "I see that he has the aptitude."

July 9 and 16, 2007

Any Drop to Drink

It had been a hot spring day, and the doors on one side of the lecture room in the Charles A. Dana Discovery Center, in Central Park's northeast corner, swung open to a small balcony above the waters of the Harlem Meer. Thirty or so volunteers with the Central Park Conservancy and other park regulars and neighbors mingled, waiting to hear a talk about New York City's water system. Many had met before, and, if they hadn't, some established that their dogs had. Then Richard "Rick" Muller, the director of legislative affairs for the New York City Department of Environmental Protection (not to be confused with the EPA), began to speak. Muller wears glasses and has a white brush cut, a prominent nose, and a wide, can-do smile. He was dressed in a crisp white shirt patterned with a blue grid, like graph paper, and a light-blue tie with a rippled, aquatic design.

In about thirty-five minutes, he laid out the early history of water in the city: Collect Pond, downtown, a primary original water supply—people washing clothes and doing other unsanitary things there; nearby Tea Water spring, the source of the city's best water for tea; yellow-fever outbreak (1798); Asiatic-cholera epidemic (1832); the Great Fire (1835); construction of the Croton aqueduct system to bring water to the city from reservoirs about forty miles north (1842); inauguration of the system, marked by a huge civic celebration with no champagne, just pure and healthful Croton water, and a parade five miles long, with four thousand marching firemen, Governor William Seward in a horse-drawn barouche, dignitaries from neighboring states, and the presentation of a specially written ode containing the lines "Pale Contagion flies affrighted, / With the baffled demon Fire!"

"The Croton system was a marvel of engineering for its time," Muller said. "Ever since it came into existence, New York City has had some of the best—if not *the* best— drinking water in the world. And the whole New York City water system has always been gravity fed! The water comes from upstate—literally 'up' from here. The aqueducts have an average thirteen-inches-per-mile drop, which builds up pressure—called 'head'—strong enough to carry the water as high as six stories when it finally reaches the city. Only about five percent of the city's drinking water needs to be pumped, to get it to the farthest reaches of Staten Island and Queens."

Outside, it grew dark and almost chilly. A Central Park Conservancy official closed one of the balcony doors. The Harlem Meer had become so calm that the lights of Fifth Avenue reflected in it were straight lines. Above Muller's head in the high-ceilinged room hung life-size seagulls with wings spread, adding to the serenity. He asked the members of the audience if he should keep going, and they said, enthusiastically, that he should. These people knew water. When he mentioned the old Yorkville Reservoir, in Central Park, and asked, rhetorically, what later took its place, they replied almost in unison, "the Great Lawn!" Muller leaped eagerly from each water fact to the next. One could imagine him as a figure in a fountain, water gushing from an amphora on his shoulder. Someone asked if his birth sign was Aquarius; but, no, it's Sagittarius.

Right now, the Croton system remains shut down while engineers install giant UV lights in a new filtration plant to treat the water for giardia and cryptosporidium. In the meantime, the city is getting more than a billion gallons of water every day from its newer reservoir system, the Catskill/Delaware, farther northwest. Muller showed maps, and praised the Catskill/Delaware water for its clarity and its wonderful taste. One map showed ruler-straight aqueducts converging on the metropolitan area from the Catskill/Delaware system. "There's an aqueduct tunnel in the rock about seven hundred feet under the Hudson River," he said. "I went down a new water tunnel that runs under the East River to Brooklyn and Queens. The tunnel-boring machines they use now had made a perfectly circular cut through the solid Manhattan schist and the diamond cutting heads had left such beautiful striations! I was very lucky to get to see that before they lined the tunnel with concrete."

Later, the audience dispersed into the night. At the corner of 110th Street and Fifth Avenue, a group of men and boys were hanging out, commenting on one another's complicated and highly accessorized bicycles. Overhead, Venus and Jupiter, which had been in close alignment, shone in the western sky. The planets' reflections quivered and jittered on the Harlem Meer's smooth surface, as if they had broken their usual no-coffee-after-dinner rule.

July 2, 2012

Fish Out of Water

In the Shedd Aquarium, on the lakefront in downtown Chicago, there's a video display that makes visitors laugh until they're falling down. The video is in an area of the aquarium devoted to invasive species, and it shows silver carp (*Hypophthalmichthys molitrix*), a fish originally from China and eastern Siberia, jumping in the Illinois River near Peoria. A peculiarity of silver carp is that when they are alarmed by potential predators they leap from the water, sometimes rocketing fifteen feet into the air. In the video, several people are cruising in a small motorboat below the spillway of a lock or a dam while fish fly all around. The people get hit in the arms, the back, the sides. They're ducking, they're yelling, the silver carp are flying, the boat is swerving. Aquarium visitors whoop and wipe the tears away and watch the video again.

The invasion of Asian carp into the waters of the South and the Midwest differs from other ongoing environmental problems in that it slaps you in the head. Videos like the one in the Shedd are the reason a lot of people know about Asian carp. Not only are the newcomers upsetting the balance in midcountry ecosystems; they are knocking boaters' glasses off and breaking their noses and chipping their teeth and leaving body bruises in the shape of fish. So far, apparently, there have been no fatalities. And while threats to the environment tend to be ignorable (if only in the short run), this one is not, because millions of people go boating and the novelty of being hit by a fish wears off fast.

Right now there are actually two kinds of Asian carp to worry about: silver carp and their nonjumping companions, bighead carp (*Hypophthalmichthys nobilis*). Bigheads, which can grow to a hundred pounds, are bigger than silvers. Neither really has the appearance of a carp, because their mouths are not the downward-pointing mouths of bottom-feeding fish. Unlike the common carp, which we think of as an American fish although it was introduced here in the 1880s, silver carp and bighead carp feed not on the bottom but in the top few feet of the water column. These carp eat only plankton, which they filter from the water with rakers in their gills. They are highly efficient feeders, outconsuming other fish and leaving less for the fry of such game fish as bass, crappies, and walleyes. The fear is that when they get in a lake or a river you will soon have nothing else.

In the United States, the Asian carp started their journey from a place of formerly ominous reputation: Down the River. As long ago as the 1970s, bigheads and silvers escaped into the lower Mississippi River from waste-treatment plants and commercial catfish ponds in Arkansas and Mississippi. Down south they were worker fish, imported to clean up enclosed areas by eating algae. Presumably, Mississippi River floods gave them the chance to get away. Once at large, the carp headed north, eventually turning up in the Missouri, the Tennessee, the Ohio, the Des Moines, the Wabash, the Illinois. For the long term, they seem to have their sights set on Canada. Today, just a few decades after their escape, they are almost there.

Not to get too sentimental about it, but the Mississippi

River is us, and vice versa. It's our bloodstream. Last summer I was driving along the river in western Illinois thinking how horrible the Mississippi had been lately, with its outsize floods and its destruction of New Orleans, and I noted the recent flooding still in progress along the Illinois shore—the miles of roads and fields submerged, and the ferry landing at Golden Eagle, Illinois, now separated from dry land by seventy feet of mud and water, and low-lying parking lots full of river mud cracked like pieces of a jigsaw puzzle curling in the sun. In the sprawl of standing water over parts of the landscape no actual river could be found. Then the road I was on descended from a ridge to the mostly unflooded river town of Hamburg, Illinois, and the Mississippi itself was running fast beside the main street, and just across the shining expanse were the houses and church steeples on the Missouri side. An old and powerful emotion hit me; my blood leaned with the current and I let the recriminations go by.

The fact that Asian carp are now in this river and many others, sucking in plankton and growing big and reproducing and waiting to smack a Jet Skier's face, is really not good. Possibly, these carp will change large parts of our national watersheds forever. We may be infected with a virus for which there is no cure.

• •

Among Asian-carp-infested rivers, the Illinois has it worst of all. This river is formed by the junction of the Kankakee and the Des Plaines about fifty miles southwest of downtown Chicago. It runs at a diagonal partway across the state and then turns due south, meeting the Mississippi north of Saint Louis. Via the Des Plaines, most of the treated wastewater of Chicago flows south into the Illinois. It's the main industrial river of the state. The fields of corn and soybeans through which it passes are the factory floor, the river is the conveyor. If there's any stretch of this river that doesn't hum and throb—with barges, tugs, grain elevators, power plants, coal depots, refineries—I didn't see it.

One morning in August I was fishing in the Illinois by the boat-launch ramp in a riverfront park in Havana, Illinois, a town whose full name is pleasant to say. Not much water traffic was passing at this early hour. A light breeze interfered with the deep-green reflection of the trees on the far shore, and the echoes of car tires rolling on the brick ramp bounced off some barges parked over there. Fish were rising near the bank in the brown current. I cast to them with a dry fly, but they wouldn't bite. Later, a guy in a sporting-goods store explained that these were Asian carp feeding on grain dust from the elevators upstream. In fact, because of the tininess of what they eat, Asian carp are almost impossible to catch with hook and line.

I quit fishing as the sun rose above the trees and the day became stifling. Two fishermen came to the boat launch from upriver in an eighteen-foot bass boat with a twenty-five-horsepower outboard. They had on camo hats and blue-jean bib overalls. As they were winching their boat onto the trailer, one of them fanned himself with his hat and yelled to me, "Hey, turn down the heat!" I went over and said hello and asked how they had done. They opened their cooler and showed me a beautiful catch of crappies and a medium-size striped bass. I expressed surprise at their success and said I had heard that the Asian carp had depleted this fishery. Not necessarily, the guys said, adding that there were so many little Asian carp now that the other fish had more prey to feed on. I asked if they thought Asian carp were a serious problem.

"Oh, hell yes, they're a problem," the smaller of the two guys said. "They jump up and hit you all the time, and they get slime on you, and they shit all over your boat. And *bleed*—oh, they bleed like no sonsabitches you've ever seen. Yesterday, a carp hit Junior in the chest—I thought it would go into his bib—and it left a trail of shit and slime and blood all down the front of him."

"Hey, look—there's my nephew!" Junior interrupted. A blue-and-white striped tugboat was going by with a young fellow in jeans and a T-shirt standing in the wheelhouse at the top. "My nephew's the youngest pilot on the river— became a pilot right out of high school," Junior said. He and the other guy waved and the pilot waved back, the happiest man in Illinois. A large American flag fluttered at the tug's stern. All around the boat, from the roiled wake and from the curls of foam at the bow, carp of mint-bright silver were leaping in the sun.

••

In the parking lot of the local field station of the Illinois Natural History Survey, just up from the boat launch, two big outboards with twin motors sat dripping on their trailers. After a thorough hosing down, the boats still smelled of disinfectant, and a few fish scales clung to the aluminum structures in their bows. At a desk in the field-station office, Matt O'Hara, a tall, broad-shouldered fish biologist who had just come in from the river, sat and talked with me, while at an adjoining desk a colleague talked to a film crew from an outdoor channel. Another reporter and a film crew from ESPN were expected shortly. During a recent fish survey, Matt O'Hara said, so many fish jumped out of the river at the first jolt of electroshocking that a camera filming from the nearby shore was unable to see the boat. In fact, the visual craziness of the leaping-carp phenomenon, propagated in Internet videos, had been drawing TV crews from all over. Dealing with crews from every major channel, from cable shows, and from Canada, Russia, England, France, and Japan had become part of these biologists' job.

Their actual and more important job is keeping track of what's in the river. North America's two largest watersheds, the Mississippi and the Great Lakes, connect in one place: Chicago. Boats travel from the Atlantic Ocean into the Saint Lawrence Seaway, go through the lakes, turn into the Chicago Sanitary and Ship Canal, continue through the canal into the Des Plaines River, enter the Illinois, and head onward from there to the Mississippi and the Gulf of Mexico. This means that invasive species can travel the same route in either direction. All of them must pass by the Havana field station's door, and Matt O'Hara and others at the station check the river continually to see if they do. These days, the watchers' eyes are on the Asian carp, whose dense population in the Illinois—eight thousand or more silver carp per river mile—exerts a seemingly inexorable pressure northward, toward Chicago and the huge, Asian-carp-free (probably) watershed beyond.

Like other scientists who grasp the threat, Matt O'Hara becomes severe when he talks about it, though in a quiet and Midwestern way. "I don't know if silver carp and bighead carp would necessarily thrive in the Great Lakes," he told me. "Lake Erie is one of the biggest fisheries in the world—the lakes together are a seven-to-ten-billion-dollar fishery annually, and most of that catch is from Lake Erie—and it does look as if the carp would do well in that particular lake, and probably trash it. What I'm even more concerned about in the shorter run is the rivers. The Illinois became seriously infested just in the last seven years. A study has identified twenty-two rivers in the Great Lakes system that might be as vulnerable as the Illinois. Some of these

are major rivers with important salmon runs, like the Pere
Marquette and the Manistee, in Michigan. Asian carp in
those rivers could become a disaster really fast.

"You can eat Asian carp, and they're good. Score the
fillets crossways with a sharp knife and cook them in hot
oil, and it dissolves a lot of the bones. But given what they
do to an ecosystem, I can't say I see any advantage at all
with these fish, definitely not if they get in the lakes. They're
terrible for the aesthetics and they certainly make people
leery of going out in a boat. Even today, it is still legal to
import bighead carp, although silvers are now illegal. And
there's another kind of carp, the black carp, that's also in
Southern catfish ponds and is legal to import and could
be an additional disaster if it moved north. Black carp eat
snails and mussels and would probably strip our native
mollusk and shellfish populations, with all kinds of consequences. That's a danger people should think about, too.
We knew fifteen years ago the silvers and the bigheads were
going to be a problem, but nothing was done about them.
Until recently, nobody paid attention to carp."

• •

Well, okay, let's eat them. This solution has already occurred to the state of Illinois. Americans in general are not
keen on eating carp, so, looking elsewhere, the governor
of Illinois recently announced an agreement to sell local
carp to the Chinese. Big River Fish Corporation, of Pearl,
Illinois, would harvest, package, and ship carp to the Beijing
Zhouchen Animal Husbandry Company, while the state
would invest $2 million in Big River to improve its facilities
and processing capacity. The Chinese had already inspected
the product and announced their complete satisfaction with
"the wild Asian carp" of Illinois. Zhouchen said it would

buy thirty million pounds, and possibly more, by the end of 2011.

Pearl, Illinois, by the Illinois River in the west-central part of the state, is on Route 100 and has 187 residents. A small post office makes up about a quarter of its downtown. Big River Fish, around a bend on Route 100, announces itself with two hand-painted wooden signs, one facing north and one south, against the trunk of a maple tree. The signs show the profile of a long-whiskered catfish done all in black and shades of gray except for the hypnotic yellow eye. Rick Smith, Big River's president, was not in his office the morning I drove the eighty-some miles down from Havana. He had just left for the big motorcycle rally in Sturgis, South Dakota, towing his fried-fish cook shack. Rick Smith belongs to the very small number of motorcycle-rally food venders who also ink multimillion-dollar deals with the Chinese.

Mike Houston, a Big River employee, was locking up as I arrived. The company would close for about a week, until the boss returned, he said. Mike Houston had a red pony-tail, gray hair at the temples, blue eyes, a ginger-colored beard, a red Ohio State baseball cap, and a T-shirt with a saying about beer. Accompanying him was another employee, a wiry bald man with tattoos and a walrus mustache. "Yeah, we've already sold our first load of Asian carp to the Chinese," Mike Houston said. "They're also buyin' yellow carp, grass carp, catfish. Thirty million pounds is a lot of fish, but they say it will feed one city. We get the fish in the round—that means whole—and then we gut 'em and power-wash the cavity. That cavity's got to be completely clean before you can ship 'em. The Chinese want the carp with the tails, heads, and scales still on. We flash-freeze 'em in our forty-below-zero freezing chamber and then bag 'em individually and put 'em in big plastic shipping bags that hold twelve or fifteen hundred pounds of fish.

"We're expanding our operation, but right now we can move a hell of a lot of fish out of here. We can operate year-round, because there's no restrictions and nobody cares how many carp you catch. Guttin' these fish is hard work. Some of the Asian carp go fifty, sixty pounds. Just liftin' 'em is hard. I used to be a chef, I can work a knife, and I've had days when I've gutted and washed twenty thousand pounds of fish. These Asian carp, what they eat, basically, is muck. You'd be surprised, though—their meat is all white meat, and it's good. I've eaten it. People say it's difficult to find Asian carp in China because they're all fished out. I like to think, sellin' silver carp and bighead carp to the Chinese, that we're sendin' their own product back to 'em. And I'll tell you, even with all the fish we move, we ain't makin' a dent in the Asian carp that's out there. There's commercial fishermen in Havana and in Beardstown that we can call up and say we need a hundred thousand pounds of fish right away, and those boys can get a hundred thousand pounds to us in a day or two. And a day or two later they can have a hundred thousand more. No, we ain't makin' a dent."

• •

The town of Bath, nine miles south of Havana on a long slough of the Illinois, takes a sporting approach to the problem. Every year in August, the Boat Tavern, a waterfront bar in Bath, holds a fishing tournament in which teams of anglers catch silver carp. It's called the Redneck Fishing Tournament; the first was in 2004. Prizes are given for the most fish and the best costumes. This year, 105 boats (at a $50 entry fee apiece) competed before a crowd of about two thousand in the event's two days. The method of fishing was straightforward: flush the carp from the water with boat engines and snatch them from the air with nets. There was also barbecuing, beer drinking, karaoke singing, games for children and teenagers, bluegrass bands, booths selling T-shirts, etc. Among the crowd, T-shirt adages were on the order of FRIENDS DON'T LET FRIENDS FISH SOBER and WHAT HAPPENS IN THE BARN STAYS IN THE BARN.

From the top of the boat ramp leading to the event, the Redneck Fishing Tournament smelled like ketchup and mud. This was on Saturday afternoon, the event's peak. Spectators milled, media swarmed. At occurrences of even slight interest, a forest of boom mikes converged, while video cameras pointed here and there promiscuously. A notice on a telephone pole announced that just by entering the premises you were granting a production company called Left/Right the permission to use your voice, words, and image in a project temporarily called "Untitled Carp" any-where on Earth or in the universe in perpetuity.

Tall cottonwoods, ash trees, and maples shaded the shore, which was rutted black mud firmed up in places with heaps of new sand. Crushed blue-and-white Busch beer cans disappeared into the mud, crinkling underfoot. Aluminum johnboats, some camo, some not, lined the riverfront in fleets. Fishing costumes involved headgear: army helmets, football helmets with face guards or antlers or buffalo horns, octopus-tentacle hats, pirate bandannas, Viking hel-mets with horns and fur, devil hats with upward-pointing horns, a hat like a giant red-and-white fishing bobber, a Burger King crown. Competitors had their faces painted camo colors or gold or red or zebra-striped. Bath, Illinois, was first surveyed by Abraham Lincoln, and on August 16, 1858, while campaigning against Stephen Douglas in the race for the U.S. Senate, Lincoln delivered his famous "House Divided" speech to a large crowd in Bath. He took as his text the New Testament verse "A house divided against itself cannot stand." A hundred and fifty-two years later, the Confederate-flag halter tops mingling with the American flags among the tournament crowd would have puzzled him; likewise, the pirate flags.

The competition took place in heats that lasted two hours. Before each start, boats put off from shore with their engines idling and waited for Betty DeFord, of the Boat Tavern, to give the signal. This honor belonged to her as the inventor and organizer of the tournament. At the air-horn blast, the boats raced off, net-men and -women holding extralarge dip nets at the ready. Soon you could see people plucking fish out of the air. Most of the boats then careered away and out of sight. Two hours later, they eased back to the riverbank, many of them heavily loaded. Grinning competitors carried big heavy-duty plastic barrels of silver carp, a man on each side, to the counting station, where festival officials counted the fish one by one and threw them into the tarpaulin-lined bed of a pickup truck. Among participants and onlookers, a cheerful giddiness prevailed. I had never seen so many fish. It was like an old-time dream of frontier bounty.

Randy Stockham, of Havana, won first prize, $1,400. He and his team caught 188 fish. Second prize of $1,100 went to Ron St. Germain, of Michigan, with 186. Mike Mamer and his Sushi Slayers, of Washington, Illinois, were third, at 153 fish ($800). Top prizes for costumes were awarded to devils from Greenview, Illinois, and cavemen from Michigan. The tournament also donated $1,500 to help local children suffering from developmental disorders and cancer. A total of 3,239 fish were caught, all of them silver carp. They ended up as fertilizer on Betty DeFord's thirty-acre farm.

"I'm just a grandmother and a bartender," Betty DeFord

said when I called her at the Boat Tavern a week later for a final recap. "I don't even own this bar. I started the Redneck Fishing Tournament because I want to warn other parts of the country about what these carp will do. I remember when this water had no Asian carp, and you could go frog gigging with a flashlight and a trolling motor on a summer night. The way these fish attack, that's impossible now. We just finished our tournament, and the carp are jumping more out there than they ever were. I want everybody to know: these fish need to be gone."

••

As you proceed northward toward Chicago on the Illinois, the industrial noise along its banks increases. Turning into the Des Plaines River south of Joliet, you might feel you're in the clanking, racketing final ascent of a roller coaster's highest hill. After Joliet, the machinery of greater Chicago multiplies along the riverbank until, in the municipality of Romeoville, white refinery towers in ranks send white clouds spiraling skyward, and a mesa of coal like a geological feature stretches for a third of a mile, and empty semi-trucks make hollow, drumlike sounds as they cross railroad tracks, and other vehicles beep, backing up. The place is a no-man's-land. Here the channelized Des Plaines and the Chicago Sanitary and Ship Canal, which have already met up some miles to the south, run parallel, about three hundred yards apart. The water in both of them is the color of old lead.

Romeoville is where the Army Corps of Engineers and the state of Illinois think they can stop the carp. At two locations on the ship canal, electric barriers zap the water. The canal, a rectilinear rock-wall ditch 160 feet wide and about 25 feet deep, passes through Romeoville behind chain-link fences topped with barbed wire and hung with signs: DAN-GER: ELECTRIC FISH BARRIER and ELECTRIC CHARGE IN WATER/ DO NOT STOP, ANCHOR, OR FISH and CAUTION: THIS WATER IS NOT SUITABLE FOR WADING, SWIMMING, JET SKIING, WATER SKIING/TUBING, OR ANY BODY CONTACT. At the fish barriers, steel cables or bars on the bottom of the canal pulse low-voltage direct current. The electric charge—according to the navy, whose divers tested it, somehow—is strong enough, under some circumstances, to cause muscle paralysis, inability to breathe, and ventricular fibrillation in human beings.

What it does to fish is less clear. Entering Chicago, the plucky Asian carp swims into a whole cityful of complications, and it continues to swim single-mindedly while questions of politics, bureaucracy, urban hydrology, and interstate commerce work themselves out. To put it another way: Chicago is a swamp. Various watercourses, only temporarily subdued, thread throughout the metro area. The engineers who caused local rivers to run backward a hundred years ago to send Chicago sewage south to the Mississippi rather than into the city's front yard—Lake Michigan—did not have too hard a job, because the underlying swamp could do the same thing itself when in flood. Given enough rainfall, the waters of swampy Chicago become one. The Des Plaines River needs no electric barrier because its Chicago section does not connect to the lake; however, when the Des Plaines floods, it sloshes into the ship canal at points above the canal's electric barriers. And the Des Plaines is very likely to have Asian carp.

Meditating on the complications of the carp's presence in Chicago can disable the brain. Do the electric barriers actually stop all the carp, or are the little ones able to get through? Do stunned fish sometimes wash through in the occasional reverses of flow in the canal? Does the electric charge remain strong and uniform when ships and barges go by? (Probably; instruments in tollbooth-like buildings beside the canal adjust the charge when necessary.) Does the electric field have weak spots where fish can pass? Does a wintertime influx of road salt in the water cause the charge to fluctuate? What about when the current must be turned off for maintenance of the bars or cables? Is the rotenone chemical fish killer administered when the current is off effective without fail?

The Chicago waterway system has several locks—why not simply close these and be done with it? Would closing the locks have a negligible effect on the economy of Illinois, as a study commissioned by the state of Michigan has claimed, or damage its economy irreparably, as demonstrated in a study preferred by Illinois? Would closing the locks risk flooding thousands of Chicago basements, as local officials say? How about the part of the waterway where there is no lock at all? Wouldn't the carp simply go that way? Will the new thirteen-mile barricade of concrete and special wire mesh designed to keep carp from swerving out of the Des Plaines and into the ship canal during flood times actually work? Will uninformed anglers introduce Asian-carp minnows while using them for bait? And what about immigrant communities from Asia who are known to perform ritual releases of fish and other animals during certain religious ceremonies? Might they have performed such rituals involving Asian carp already? Might they do so in the future? Will all this bring prevention to naught?

The Illinois Department of Natural Resources addresses itself to many of these questions, as does the U.S. Army Corps of Engineers (Great Lakes and Ohio River Division), the Metropolitan Water Reclamation District of Greater

Chicago, the U.S. Fish and Wildlife Service, the Senate
Great Lakes Task Force, the Congressional Great Lakes Task
Force, the White House Council on Environmental Qual-
ity, the interagency Asian Carp Rapid Response Team, and
the interagency Asian Carp Regional Coordinating Com-
mittee's Asian Carp Control Framework. The Illinois
Chamber of Commerce, the American Waterways Opera-
tors, and the Chemical Industry Council of Illinois put in a
word for industry, while the Natural Resources Defense
Council, Freshwater Future, the Sierra Club, Healing Our
Waters Great Lakes Coalition, and the Alliance for the
Great Lakes offer perspective from the environmental side.
The Chicago Department of the Environment, the Great
Lakes Fishery Commission, the Great Lakes and St. Law-
rence Cities Initiative, and the University of Toledo's Lake
Erie Center are heard from as well. For legal guidance, con-
cerned parties refer to the Nonindigenous Aquatic Nui-
sance Prevention and Control Act of 1990 (revised as the
National Invasive Species Act of 1996, revised as the Na-
tional Aquatic Invasive Species Act of 2007); also, to the
Asian Carp Prevention and Control Act of 2006.

Man proposes, carp disposes. Through waving weed
beds of bureaucracy and human cross-purposes, the fish
swims. Starting in 2009, tests for Asian-carp DNA in Chicago waters indicated that the fish might have moved beyond the barriers. In February 2010, the state of Illinois,
hoping to calm its neighbors, began an intensive program
of fishing for actual fish with electroshocking and nets,
while the DNA tests continued. These efforts turned up
more DNA but no fish. In March, the Illinois DNR announced that six weeks of searching had found no Asian
carp throughout the entire Chicago Area Waterway System.
Then, on June 22, a commercial fisherman working for the
DNR netted a nineteen-pound-six-ounce bighead carp in

Lake Calumet, thirty miles beyond the electric barrier and six miles from Lake Michigan. Between this well-fed, healthy male Asian carp and the Great Lakes no obstacle intervened.

If the neighbors had been worried before, they began to sweat and hyperventilate now. Outcries of alarm came from officialdom in Minnesota, Wisconsin, Michigan, Ohio, Pennsylvania, and New York, as well as from Canada. Michigan's attorney general, Mike Cox, brought suit in federal district court to force the Corps of Engineers and the city of Chicago to close the locks immediately. Four other Great Lakes states, but not New York, joined on Michigan's side; two previous lawsuits for the same purpose had already failed. The Senate Energy and Natural Resources Subcommittee on Water and Power held hearings on the federal response to Asian carp. The governor and the attorney general of Ohio called on the president to convene a White House Asian Carp Emergency Summit. Dave Camp, a congressman from Michigan, proposed a piece of legislation he called the CARP Act, for Close All Routes and Prevent Asian Carp Today.

Senator Dick Durbin, of Illinois, announced that he had asked the president to appoint a Coordinated Response Commander for Asian Carp, and the president had agreed. This so-called carp czar was to be chosen within thirty days. The president made clear that he had a "zero-tolerance" policy for invasive species. Senator Kirsten Gillibrand, of New York, announced her support for another anticarp bill, the Permanent Prevention of Asian Carp Act. Michigan's Mike Cox accused Obama of not doing enough about the problem because he sympathized with his own state of Illinois. (Cox, a Republican, is running for governor.) Senator Carl Levin, Democrat of Michigan, sent Obama a letter asking him to act quickly to protect the Great Lakes from Asian carp, and thirty-two representatives and fourteen senators added their names.

••

Unlike Romeoville, the place where the apocalyptic bighead was caught is quiet. To some, it might even be paradise. The part of Lake Calumet in which the commercial fisherman netted this carp doubles as the water hazard beside the concluding holes of a luxury golf course called Harborside, rated by *Golfweek* as the third-best municipal golf course in the country. One afternoon, I walked some of the course. To play eighteen at Harborside on a Saturday or a Sunday costs $95; new SUVs filled the parking lot. Several of the raised tees provided a panoramic view of the Chicago skyline, while the surrounding Rust Belt ruins and ghetto neighborhoods of south Chicago just beyond the fence seemed far away. I asked employees at the clubhouse golf shop, waiters in the restaurant, a bartender, and a man tending the greens, but none had heard of the nation-shaking carp netted here two months before.

The reason the fisherman happened to be fishing here in the first place was that a team of scientists from Notre Dame had already found bighead carp DNA in the water. Working for the Corps of Engineers, the university's Center for Aquatic Conservation has been doing DNA tests for more than a year. As part of the increased tracking of Asian carp, the Notre Dame scientists collected samples from bodies of water all over Chicago. David M. Lodge, a professor of biology, heads the center. I stopped by South Bend to see him on my way back from Illinois.

Professor Lodge is a tall and genial man in his fifties, with a Southern accent, blue eyes, and a DPhil in zoology from Oxford University, which he attended on a Rhodes. He wore a yellow tennis shirt with his ballpoint pen and mechanical pencil stuck neatly in the button part of the neck, an innovation I admired, because I was wearing the same kind of shirt and had compensated for its lack of breast pocket by putting my pens in my pants pockets, always an awkward deal. He asked if I was writing something funny on carp. I said I probably was. "I know you can't not laugh when you see the silver carp jumping all over the place, but it's really not funny," he said. "It's a tragic thing, and people are wrong to trivialize it. We should focus on these fish's potential environmental and economic impact. In the Great Lakes—just as we're seeing now in south Louisiana—the environment *is* the economy. Look how the degrading of Lake Erie in the sixties and seventies contributed to the decline of Detroit and Cleveland and Buffalo. To people who say this is a question of jobs versus the environment, I say it's not either-or.

"The bigger issue is how we as a country protect ourselves against invasive species. At the moment, we are not very good at preventing invasions. We're constantly reacting after it's too late. Most invasions, if detected early, can be stopped, because establishing an organism so it's viable in a new environment is not automatic. Our current approach is more or less open-door. Right now, the canal-and-river passage across Illinois from the lake to the Mississippi is a highway for the dispersal of organisms. The Great Lakes is a hot spot for aquatic invasions. In the lakes there are a hundred and six species nonnative to North America that are not in the Mississippi, while there are only fifty in the Mississippi that are not in the Great Lakes. An even greater threat, really, is of invasions going in the opposite direction from the carp's—that is, going from the lakes to the Mississippi. The Mississippi system holds the richest heritage of biodiversity in North America. The electric barrier at Romeoville was built originally to stop a small

invasive fish called the round goby from coming south—
too late, as it turned out, because today the round gobies
are established in the Illinois. A later invasive, the tube-
nose goby, does appear to have been stopped. So the barrier
may have helped. But over time it will not be able to stop
everything.

"As for the Asian carp and the lakes, worst case is they're
already established there. We wouldn't necessarily know.
Usually, the first sign we have that organisms are invading
is that members of the public see them. But people aren't
underwater, and netting and electroshocking are not good
tools for finding out what's going on in a body of water,
especially not in one as big as Lake Michigan."

To explain more about how DNA testing for Asian carp
works, David Lodge led me to the office of his colleague
Christopher Jerde, a brown-haired South Dakotan who
helped develop the technique. I did not follow all the science of it. Essentially, the technique uses DNA found in
water samples to determine what species might have been
present, just as DNA evidence can suggest that a person
was at a crime scene. The DNA sequences in water samples
are not followed to the point where individual fish are
singled out, but that could be done, too. Christopher Jerde
said that people who wanted to ignore the carp problem
kept pooh-poohing Notre Dame's DNA findings before
the confirming bighead carp was caught. They argued that
the DNA could have been carried in on a duck's feathers,
or something. But in places where his team got multiple positive hits, he knew the fish had to be there. When he was
proved right, he took no pleasure. The carp invasion only
makes him mourn.

Some planners who take a long view believe that the
Midwest's invasive-species problem requires a bold solution:
the complete separation, or reseparation, of the Great Lakes

from the Mississippi at Chicago. This huge infrastructure project would consist of concrete dikes, new shipping terminals, new water-treatment facilities, maybe barge lifts to transfer freight, maybe the re-reversing of Chicago's wastewater flow so that it no longer goes south. Business interests tend to hate this idea. I asked Jerde about it, and he said, "Right here is where you could put something like that," and called up a Google Earth photo of Chicago's South Side on his computer. "This empty area here is a Rust Belt nowhere left over from old Chicago," he said. "The main hub of a new shipping and hydrological arrangement for Chicago could go right here." As it happened, the brown and empty region he indicated on the satellite photo was not far from the green oases of the Harborside golf course.

"Well, we don't have opinions on policy," he continued. "We just provide the data. We give it to the corps or the DNR, and they present it to the people who make the decisions, and it's out of our hands. When people were coming up with all those supposed rebuttals to our findings, we couldn't defend ourselves. It's frustrating. People either say we're wrong or exaggerating, so there's no problem and there's nothing we need to do, or else they turn around and say it's too late, the carp are already here, so there's nothing we *can* do. I don't know whether we can stop these fish, but if we do nothing I can guarantee this problem and plenty of others will get worse.

"Now, let me just show you a few of the places where we've had positive DNA hits for Asian carp." He touched a button on his computer and little yellow thumbtack-like circles appeared on the Google Earth photo. They followed the ship canal, they appeared in the Grand Calumet and Little Calumet Rivers, they clustered at the south end of the Romeoville electric barrier—proof that it was stopping fish, he said. "Last summer, we had a positive hit here, in Calumet Harbor, which is separated from the lake only by a breakwater," he said. Then he moved in to a closer view of Chicago's downtown. "We also got a positive right here." He pointed to a yellow thumbtack at the Chicago River Lock and Dam, under Lake Shore Drive, about a mile and a half north of the Shedd Aquarium.

October 25, 2010

Passengers

Before Salvatore Siano, known as Sal, retired, last December, he had driven a bus for the DeCamp bus company, of Montclair, New Jersey, for forty-two years. DeCamp has eight or ten routes, but Sal mostly drove the No. 66 and the No. 33, which wind among West Caldwell and Bloomfield and Clifton and Nutley before joining Route 3 and heading for the Lincoln Tunnel. Unlike some bus drivers and former bus drivers, Sal himself is not bus-like but slim and quick, with light-gray hair and eyebrows, and a thin, mobile face. In a region where the most efficient way to commute is by train, the bus can be cozier, more personal. When he drove, Sal reconfigured his bus as his living room, lining the dashboard with toy ducks, chatting over his shoulder with passengers, and sometimes keeping snowballs handy to throw at policemen through the open door. He used to caution children, "I am not a role model!" His travel-guide monologues upon arrival at the Port Authority Bus Terminal—"Welcome to sunny Aruba! Don't forget your sunblock! *Cha-cha-cha!*"—won him minor fame.

On the morning of September 11, 2001, Sal was driving a No. 66 bus that began its run at eight twenty-five. As he headed for the city on Route 3, he saw the smoke rising from downtown. By the time he reached the tunnel, it had been closed, and Sal had received a call from another driver telling him about the first plane. Wedged in heavy traffic, Sal managed to back the bus onto an entrance ramp, turn around, and retrace his route, dropping the passengers at their stops and returning their tickets or cash fares along the way. Six hundred and seventy-nine New Jerseyans, many from towns that Sal drove through, died in the attacks. Afterward, Sal stopped joking around on the bus. When asked why, he grew sad and dispirited, and said that he was too emotionally caught up in the tragedy. Eventually, he began to joke again.

Among his passengers, Sal had many fans. Once, when he pulled up to the Bellevue Plaza stop, in Upper Montclair—this was years ago, before September 11—he saw such a crowd that he thought he would have to order another bus. But then everyone yelled, "Surprise!" They had been waiting there to give him a party. He had great affection for his riders and considered 99 percent of them to be wonderful people. He never asked anyone's name or occupation, but he learned a lot about his regulars anyway. He believed that he had a skill for picking out the ones who would succeed and, as an example, cites a boy named John Miller, then a Montclair high school student, who became a well-known journalist and one of the only Americans to interview Osama bin Laden.

Sal lives by himself in a garden apartment in Clifton. In his retirement, he sometimes works for an auto shop, driving to pick up parts. Afternoons, he goes to Brookdale Park, in Montclair, and spends a couple of hours playing tennis or reading the newspapers. Recently, one of his fan-passengers—who can recall many drab morning walks that were improved by the sight of Sal waving to him from the driver's seat of a passing No. 66—stopped by the park to say hello. Sal was sitting in his car, taking shelter from the rain. A gloomy, apocalyptic quality of the light, maybe caused by the approaching hurricane, led to thoughts about the upcoming anniversary of September 11. Sal said, "The other day, I was remembering this one passenger from Upper Montclair who always got on at the Norwood Avenue stop, by the public library. After the attacks, I read in the paper—someone must have told me his name—that this man had passed away. He was such a pleasant human being. A man about my height, wore glasses. I had seen him just the week before. The obituary in the *Times* said this man volunteered to work in homeless shelters and sometimes slept in them to experience what they were like." (Here Sal began to cry.) "When I read that, I knew that my instincts about him had been right. I remember him whenever I go by Norwood and the library."

The passenger's name was Howard L. Kestenbaum. Along with the names of nearly three thousand other people who died that day, his is inscribed on a granite wall at the edge of the memorial garden in Eagle Rock Reservation, a county park in nearby West Orange, at the top of a ridge with a clear view of lower Manhattan. "He had a wife and daughter, and they are special people, too," Sal continued. "I still see them around Montclair on a regular basis. Whenever I do, I embrace them and give them a kiss on the cheek."

September 12, 2011

Sal Siano died in December 2014.

The Rap

Derrick Parker is the hip-hop cop. Although he no longer serves on the police force—he retired from the New York Police Department in 2002, as a twenty-year veteran with the rank of detective, first grade—that is still how people think of him. For years, Detective Parker was the department's hip-hop expert, and, starting in 1999, he headed a special intelligence unit that focused on rap and hip-hop crime. Now he has his own security firm in midtown. When a crime takes place in the rap and hip-hop world (a not uncommon occurrence) and no leads or witnesses can be found (ditto), Derrick Parker is still the person to call. In the past, he has consulted with police not just from New York but also from Miami, Orlando, Atlanta, Las Vegas, and Los Angeles. Some of rap music exists in a strange symbiosis with crime, and those close to the music are usually unwilling to talk to the police. This combination makes Derrick's skills unique; he probably knows more about crimes in the rap and hip-hop community than anybody but the perpetrators themselves.

His company, Styles Security and Executive Protection, on West Twenty-seventh Street, provides security for concerts, nightclubs, retail stores, and construction sites, along with executive protection and private investigation. The work allows Derrick to expand a circle of acquaintance already staggeringly large. He seems to know everybody. In the rap world, this familiarity extends from stars like Jay-Z and Foxy Brown to the dancers in the videos to Steve, the guy on the sidewalk who hands out rap-show flyers from a shopping bag. Derrick can tell you who shot Tupac Shakur and Jam Master Jay, and he has a fair idea of who killed Biggie Smalls. Just because a murder is unsolved doesn't mean nobody knows who did it. Information seeks out Derrick through the air, arrives with the R & B ringtone of his cell phone. "The street will tell you everything you need to know, if you wait patiently," he says. "The street knows everything."

Derrick turned forty-seven last May. He still has a kid's round, unlined face and a kid's openmouthed smile—the kind that goes up and down as much as it goes across. The expression conveys total delight; for all the mayhem and wickedness he has dealt with in his professional life, he is a remarkably lighthearted guy. Derrick stands six feet three and weighs about three hundred pounds. With his size and presence, you tend to see only angles of him, not all of him at one time. He is black, but now and then people mistake him for Indian or Latino, and he can get away with Italian, too. Strangers sometimes come up to him and start right in speaking Spanish, of which he knows only a few words.

He favors well-tailored suits in black or charcoal gray, purple shirts, and lavender ties. When called to testify in court, he dresses in a gray pin-striped suit, a white shirt with collar and cuffs of a creamier shade, and a tie striped white, light blue, and gray. A single-carat diamond-stud earring highlights his left earlobe. On occasion, he wears on his right hip or under his left arm a .40-caliber Glock automatic, a pistol he likes for its stopping power. "If you are shot with a forty-caliber you will definitely be wounded, possibly seriously enough to lead to your demise," he says. But in twenty years with the NYPD and five in private security he has never fired his gun except at the range.

His hands are large and thick, and he knows certain things like the back of them. To underscore this point, he will hold up one hand and tap its back significantly with the other, meanwhile tucking his chin into his collar and looking at you through his eyebrows. The gesture is that of an experienced interrogator. One particular thing he knows like the back of his hand is the Bedford-Stuyvesant neighborhood of Brooklyn. He was born there, in St. John's Episcopal Hospital (now Interfaith Medical Center), and both sets of his grandparents lived there. Later, his father, Lionel, a cop with the Sanitation Department, moved the family to St. Albans, in Queens. From visiting his grandparents back in Bed-Stuy, growing up in the black middle class of St. Albans, and attending mostly white Bayside High, to which he was bused, Derrick absorbed a cross section of New York. With this background, he can talk to anybody. White cops saw him as black, but fellow black cops used to tease him, "You ain' black, you're from Bayside!"

Derrick's mother, born Dolores Bryant, came from black show-business aristocracy. Her father, Willie Bryant, was the leader of a well-known swing band in the thirties and forties. He was also an uptown celebrity, then and into the fifties, as the master of ceremonies at the Apollo Theater. The city named him "Mayor of Harlem" (an honorary position) in 1952. Later, he moved to California, where he worked as a disk jockey and an actor for several years. Willie Bryant was light-skinned and could play nonblack roles. Dolores says that Derrick reminds her of her father—"especially when he quirks his eyebrow at you after he tells a joke. My daddy used to do his eyebrow just that way." For complicated reasons involving his grandparents' divorce, his grandmother's remarriage to a man whom Derrick knew as his grandfather but who was really his step-grandfather, and Willie Bryant's early death, in California, in 1964, Derrick never saw him face-to-face. But as a boy he did watch him in reruns of *The Untouchables*. Dolores remembers that in one episode her father played a crony of the gangster Frank Nitti and in another he was a detective helping Eliot Ness.

··

On an October night a couple of years ago, two crimes took place on the same block of West Twenty-first Street in Manhattan. At about midnight, a gold-and-diamond chain reportedly worth $50,000 was snatched from the neck of Sebastian Telfair, a professional basketball player then with the Boston Celtics. The theft occurred outside Justin's, a bar and soul-food restaurant frequented by rap stars. Telfair did not call the police or ask anybody else to, but by some accounts he was seen talking on his cell phone afterward. Then, within the half hour, somebody shot Fabolous, the rap star, in the thigh as he stood in a parking lot just up the street. On the way to Bellevue Hospital, the car in which Fabolous was riding was pulled over by the police, who found two handguns in it.

Logic suggested that the shooting and the theft were connected. Two weeks after the crimes, the *Daily News* sought out Derrick Parker (reporters, too, sometimes turn to Derrick to help them understand what's going on), and he explained that Fabolous grew up in Brooklyn's Brevoort projects, home to a number of dangerous thugs who belong to a gang called the Commission, or the Street Family. Some of these guys are part of Fabolous's crew, according to Derrick, and he even gave the Street Family a shout-out in one of his performances. In the past, this gang has robbed the rappers Busta Rhymes, Ol' Dirty Bastard, and Foxy Brown, Derrick told the *News*. Of the Telfair robbery, he added, "If the Commission members didn't do it, they know who did do it." Telfair, who comes from a project in Coney Island, has had his own run-ins with the law; Derrick speculated that after the Fabolous shooting there might be retaliation against Telfair. In any event, neither the theft nor the shooting was (or is) likely to be solved by the police. Neither victim gave the cops much useful information, and because gun charges against Fabolous were eventually dismissed, even those couldn't be used against him. (Fabolous's attorney says that the Street Family is a group of artists, and that his client "is not involved in any illegal activity.")

With no forthcoming witnesses, solid suspects, or arrests, Derrick's explanation seemed the closest to a resolution that these murky events were likely to have. As an average uninformed observer, I found myself grateful even for that slim shaft of clarity. The *News* article also mentioned that Derrick had a book out. It's called *Notorious C.O.P.: The Inside Story of the Tupac, Biggie, and Jam Master Jay Investigations from the NYPD's First "Hip-Hop Cop,"* by Derrick Parker, with Matt Diehl. Mainly, it concerns Derrick's NYPD career, especially his years working in rap intelligence, with long sections about the famous rap murders in the title. I enjoyed the book a lot; Derrick says that it has received praise from street thugs as well as from veterans of the NYPD.

The first time Derrick and I met, at his office, he held forth for six hours straight. Detective work is about narratives, and Derrick has hundreds of them. On top of that, he's naturally outgoing. Over the next couple of months, I hung out with him now and then—or, rather, I followed along while he did what he does. Being with him was almost always relaxing, like traveling with a citywide all-access pass.

••

One night in May, Derrick was manning the door at Spotlight Live, a nightclub on Broadway at Forty-ninth Street. Not much was going on when I arrived, at about eleven. Derrick stood by the velvet rope with other bouncers, some of them his employees, some the club's. One or two were even bigger and wider than he; a guy called House looked the part, all the way up to the rooflike black ski cap on top. Under a black suit coat, Derrick wore a heavy brown-and-black turtleneck against the chilly night air. Rain was falling straight down and a flashing advertisement that covered many stories of a nearby building was changing the rain from silver to red to blue. Derrick stayed dry under the marquee. I had an umbrella.

Derrick and the promoters he works with divide their nightclub events into categories. They are: Gay, Bridge & Tunnel, Latino, Italian, Asian (usually Chinese or Korean), Jewish, and Urban. Urban means black. Tonight was to be an Urban party, and the promoters, for security reasons, wanted an upscale crowd without too many gangster overtones. In dress-code terms, that ruled out baggy jeans, white T-shirts, gold chains, hooded sweatshirts, flat-brim fitted baseball caps ("fitteds"), do-rags, gang colors, and Timberland boots. The guidelines had some flexibility, naturally, and on a person-by-person basis Derrick was to be the arbiter. Practically speaking, that put him in charge of turning actual gangsters away. Before I arrived, a kid he didn't let in told Derrick that he was going to get his gun and come back and pop him. Derrick laughed this off.

By midnight, the crowds were lining up. Kids—everyone

there was a kid, it seemed to me, though some might have been in their thirties—came in groups of two or five or a dozen. Some of the young women were so beautiful that a force field around them dematerialized the raindrops before they hit. On this raw night, a few of these women were wearing, basically, handkerchiefs; unshivering, they stepped neatly on their pinpoint stilettos around the subway gratings without looking down. Nobody on city streets is as sweet and winsome as a young person trying to pass muster at a nightclub door. The wrongly dressed ones whom Derrick had questions about carried their appeals to bystanders, including me: "Yo, man, see—these boots *ain't* Timbalands, man, they jus' *look* like Timbalands!" And when Derrick approved of a particular ensemble, its wearer nodded with satisfaction and pride. To a woman who had on a zebra-stripe dress, House, the bouncer, said, "I *agree* with that!" The woman beamed.

An odd-looking older white guy walked up carrying a stick of firewood. It was good-sized, prism-shaped, with bark on one side. When told he could not take that into the club, he replied that he expected to have the firewood returned to him when he left. A tour bus stopped on Broadway and a full load of British tourists poured out. They thronged around Derrick, pleading to be let in free, their heads upturned like baby birds'. Two of them sheltered under my umbrella. They were from the city of Rochdale, in Lancashire, they said, and visiting New York on an all-expenses-paid tour sponsored by their company. Just for variety, Derrick let in all the Britishers. Streams of people, mostly women, kept showing up for a private birthday party on the club's third floor for somebody named Raheem. They also got in free.

All the while, Derrick provided a commentary for me, sort of out of the side of his mouth: "That dude there is DJ

Clue, from Power 105 FM. He's doin' the music tonight. He's the one whose car got shot up in front of the Hot 97 radio station a few years ago. Those guys behind him look pretty thugged-out, it's true, but I gotta let 'em all in, 'cause they're with him . . . That big guy is Al Harrington, the pro basketball player, with the Golden State Warriors . . . That's Donnell Rawlings, the former 105 FM DJ . . . O'Neal McKnight, the rhythm-and-blues guy; next week, he's doin' a bar mitzvah for a friend of mine . . . Glenn Toby, a good friend of mine from Queens back in the day, you gotta meet this guy. Glenn is the hottest sports agent around right now. He just moved Asante Samuel, of the New England Patriots, to the Philadelphia Eagles for I don't know how much money . . . That guy with the fade haircut is Kenny, a friend of Foxy Brown's brother, Gavin. [To Kenny:] Yo, man, I don't want you callin' your crew in Brownsville, sayin', like, 'Yo, it's hot over here at Spotlight, you better come over here!' I don't want to see any of your Brownsville crew around here tonight! . . . That huge guy, wearing the Cadillac medallion around his neck, he's called Escalade; he runs a charity basketball tournament uptown . . . The dudes with those slinky women are the founders of FUBU clothing . . . That sharp-looking guy with his hands in his pockets is Chris Gotti, of Murder Inc. Records, a big-time producer. He was cleared of federal money-laundering charges, got a not-guilty verdict a couple of years ago. We've done a lot of security work for Chris and his brother, Irv. Their real last name is Lorenzo. They're both really good guys.

"Sometimes in the clubs I see people from twenty, twenty-five years in my past," he went on, during a lull. "Guys I arrested back in the day are surprised I still remember their real names, their priors, what they did time for, the names of their baby mamas—all the data you store up in your head when you're a detective. A couple of years ago, at this club called Avalon, this dude tried to slip by with his hat down over his face, and I looked and I recognized him. It was a guy who'd been an enforcer for some Brooklyn drug dealers called the Ortiz brothers, Dominican guys. While he was working for them, this guy had a guy handcuffed in a bathroom and he was beatin' him, tryin' to find out what he'd done with some money he owed the Ortiz brothers, and this guy gets carried away and he kills him. So now he doesn't know what to do, so he cuts the guy up into parts, and later the victim's bones were found in trash bags beside the highway. The guy eventually got arrested for something else, and he turned state's evidence for the Feds, and helped convict a lot of other criminals, so the Feds gave him a reduced sentence, and he was out in eleven years.

"Anyway, as he was goin' by me at Avalon, I said to him, 'So, do you still like to use cutting tools?' and he said, 'Aww, Parker, *man*, don' be bringin' that old stuff up, all that's in my past, I did eleven years, I got my life back now.' Later, I told the promoter who this guy was and the promoter said, 'You mean you let a convicted murderer and dismemberer into my club?' I said, 'What can I do, man? He was dressed properly. According to the U.S. government, he's paid his dues.' "

By three in the morning, the night was winding down. A few people still came but no line accumulated at the door. The rain had stopped. Sometime after three, a small, mild-looking man asked to be let in with no cover charge. He said his name was Raheem. "Raheem, the dude with the birthday party?" Derrick asked; it was the very same. "Man, what're you doin' comin' so late to your own party?" Derrick remonstrated. "There's dozens and dozens of fine-lookin' women up there waitin' for you!" Raheem hurried in; rarely had I seen a happier man. The guy who had been compelled to check his piece of firewood came out and claimed it from beside a phone booth, where it was still sitting on the curb. The British tourists also began to emerge, in twos and threes, a few of them knee-walking drunk and being steered by their companions. The number of police cars parked out front on Broadway, which had never been fewer than two, increased to five. Standing beside them was Lieutenant Walter Mayerback, the NYPD officer with special oversight of all nightclubs in the Midtown North Precinct. Under a streetlight, he looked on with his arms crossed. Derrick took ten minutes and went over and talked cordially with him.

· ·

Derrick got into the security business in this way:

After high school, he went to St. John's University, then dropped out and joined the Police Academy. He graduated and became a cop in 1982. First, he worked street patrol in Times Square, and then the department assigned him to undercover narcotics in the Bronx, where he grew a bushy beard and spent his days buying drugs from street dealers and assisting in arrests. This was at the height of the crack-cocaine boom, when a single team might make thirty arrests in a day. For his success working undercover, Derrick received a promotion to detective, third grade, in 1986. Out of nearly thirty-eight thousand New York City cops, only five thousand are detectives, and to become one at the age of twenty-five is rare.

From the Bronx, Derrick went to the detective squad of the Seventy-fifth Precinct, in the East New York section of Brooklyn, and then to the Eighty-first Precinct, in Bedford-Stuyvesant. Both were experiencing an unprecedented surge in murders. In the Eighty-first, he regularly led the precinct in the number of murder cases closed. When his boss there,

Lieutenant Commander Joseph Pollini, was given the job of running the NYPD's Cold Case Squad, in 1996, he took Derrick with him. Some of the city's best detectives work at Cold Case. They have more freedom and use more personal initiative as they track down long-uncaught murderers, sometimes traveling out of state or even out of the country.

Throughout his years in the department, Derrick also moonlighted at other occupations. Police regulations allow New York City cops to work up to twenty hours a week at outside jobs, provided the jobs meet certain criteria. Derrick was the assistant promotional director and then the promotional director for a magazine called *Chocolate Singles*, a publication aimed at young single black people. In that capacity, he arranged parties, dances, group vacations, and musical events, putting in ten hours or so a week for about six years. Sometimes he also sang backup for musical acts in nightclubs, and in 1988 he even cut his own record, "Single Man," with Jump Street Records. He had always loved rap music, from back when it almost didn't have a name and he used to listen to local rappers who wired their amps into the bases of streetlights in places like O'Connell Playground, in Queens. As rap grew in popularity and crimes became more common in the hip-hop world, he tried to alert his superiors in the department to the problem.

They didn't have much interest until 1997, with the murder of Biggie Smalls. After the rapper and Bed-Stuy habitué was shot, in Los Angeles, Derrick told his superiors that Biggie's funeral, in Brooklyn, would be huge. By then, Derrick was known in the department as the authority on questions regarding rap. Partly because of his counsel, the department assigned thousands of officers to escort the funeral procession, he says. Though the crowds showed up as predicted, the event went off without major violence. After that, the NYPD decided that rap crime should have its own unit within Gang Intel. In 1999, Derrick was moved from Cold Case to head the new rap-intel squad.

Two high-profile New York City rap-related crimes followed not long afterward. In December 1999, there was the Club New York shooting, when Sean "Puffy" (at the time) Combs got into an altercation in a midtown club that left three patrons shot, one seriously. Combs, with his bodyguard, his driver, and his then girlfriend, Jennifer Lopez, was picked up in his SUV on Eighth Avenue after fleeing the scene. A high-ranking police boss called Derrick at home on Long Island at two in the morning and told him to go to the Midtown North Precinct right away. Dozens of reporters, photographers, and miscellaneous people were at the precinct house by then.

Derrick recalls the lawyers for the parties under arrest applauding when he walked in; they were glad to see someone who knew what he was doing. He took over from the duty chief and straightened things out, allowed each person to see his or her attorney, and unlocked Jennifer Lopez's arm from a pipe where somebody had handcuffed her. When all the principals in the case were taken to Midtown South, the precinct of the shooting, he says he rode in the car with Jennifer Lopez.

Among the witnesses who had been at Club New York was a man named Glen Beck, who was doing security for the promoter. Beck had been standing at his station just outside the club's entrance when he heard shots. He looked inside, and seconds later he saw Combs and others hurtling down the club's stairs, tripping on a broken step, and sliding around the curved wall at the bottom, like when a roller coaster goes around a turn on its side. Then they ran out the door. Along with other witnesses, Beck gave a statement to the police. As it happened, he and Matthew Bogdanos, the ADA prosecuting the case, had both been in the Marine Corps. Bogdanos introduced Glen Beck to Derrick, recommending each man highly. Glen and Derrick hit it off right away.

The next rap crime to make news was the Lil' Kim shoot-out. In February 2001, Lil' Kim's entourage and sympathizers of her rival, Foxy Brown, fired more than twenty shots at each other on the streets of a commercial and residential neighborhood downtown. The fact that the shoot-out took place where it did—a woman with a baby stroller appears on the security tape just before the gunfire starts—upset the police. Derrick had recently switched to celebrity bodyguarding as his off-duty occupation, and when the shooting occurred he was in Las Vegas escorting the Rock, the actor and World Wrestling Federation star. An urgent call from the chief of detectives brought him back to New York, where he met with Police Commissioner Bernard Kerik, who, according to Derrick, yelled, "Derrick, I want those fuckers! And I want those fuckers *now!*"

One result of this incident was that the chief of detectives ordered Derrick to compile a dossier that included every person in the rap-music business who might be of interest to the police. Derrick says he thought that the idea was unsound, because people in the hip-hop world might somehow obtain the information in the dossier and use it against each other. Also, such a plan seemed close to racial profiling. He was told to make the dossier anyway, and he did, and it became known in the department as the Binder. Newspapers later found out about the Binder, quoted people who were outraged to hear about it, and identified Derrick as the one who had compiled it.

In May 2001, police detectives in Atlantic City asked Derrick to come down and help them gather intelligence during a rap event there. He agreed, and took his brother along, because he thought he might enjoy the trip. Two detectives who were working the Lil' Kim shooting heard about the trip and asked if they could meet up with Derrick in Atlantic City. They hoped they might find some leads there. He said that would be okay. But in Atlantic City, when the detectives walked up to him and asked where they might find a guy they wanted to talk to, Derrick just shrugged and smiled. The guy in question was standing right next to him.

Afterward, the detectives complained to the department that Derrick wasn't helping them. They also said that Derrick's brother had represented himself as a New York City cop while in Atlantic City. Because of this charge, and an earlier one alleging that Derrick had leaked information to the defense in the Sean Combs trial, Derrick became the subject of an investigation by the department's Internal Affairs Bureau. After examining the facts, the IAB concluded that the charge of leaking information was groundless, and that Derrick's brother had not represented himself as a policeman in Atlantic City. The IAB did, however, give Derrick a ruling of "warned and admonished" for bringing his brother along while he was on the job. Derrick recalls that his punishment was the loss of one or two vacation days.

This series of events persuaded Derrick that he should retire. His high profile and his friendships with rappers had brought him enmity in the department, and he feared that another IAB investigation might cost him his pension. A number of precinct chiefs asked him to join their homicide squads. Joseph Pollini, his former boss at Cold Case, offered him his old job back. Derrick thanked them but said no. By now he was making a hundred thousand a year as a detective, first grade. His pension would be half that plus health insurance and adjustments for cost of living.

He had no big expenses—no wife or children to support—and he could think of lots of other things he'd like to do. He left the force in January 2002.

In the meantime, a jury had acquitted Sean Combs of gun possession and bribing a witness in connection with the Club New York shooting. "It made no sense for Bogdanos to claim that Puffy had a gun," Derrick said. "Puffy has people to do that for him." Glen Beck's description of Combs coming headlong down the stairs, tripping, and turning sideways along the wall argued against Combs possessing a gun at the time, because it would have fallen out in the tumble. Beck testified for the defense, and as a result his friendship with Bogdanos grew strained.

Derrick and Glen Beck, however, had become close friends. Each had skills that complemented the other's. Beck, the former marine, is a jujitsu fifth-degree black belt, and a direct, confrontational type who doesn't hesitate to fight, while Derrick has a more laid-back and diplomatic style. By temperament, the two make up the classic hard-cop, soft-cop duo. Eventually, they decided to pool their experience and go into business together. The year after Derrick retired, he joined Styles Security, which Beck had recently founded. Some of Derrick's former colleagues told him that he had gone over to the "dark side." But he found that he liked his new career better, all in all, than being with the police.

••

On the walls of Derrick's office hang a cloth dartboard for Velcro darts, several plastic security IDs on lanyards, a poster-size blowup of a *Village Voice* front page featuring him, and his Certificate of Retirement from the NYPD. On one side of his desk is a squat floor safe and a paper shredder, and in a corner stands a fingerprinting table with ink pad, fingerprint blanks, and alcohol swabs. About fifty guys work for him; during the busier months, at the end of the year, he might employ eighty or a hundred. Each employee is fingerprinted, and then vetted and licensed by the state. Each also has to take a total of twenty-four hours of state-administered training and an annual eight-hour refresher course.

Sometimes the top document on the piles on Derrick's desk is a letter on impressive stationery from a law firm informing him that he is being sued. Bouncers can't legally do much to you besides intimidate you. If they use physical force and injury or damage results, they can be arrested or (as more often happens) sued. Derrick's company gets sued all the time. He has never lost a trial and he doesn't mind going to court. At the moment, four plaintiffs are suing him. Two of the suits involve deaths: first, he says, by the family of a young man who died of stab wounds across the street from Spotlight, in January, because the family claims he was stabbed inside the club when Derrick and his guys were on duty; and, second, by the family of a man who allegedly assaulted one of Derrick's off-duty bouncers with a pipe and the bouncer punched him and the man died.

No one who has worked for Derrick's company has been seriously injured or killed in his employ. However, a longtime employee named Israel Ramirez, called Izzy, died of a gunshot wound while working for somebody else. Izzy was a cheerful guy, twenty-nine years old, with three kids. Both Derrick and Glen liked him and considered him a friend; Glen had known Izzy since he was a teenager. In February 2006, Izzy was working as a bodyguard for the previously robbed Busta Rhymes at the filming of a video at a warehouse in Brooklyn. An argument started between people at the event when a group of guys with the rapper Tony Yayo got kicked out. As the dispute continued on the street, somebody shot Izzy in the chest. Of the hundreds in attendance at the video session, nobody would say who killed him. Busta Rhymes, who is presumed to have seen the shooting, expressed condolences to Izzy's family but did not tell the police much of anything.

Other bodyguards and bouncers, Derrick and Glen included, reasoned that any one of them could have been Izzy. Some security firms were so disgusted by Busta Rhymes's unhelpfulness to the police that they said they would no longer work for him. Derrick took a more lenient view. "If Busta goes to the cops, he's a snitch," Derrick says. "His popularity and his record sales go way down. It would be impossible for him—career suicide. The detectives on the case should realize that fact and start coming up with other witnesses. They won't make any progress if they keep focusing on Busta." Derrick adds that his company has not boycotted Busta Rhymes.

When I mentioned this opinion of Derrick's to a detective who had worked with him and is still on the force, the detective said, "I think that's bullshit, honestly. So Busta's record sales do go down ten percent. So what? If Busta saw who killed his bodyguard, he should come forward, because it's right. Forget about the record sales. There's a principle involved here. Busta should come forward because it's right.

"Derrick is a good man, and somehow he gets along with and understands and even likes these people he works for," the detective said. "Well, Derrick does what he does. You dance with the devil and hope you don't get burned."

• •

Going to meet Derrick at the Eighty-first Precinct station house in Bedford-Stuyvesant one morning, I took a round-about way through the neighborhood. I'd walked a lot in

Brooklyn, but not much in or near Bedford-Stuyvesant before. The day was hot, and by eight o'clock I had sweated
through my shirt. A school crossing guard looked at me
and said, "Mm-hmm, sweatin' already!" At the corner of
Myrtle and Vanderbilt Avenues, a few blocks past the Walt
Whitman Houses, I came upon a memorial mural on the
brick wall of a building. It showed the face of a bright-eyed,
sincere-looking, mustachioed fellow superimposed on a
blue sky above a seascape with palm trees. I recognized the
name—Benjamin C. O'Garro—from Derrick's book. That
would no doubt be the same Benjamin O'Garro (or O'Gara)
also known, Derrick says, as Killer Ben. The memorial did
not mention this street name, or Derrick's theory that he
had been killed for stealing a chain from a Biggie Smalls
associate at a music-awards show. As I walked, I noticed
other street-corner murals. Most depicted painfully young
and fresh-faced men, often in an elongated, El Greco–like
portrait style. Many of the murals are fading in the weather
and need to be restored.

At the corner of Myrtle and Marcy, I turned left and
wandered into the paths through the Marcy Houses, a
public housing project of apartment buildings spread over
six full blocks. None of the windows in the buildings were
broken, community gardens flourished among the lawns,
police cars proceeded slowly along the paths, and there was
almost no trash. I asked a maintenance person sweeping
something into a long-handled dustpan, "Who would you
say is the most famous person ever to come from the Marcy
Houses?" She answered, "Jay-Z," with no pause, as if the name
were her own. Then, looking up and smiling, she said, "Jay-Z
grew up here, and there's other famous rappers from Marcy,
too—Papoose, Memphis Bleek . . ."

That day Derrick and I spent doing what he referred to
as a "ride-around." "I'll call you back—I'm on a ride-around

with this writer," I heard him tell somebody on his cell phone. Our only purpose was looking at out-of-the-way places of interest in Brooklyn, Queens, and the Bronx. On some of the streets we went down, the kids hanging out smiled and pointed at us. Derrick laughed. "They see a black guy and a white guy in an unscript car and they think they've spotted the po-po," he said. His driving might have been another clue. He drove like a cop, with a taken-for-granted authority, talking to me or on his cell phone all the while. If another car wanted to go ahead, he graciously let it, then swooped where he wanted to go.

"I asked you to meet me in the Eighty-first because I learned to be a detective mostly here," Derrick said. "When I was assigned to the Eighty-first, I already knew the neighborhood, because of my grandparents. I worked in the Eighty-first for eight years and I solved a lot of murders here. You gotta remember this was back in the crack era, when New York had many more murders than it has now. In the precinct where I was before this one, we had six murders in my first week. One year in that precinct, the Seventy-fifth, there were a hundred and twenty-eight murders—an average of more than two murders a week. The Eighty-first is smaller and not as bad as the Seventy-fifth, but, still, here in the Eighty-first we had fifty-one murders one year. I saw people who'd been killed every way you can be killed—shot, cut up, stabbed, face blown off by a shotgun, poisoned, shaken-baby syndrome, strangled, stuffed in a closet, smothered, decapitated, drowned. I don't know why seeing all that didn't affect me more. I mentally removed myself from it, I guess. I always loved to catch the guys that did it, though.

"With so many murders, you had a very high rate that were going unsolved. Some of the detectives here were just walking through the motions—they couldn't catch Charlie the Tuna on a tuna-fish can. I was lucky here in the Eight-one because I had an older detective that helped and taught me, Lloyd Henry. He was my father's age, and I was twenty-five, and Lloyd told me, 'I'm as old as your father, and I'll beat you like your father, too!' Lloyd Henry rode me like Seabiscuit, but he made a good detective out of me."

Derrick then called Lloyd Henry, who still lives in the neighborhood, and asked if we could stop by. Lloyd Henry was just going out for a jog. He said he would wait for us and came out in his running gear. We talked on the front steps of his brownstone. Lloyd Henry is a slim, light-eyed black man who ran a 47.4-second quarter mile in college and almost looks as if he could do it again today. He retired from the NYPD in 1995, after thirty-eight years. "Derrick had all the street skills and all the people skills you need to be a detective when he started out," Lloyd Henry said. "I didn't teach him any of those. I *did* teach him something about paperwork. That's mostly what being a detective is—paperwork, typing, filling out forms. People used to ask me what I did for a living and I'd say, 'I'm a clerk-typist.' That was really my job, more than anything else. On TV shows like *Law & Order*, when a detective brings a witness to the station house, he tells him, 'The sergeant will take your statement now.' That is completely untrue to life. No sergeant will take that statement—*you*, the detective, take the statement yourself, and then you type it up and get the signatures on it and photocopy it and file it and all the rest. Typing, neatness, spacing, making good reports—most of the young detectives and a few of the older ones were terrible at that."

"Remember Ernie Bostick, that couldn't type at all?" Derrick put in. "Ernie would triple-space his reports, so he had to run over onto extra pages that he'd staple to the original, and he made typos practically every other word.

One time, Ernie was trying to type 'homicide' and he messed it up so bad it came out 'yomice.' When we read the report we couldn't believe that typo. So that became the word we used. We'd say, 'Hey, how many yo-mice did we have in the precinct this month?' or 'Hey, Lloyd, did you get any leads on that yo-mice on Gates Avenue?' "

Lloyd's wife, Geraldine, appeared from inside to give Derrick a hug. She joined us as Derrick and Lloyd talked about the robbery at the Shoe King store where a cop was shot five times and an accomplice of the robbers, shot in the leg, bled to death while the paramedics were taking care of the cop, and about the detective who used to fall asleep on the job while he drove, and about the suspect who agreed to take a lie-detector test and then showed up at the precinct house in the stolen car used in the crime. "Lloyd and Geraldine are like my family," Derrick said as we walked back to his car. Later, I noticed that many of the people he talked about, and almost everybody he introduced me to, he described in this way.

Every sight that passed by his windshield in Bed-Stuy seemed to be connected to him and to have a long caption. On Lewis Avenue, I glimpsed another memorial mural, this one to somebody named Larry Low-Top. "Oh, yeah, I knew Larry Low-Top," Derrick said. "I forget what his real last name was. He lived over past Decatur Avenue. I questioned him a few times. I don't think I ever arrested him, though."

"What was he like?"

"Larry? Well, he was a black male, about five nine, box-cut haircut like Wesley Snipes in *New Jack City*, always wore low-top sneakers, rocked a pink suit sometimes. He was shot to death outside his own birthday party at the Toy Factory, at Fifth Avenue and Twenty-fourth, in Manhattan."

Certain storied housing projects went by—the Tompkins Houses, the Sumner Houses, the Brevoort Houses. "We took a lot of bad guys out of here," Derrick said, as the Brevoort's many buildings came up on our right. He started talking about names from the past, recalling Kendu, and Da Kommander, and D-Nice, and Nubbs, and King Tut, and Big Born, and Sequan, and D-Wiz, and JuJu, and Franklin Frias, and Kool Aid and his even more dangerous brother Glaze, and Bey Allah. Our wanderings continued through East New York, past the Seventy-fifth Precinct House ("Home of the Brave") and along Jamaica Avenue into Queens. I have trouble grasping sometimes how huge New York City is. Queens alone is endless. We saw the house Derrick grew up in and the park where he heard his first hip-hop music. On a residential street in one of the borough's far reaches, four guys in the middle of the street were leaning into the open window of a waiting car. As Derrick eased his car past, he recognized a couple of them. They were guys he'd seen a few times at a club where he works in Manhattan. He waved his arm out the window and said, "Yo, what up?" They registered considerable surprise and asked what Derrick was doing way out here. "Man, I'm everywhere," Derrick said.

••

Near the corner of Merrick and Linden Boulevards, in Queens, we passed the African Methodist Episcopal church where the family of Jam Master Jay held his funeral. Derrick said how bad he felt about Jay's murder, and how his one regret about retiring was that he would have liked to lead the investigation. He criticized the overaggressiveness of the Queens police—the "Queens Marines"—who handled the case, and especially the way they dealt with the witnesses.

Derrick thinks that Jay had become involved with drugs to supplement a declining income from his music, that he got into a dispute over payment, and that he knew his life was in danger. On his last day, he was at the Queens music studio where he often worked. He showed no signs of distress, but he had a loaded pistol on the couch beside him when he died. The receptionist at the studio, Lydia High, probably saw the killers. They went past her desk and into the room where Jay was playing video games and shot him in the head. Based on what Derrick has heard, he believes that the killers were a man named Ronald "Tinard" Washington, who is in prison for robbery, and a father-son team. (Federal prosecutors agree with Derrick's opinion about Washington, though his lawyer points out that he has never been charged in the killing.)

Neither Lydia High nor other witnesses who were in the studio have identified the person who pulled the trigger. Not long after the murder, Lydia High received a telephone call that she took to be a threat on her life. She was afraid to go to the funeral without a bodyguard, but she couldn't afford one, so she asked Derrick. He agreed and escorted her, armed with a pistol. After the graveside ceremony, as he was driving her and her girlfriend home, they were pulled over by Queens detectives. He says that one of the detectives yelled at Lydia through the car window and yanked on the door handle and tried to get her out of the car. The tactlessness of this further upset her and reduced the chances of getting her to cooperate. Eventually, she did cooperate, reluctantly. Later, she decided she would be better off if she left the state, and Derrick helped her with $500 from his own pocket in moving costs. Tinard Washington is serving a seventeen-year sentence, but, as far as Derrick knows, the father and son are still out walking around.

I asked Derrick whether, given the difficulty of finding solid information and witnesses willing to testify, he had ever actually caught a criminal in a rap-related crime and had later seen that criminal go to prison.

His answer was long and amounted to not many. It touched on the ignorance of the Police Department as regards hip-hop and rap, his own desire when he was a cop to educate his fellow cops on the subject, the resistance of some of them to being educated, and the persistence of an us-versus-them attitude among the police. "Some cops didn't trust me because of people I hung out with, and some of the people I hung out with didn't trust me because I was a cop. Actually, though, I wasn't *against* either side. What I was doing at rap intel wasn't against the hip-hop community at all. There are plenty of people in rap who don't like the thug element and the violence that got involved in the scene. After crack pumped so much money into poor neighborhoods, and little thug dealers thought they were something big, they saw the money the rappers were making and they wanted some of that. And after the thug element got in, it was hard to remove. Take someone like Fabolous, who grew up with thugs and gang guys. When Fabolous becomes a star, is he going to say to them, 'Yo, get lost, I'm famous now'? No, because they're his guys. Even if you weren't afraid that they'd kill you, you might do the same.

"Obviously, over the long run the violence has been bad for rap's image. Last week, I heard on the radio that a tour had to be canceled because, with two hard-core rappers on the bill, the venues were scared to book it and the promoters couldn't get liability insurance. Seventy percent of rap's audience is white suburban teenagers. When the violence gets too bad, that audience is going to drift away. It's starting to do that already. So, no—my goal was never just to arrest and convict rappers. I wanted to let law enforcement know about rap's inner workings, and show the majority, nonviolent element in rap that there were law-enforcement people on their side. My basic goal was to protect rap music from itself."

• •

Derrick had a rough summer. In June, an irate patron of the World Famous Bada Bing, a South Bronx strip club for which Derrick provides security, tried to run him over on the sidewalk outside the club. Derrick and Edgar Ramos, one of the managers at the time, dodged the vehicle, which then rammed Derrick's brand-new black Nissan Murano, parked nearby. The police later caught the guy, he said. The Murano spent a long while in the shop. In July, Derrick's father, with whom he lived, died suddenly of a heart attack. The death and the accompanying family difficulties shook Derrick. When I called him, he sounded stunned and miserable. The change made me notice how, up till then, I'd never known him to be in any mood other than happy and easygoing.

In August, a man was murdered on the same stretch of sidewalk outside Bada Bing where Derrick had dodged being run down. Another man, shot in the chest and leg, survived. Police arrested three suspects in the killing. Derrick wasn't at Bada Bing that night, but one of the shots grazed Terence, a very wide guy who works for him, in the back and side. Afterward, Derrick visited Terence in the emergency room at 5:00 a.m. And that same night, after Derrick finished tending the door at Spotlight for a big blowout birthday party for Lil' Kim, a young woman was murdered on Spotlight's roof. The body wasn't found for a couple of days. Police questioned Derrick and all the guys he had working at Spotlight for that event. A "bar back"—a club employee who brings supplies to the bar—later confessed to the killing, according to police. (He has since pleaded not guilty.) Inspectors descended on the club and found violations, and the club closed indefinitely.

On the night Barack Obama made his acceptance speech at the Democratic Convention, I went to the Bronx to see Derrick at Bada Bing. The club is in a low gray brick building with black security gates, and it covers most of an irregularly shaped block below a span of the Bruckner Expressway. Railroad tracks in a sunken road cut run alongside, and the wider neighborhood offers auto junkyards of crashed vehicles with their air bags deployed, vast no-name warehouses, and chain-link fences grafted to thickets of ailanthus trees. The trucks on the Bruckner, the surface streets' unmuffled cars and motorcycles, and the airplanes overhead all speed past as if they were atoms dissipating rapidly from the city into the pink-tinted sky.

Derrick wasn't there when I arrived. I found Edgar Ramos, and he led me into the DJ booth, where he was filling in until the real DJ arrived. To get to it, we had to pass through a room where about thirty young women in almost no clothes were waiting to go on. Most were tattooed. I saw a striking tattoo: two staring eyes, with long eyelashes. What made the eyes striking was that they were at the very base of the back. The club was large, dim, and fogged with artificial smoke for atmosphere. There were enough dancing platforms so that a number of dancers could perform simultaneously. I watched Barack Obama's speech, closed-captioned above the painfully percussive music, on ceiling TV monitors through a writhing forest of dancers on poles.

When Derrick showed up, at about midnight, we stood around outside. He showed me the place on the sidewalk where the guys had been shot; one of them had failed to escape because his low-riding jeans fell down and tripped him. On this slow Thursday, not so many people were out, but almost everybody who came by greeted Derrick, and he introduced me to them all. I met more guys he knew from Queens, and other bouncers, and dancers coming to work the later shifts, and Terence, the bouncer who was grazed, and a guy named Julio who had just taken the police exam and who wanted Derrick to write him a recommendation, and a guy who said he had just talked to a cop who was carrying around an Intel gang chart written in Derrick's handwriting.

Derrick leaned back against the wire cables that braced a telephone pole and he talked about what he would like: a job with the NYPD where he had complete freedom and no responsibilities other than catching bad guys, or maybe a consulting job going around to police departments and teaching them how to close out homicides. He said his company wasn't making money yet, really, but he expected it to start doing that soon. Companies don't usually earn money until their fifth or sixth year, he said, and this was only the fifth year for his. The night got late enough so that the rats came out in the parking lot of the McDonald's across the street. Derrick said, "Hey! A rat!" cheerfully pointing out the rodent as it came hopping from beneath a parked car into the restaurant's orangish light.

Occasionally when I'm with Derrick, I think again about his grandfather Willie Bryant. Some of the shows Willie Bryant MC'd at the Apollo are on video at the Library for the Performing Arts, at Lincoln Center, and I've seen one or two of them. (Derrick, as it happens, has never seen them himself.) The program is a musical-variety revue that was taped at the famous theater. Willie Bryant introduces the acts and provides entertainment and banter in between. At that age, he looks surprisingly like Derrick, except that

Willie Bryant's hair is straightened and flat in the then popular painted-on style.

Willie Bryant comes out, talks to the audience, and exchanges fast jokes with the comedian Nipsey Russell. He lounges against the proscenium arch, compliments Dinah Washington before she sings, dances a few steps of a Cab Calloway–style shuffle, plays some air piano when moved by the fast boogie-woogie of Amos Milburn, and eases back into the wings to give Duke Ellington some room. Leonard Feather, the jazz critic, once wrote that Willie Bryant MC'd an Apollo show "in his usual flawless manner." He "followed the unusual policy of introducing every man in the band by name, and did it in such a manner that it bored nobody."

That's sort of what Derrick does, too. There's this cool nighttime world, and he's part of it, and everybody in it is, if not necessarily good, at least worth knowing about. "I don't care who they are," Derrick says. "I don't talk down to anybody."

December 8, 2008

The March of the Strandbeests

If you're like many people, you know about Theo Jansen already. You may not *know* you know, but on reflection perhaps you realize you do. You've come across his kinetic sculptures in videos online, or a kid has shown the videos to you, or you've been with friends who were watching them. Once seen, they are remembered. Theo Jansen is a Dutch artist who lives in Delft, near the North Sea. He could almost be a single-name artist, because everybody calls him Theo, pronounced "Tayo." For the past twenty-one years, Theo has devoted himself to constructing animals that can walk on the beach powered only by the wind.

His name for his animals is Strandbeests, which means "beach animals" in Dutch. The first time I saw them, I was in a restaurant in Manhattan having lunch with friends and somebody brought out a laptop and we watched and re-watched them. The creatures were many legged, they seemed as at home on a beach as sandpipers or crabs, they high-stepped with the vivacity of colts, they fit perfectly next to the waves and sky. Some had batwing-like sails, one was made of plywood, but basically they were accumulations of stiff plastic tubes. To see inanimate stuff come to life that way was wild, shiver-inducing—like seeing a haystack do the Macarena.

At this lunch, people said how great it would be if the Strandbeests came to New York. And they might, because Robert Kloos, the director for Visual Arts, Architecture, and Design at the Consulate General of the Netherlands, has been working with other fans of Theo's to find a venue and funding for a show in the city in 2013, and has described such a show as "a dream come true." The photographer Lena Herzog, one of Theo's fans, who was at the lunch, said the show would draw a big audience, because a commercial for BMW cars featuring Theo and his Strandbeests had already received more than four million hits on YouTube. Then she told me that Theo would be bringing out some new Strandbeests for a trial run, or walk, on a beach near Delft very soon, that she would be going over to photograph them, and that I should come along.

So in mid-May I went, and Theo himself met me at the airport in Amsterdam, holding a hand-lettered sign with my name on it at the customs exit. (Lena would be joining us in a day or two.) He greeted me warmly and we wandered off. At first, he couldn't find his white Volvo in the airport parking garage, and I set down my suitcase while he listened for his dog. Theo has a small wool-colored dog of a French Madagascar breed who goes almost everywhere with him and is named Murphy. In a minute, he picked up Murphy's bark and we homed in on it. The dog barked more the closer we got to the car.

A drive of about forty minutes brought us to Theo's outdoor workshop, on a man-made hill in the suburb of Ypenburg, near Delft. The hill is on land that used to be a military airport and serves as a sound barrier between a highway on one side and apartment houses on the other.

A sort of no-man's-zone, it remains mostly unoccupied, so local officials let Theo use it to assemble and store his Strandbeests. The yellow PVC tubing the animals are made of bleaches to bone white in the sun; wrecks of defunct Strandbeests lay in the hilltop grass like heaps of old bones. A few newer, ready-to-travel models stood in a line next to the storage container where Theo keeps thirty miles of plastic tubes for future use. Others of his more recent animals were absent, returning from an exhibition in Japan.

Theo is sixty-three. His collar-length white hair frames his head like two S shapes facing each other, his eyes are china blue, and he has a wide, guileless smile. That he is handsome contributes to the success of his videos. When he is working, and at other times, he wears a well-tailored purple corduroy jacket narrow at the waist and flared below. His jacket, unrestrained hair, long legs, and antic energy often give him the look of a storybook sorcerer. He is somewhat deaf—the result, he says, of spending so much of his forties hanging next to the loud engines of the paraplanes he loved to fly in many places, but mainly over the North Sea coastline. His country's famous landscape, intensely cultivated and flat as water, floors a vast column of cloud-filled sky, and the image of a younger Theo careening around up there in his sketchy flying machines somehow still is part of him.

In fact, Theo's first important work was a sky piece. In 1980, he made a flying saucer from plastic sheeting on a light frame. The saucer was lens-shaped, about fifteen feet across, and carried beneath it a plastic paint bucket that emitted outer-space-like beeps. One afternoon, he and some friends filled the flying saucer with helium and launched it over Delft. Immediately, a local sensation resembling the

War of the Worlds episode (if less frantic and more civilized) ensued. The object he had made looked and behaved as a flying saucer is expected to. It hovered, rose, darted (with the wind), went in and out of clouds. The police gave chase, people ran from their houses to look up, authorities reported that the object was moving at great speeds, it was said to be as big as a nuclear reactor, etc.—all satisfying developments, from Theo's point of view. After exciting the population and inscribing in thousands of memories its flight through the spacious skies of Delft, the saucer vanished in the direction of Belgium. When the author of the event was revealed, he got a lot of press. The experience ruined him, he says, for the landscape paintings he had been doing before.

I was thinking it must be strange for a landscape painter to live in a landscape that was fixed in oil and ratified permanently by the great Dutch painters of the seventeenth century. From Theo's man-made hilltop, for example, I could see several familiar-looking towers, including the fifteenth-century church steeple that appears in Vermeer's *View of Delft* (1660). I could also see a small flock of storks flapping to the horizon, and a canal lined with possibly invasive reeds, and blunt-faced trucks on the highway, and red rooftops, and rows of thin, dark trees like sawteeth. The only other structure as tall as the old steeple or the towers was the two poles holding up the golden arches of a McDonald's restaurant. With binoculars, I might have picked out the crows and ravens that throng around the sign and descend on the garbage cans in the McDonald's parking lot. My hotel was near the McDonald's, it turned out, and I observed the birds close up later.

Theo showed me around his small on-site workshop. It was filled with tools like vises, saws, clamps, and heat guns for softening the plastic tubes. On perforated wallboards, tools hung neatly inside their black Magic Marker outlines. From a workbench, Theo picked up a piece of three-quarter-inch PVC tube about two feet long. He said this was the basic element in the Strandbeests' construction, like protein in living things. "I have known about these tubes all my life," he told me. (He speaks good English.) "Building codes in Holland require that electrical wiring in buildings go through conduit tubes like these. There are millions of miles of these tubes in Holland. You see they are a cheese yellow when they are new—a good color for Holland. The tubes' brand name used to be Polyvolt, now it is Pipelife. When we were little, we used to do this with them."

He took a student notebook, tore out a sheet of graph paper, rolled it into a tight cone, wet the point of the cone with his tongue, tore off the base of the cone so it fit snugly into the tube, raised the tube to his lips, blew, and sent the paper dart smack into the wall, fifteen feet away. He is the unusual kind of adult who can do something he used to do when he was nine and not have it seem at all out of place. "I believe it is now illegal for children in Dutch schools to have these tubes," he said.

• •

Theo grew up in Scheveningen, a small port city just north of Delft. His father, a farmer, moved the family there after losing his farm during the Second World War. In Scheveningen, the family supported itself mainly by taking in German tourists who wanted to vacation at the beach, just across the street from the Jansens' apartment. Theo remembers his mother waking him and his six brothers and four sisters early in the morning during the summers so they could deflate the air mattresses they had slept on and get them out of the living room before the guests occupying the family's beds woke up. He went to primary and secondary schools in Scheveningen, studied physics at the Delft University of Technology, and left in 1974 without a degree.

After university, he became an artist and did other things, like work in a medical laboratory. His landscape paintings, which he spiced up by putting in women wearing only underwear, had some success—"They were vulgar paintings, but they sold"—and after the flying-saucer episode ended them he invented a light-sensitive automatic painting gun that he demonstrated at local fairs. The Delft city government gave him a subsidized studio in a downtown building converted for artists, which he still uses. In it he built a large pair of feathered wings and propelled himself through the air by means of them while suspended on cables. He had several shows of his work in Dutch museums and galleries, marking one opening with the launch of a twenty-foot-long rocket he'd made.

In 1990, in a column he was then writing for *De Volkskrant*, a national newspaper, he warned that rising sea levels might reflood Holland and reduce its size to what it had been in medieval times. As a solution, he proposed to build animals that would toss sand in the air so that it would land on and augment the seaside dunes. What he envisioned were self-propelled creatures that would restore the balance between water and land, the way beavers do in Dutch marshes. He promised to devote a year to the project, and it has occupied him exclusively ever since. While fooling around with plastic conduit tubes at a building-supply store, he realized that they were the perfect raw material. More even than the Strandbeests, the possibilities he saw for the tubes changed his life, he says.

He divides his different generations of Strandbeests into time periods like geologic eras. In the earliest period, he was taping the tubes together. He calls this the Gluton Period (1990–91). The first tube-and-tape creation, Animaris

Vulgaris, could not stand up, only lie on its back and move its legs. In the next period, the Chorda Epoch (1991–93), he began to connect the tubes with nylon zip strips, a great improvement on tape, and he built Animaris Currens Vulgaris, the first animal that could stand and walk. To figure out the best way to make the legs, he ran a genetic algorithm for leg design on his computer, and it suggested a foot that pivoted at the ankle and a double-jointed leg that allowed the foot to stay on the ground as long as possible before lifting for the next step. Basic Strandbeest design now uses multiple pairs of these legs set on a central crankshaft, which produces a galloping-herd effect.

Later refinements added sails, a shovel arm for tossing up sand, pneumatic power with fanlike blades pumping air into plastic bottles for pressurized storage, "nerve cells," which can detect when the animal is in shallow water, and directional cells, which count steps and cause the animal to back up when it is about to go into the sea. As of now, none of these technologies works very reliably. Theo says he envies the original Creator's supply of countless millions of years for animal evolution, and is sure he could make perfect beach animals, given that much time.

"The walking Strandbeest is a body snatcher," he told me, while disassembling one for transport. "It charms people and then uses them so they can't do anything else but follow, and I am the worst victim, you could say. All the time I think about them. Always I have a new plan, but then it is corrected by the requirements of the tubes. They dictate to me what to do. At the end of my working day, I am almost always depressed. Mine is not a straight path like an engineer's, it's not A to B. I make a very curly road just by the restrictions of goals and materials. A real engineer would probably solve the problem differently, maybe make an aluminum robot with motor and electric sensors and all that. But the solutions of engineers are often much alike, because human brains are much alike. Everything we think can in principle be thought by someone else. The real ideas, as evolution shows, come about by chance. Reality is very creative. Maybe that is why the Strandbeests appear to be alive, and charm us. The Strandbeests themselves have let me make them."

••

Theo's beach headquarters is a thatch-roofed cabaret-restaurant called De Fuut (the Grebe). Its owner, Leo Van Der Vegt, likes to have him and his Strandbeests on the sand beside his restaurant's outdoor dining area, and sometimes he picks up the tab for Theo and his entourage. The Scheveningen beach is huge. From the dunes to the water it's at least a football field, and maybe half again as far at low tide. In one direction, the beach stretches more than a mile to the piers of Scheveningen harbor, where a monumental wind turbine rotates counterclockwise against the sky. In the other direction, the beach dwindles out of sight to the faint silhouetted cargo cranes of Rotterdam. Along the middle of the sand, parallel to the shore, runs a row of metal-and-plastic trash barrels set in concrete foundations. Toward Rotterdam, these barrels extend onward until the row becomes a dotted line. As a visual reference, they are modernist and daunting, and I've noticed that photographers and filmmakers who record the Strandbeests' ramblings try to keep them out of the frame.

On a Saturday morning, Theo loaded several Strandbeests on a rented flatbed trailer and the roof of his Volvo and drove to beach ramp No. 10 with the wind whistling in the tubes. His friends Hans and Loek came along to help. Hans teaches language skills to vocational students and Loek takes photographs, teaches high school and university students about the Strandbeests, and sometimes works as Theo's assistant (paid). At the beach, four admirers of Theo's who are in the master's program at the Delft University of Technology were waiting for him: Esra, a young woman from Istanbul; Baver, a young man from Ankara; Marta, from Portugal; and Miguel, from Monterrey, Mexico. All spoke English, the language in which classes in the DUT master's program are taught. With Theo and his friends, they unloaded the Strandbeests and carried or frog-marched them half a mile from the ramp to the restaurant.

A strong onshore breeze was blowing, causing flags to point inland. Waves broke and foamed. Dark shadows of incoming clouds sped over the white sand and swept across the dunes in a blink, like the waves' secret intentions. Wind-blown sand was whipping along at ankle level and leaving little drifts behind pebbles. The few other people on the beach appeared tiny in the immensity, except for the para-surfers, whose scoop-shaped chutes bucked and pirouetted and lifted the riders sometimes twenty feet above the waves.

Theo was toting a long-handled wooden mallet of the sort usually associated with circus tents. Employing round-house overhead blows, he pounded metal stakes into the sand and tethered Strandbeests to them. One of the animals was a worm that isn't wind-powered but writhes violently when infused with compressed air; he left it unstaked. A large Strandbeest seemed about to blow over rather than walk away, and he adjusted its tether to hold it up. Another, Animaris Longus, was light and limber enough so that it appeared on the verge of trotting off at any moment on the breeze. Theo laid this one on its side and staked it down. He then went among the Strandbeests, tinkering while the blown sand hissed against them and the wind made them creak and strain. Murphy, his dog, followed him and watched everything he did.

..

Beach trials the next morning were called off owing to rain, so I took a train to Amsterdam and visited the Rijksmuseum. Much of the museum is closed for renovations, and its most in-demand paintings have been concentrated in just thirteen rooms—sort of a Rijksmuseum's Greatest Hits. I got there at opening time and for twenty minutes or so it wasn't crowded. Such a mass of visual sublimity all in one place tramples the viewer like the legs of a thousand Strandbeests, but I did have one thought, despite my dizziness, as I paused in a nook of seventeenth-century landscapes. I had never been to Holland before, but the minute I arrived I felt as if I had been. I was comfortable in it. The reason, I now saw, was that I had previously habituated myself to the place during long contemplations of Dutch landscapes in American museums. I was like those first-time visitors to New York or Los Angeles who immediately know their way around from having seen the cities so much in movies and on TV.

Soon, the visual trampling administered by the Rijksmuseum's greatest art was matched by a literal trampling from fierce tour groups speaking every language, and I caromed into Gallery No. 12, a dark room featuring the Rembrandt masterpiece *The Night Watch*. Packed multitudes stood there in the dark letting the gigantic and glorious and well-lit painting blast them. Just off that room was a smaller one, not part of the Greatest Hits, with an unassuming show of landscape sketches on paper. People were passing through it without stopping. I ducked in and took a breath. The show, "Dunes: Holland's Wilderness," was about the shore where I'd just been. The introductory label said, "Holland's landscape is man-made. Only the sands and the dunes along the coast are more or less nature's creation. They are our natural defense against the sea . . . The earliest

known drawings of Holland's landscape are views of
the dunes near Haarlem recorded by Hendrick Goltzius
around 1600. Many landscape specialists followed in his
footsteps . . . Their work shows the wide, endless space, the
quiet and the wildness."

All the drawings were sketchbook size, done in pencil,
ink, or black chalk. If the giant Rembrandt in the adjoining
room was jet-engine powerful, his little horizontal sketch
here, of a shore landscape, was moving for its simplicity
and self-effacement. Some of the dune sketches showed the
blades of windmills against the sky; the main purpose of
Dutch windmills wasn't so much to mill anything as to
pump the incoming sea back out. A Jacob van Ruisdael
sketch with a heavy shading of cloud in one corner showed
more clearly the same quality of torque that his paintings
often have. In a vitrine, a leather-bound sketchbook of
Gerard ter Borch the Younger lay open to a black-chalk
drawing of a tangled patch of brush on a hillside. Such a no-
count, charming piece of ground! The drawing dated from
1634, though it could have been done in the Scheveningen
dunes, or maybe West Texas, just last week.

••

The weather did not let up, but Theo went ahead with beach
trials the following afternoon anyway. Lena Herzog had
arrived from New York, and Alexander Schlichter, a German
documentary filmmaker who has been making a film about
Theo for ten years, had driven up from Hannover. The
four DUT students were there, and Theo's twenty-year-old
son, Zach, and his seventeen-year-old daughter, Divera, and
Loek, Theo's sometime assistant. Beach passersby and restaurant patrons and their dogs came to watch and stood
around and moved on. Almost everybody took photographs. Lena Herzog stood on a stepladder, and crawled

under the Strandbeests, and lay on her back on the wet sand for her shots. Alexander Schlichter erected a tripod for his camera, and then, since I was doing apparently nothing, asked if I would be his soundman. Taken by surprise, I gave a polite and complicated answer that was not "yes."

Theo was devoting all his energy to getting a Strandbeest he called Animaris Gubernare up and moving. This colossus had fan-blade-driven air pumps, ninety-six plastic 1.5-liter bottles to store the compressed air, and a stegosaurus-like nose. Sand had drifted over its many feet and become soggy with the rain. Blown sand had got into its joints. Theo prodded it, repaired some broken tubes, fooled with the blades, sprayed the joints with lubricant, coaxed. His hair was flying. His fingernails had become chipped and there was a scrape on his forehead. Really, all that gets the Strandbeests moving is the enthusiasm of this one guy, and he was in the middle of an agon. He said to Alexander Schlichter, "If we can get even eleven seconds of videotape today we'll be doing great."

But that was not happening. Theo had us all assemble on the sides of the monster Strandbeest to lift it out of the soft, soggy sand and take it farther down the beach to where the sand was smooth and hard. When we lifted it, it felt inert, like a heap of wet sand itself. We carried it, its legs walked stumblingly and unwillingly, we set it down, we carried it again. Two feet burrowed toe first into the sand and stuck, causing shafts on the corresponding legs to break. Theo told us to carry it back to where we had begun and the disabled legs trailed brokenly.

Theo often says that he does not know if he is a sculptor or an engineer or what. His Strandbeests have been in exhibitions all over the world—Munich, London, Taipei, Madrid, Tokyo, Seoul—and he does not care whether they are in art museums or science centers; they have appeared in both. My theory about Theo is that he is secretly a landscape artist. His flying saucer was a landscape piece that for a few minutes brought the classical Delft sky up to date. His Strandbeests, magnets for filming and photography, are really decoys to get us to notice the dunes, sea, and sky. The endless painful artifice involved in the Strandbeests' construction is his version of the great painters' technical skill. They painted windmills, he builds wild new kinds of windmills for the most acute observers to photograph.

Artists produced more landscape paintings in the northern Netherlands in the seventeenth century than in any other time or place in the world, probably. Why? I think the reason goes back to Holland's landscape being man-made. The Dutch made it and they liked to look at it. They had a good workman's justifiable pride; the landscape paintings were like the "after" pictures of a successful home-improvement project. Anyone who has stood back and admired a lawn he has just raked knows the feeling. Theo's Strandbeests, whose long-range purpose is to restore Holland's dunes, attempt to compress centuries of Dutch experience; ideally, he would remake the landscape and record it all in one career. And since the Dutch think constantly about their always challenged lowland, he falls in line with some deep historic impulses. Chances are, after all, that soon the seas really will rise. Theo's ambition is civic-minded and admirably high—to create something beautiful and save his country. Beyond that, he gets the rest of us thinking about the actual world, and what it's going to be like, and how humans will live in it.

• •

Torque: the beach at Scheveningen seemed to be ruled by it. Everything was turning, inward-spiraling. The northeast wind skimmed the waves along the beach like pinwheel blades, the giant wind turbine above the harbor rotated, the parasurfers' chutes twisted this way and that, the ropes on the masts of the catamarans in drydock beside the dunes snaked back and forth and banged their metal parts on the hollow aluminum with a racket that could frighten off wicked spirits. In shoreline indentations, heaps of sea-foam accumulated and shivered, and clumps of foam kept blowing free and spinning across the sand, assuming corkscrew shapes and in the next instant abrading themselves away. The speed of their transition from material object to nothing happened so fast it made me queasy.

Theo worked on, fixing, altering, ducking in and out of the huge Strandbeest, searching for replacement parts in plastic storage crates he had brought. On an outdoor table, the owner of the restaurant set out glass mugs of tea with fresh mint leaves. In between taking photos and standing around and occasionally pitching in to help, all of us supernumeraries had plenty of chance for conversation. Lena told me again how much she admires Theo and how he reminds her of her father, a Russian geophysicist who lives in Yekaterinburg and who has invented a revolutionary new method of petroleum exploration, which, she says, the international oil companies have resisted. Miguel, the DUT student from Mexico, said he loved living in Holland but worried a lot about the violence in Monterrey, where many of his friends and relatives are. Baver, the young man from Ankara, said that Holland's public transportation was vastly better than Turkey's. Alexander, the filmmaker, described a documentary he was working on that concerned the creation of artificial life-forms, such as a fish that contains plant DNA and can feed itself by floating in the sun and photosynthesizing.

Esra and Marta, the students from Istanbul and Portugal (respectively), said they were working together on a

research project about Theo and the importance of the sus-
pension of disbelief to the creative process. Like most other
kids who know about Theo, they had first encountered
him in videos (many of them made by Alexander) on the
Internet. In their rapt regard for him, there appeared no
disbelief, suspended or otherwise. For a moment, Theo
took a break and joined the onlookers. He was frustrated,
vexed, abstracted with technical snafus, and unhappy that
some of us had to leave soon and would not get to see
Animaris Gubernare lumber off into the sunset (as it did
successfully the following day). Then he smiled his sparkling,
camera-ready smile. He was having a wonderful time.

Theo went back to work, and the rest of us continued
standing around. Earlier in the day, he had taken the
smaller Strandbeest, Animaris Longus, and moved it onto
the smooth sand, maybe just to get it out of the way. It was
a simple, elegant construction of triangular elements in a
pyramidal shape supported by two groups of six legs on a
central crankshaft. Animaris Longus had no sails, but was
light enough so that a wind could move it without them.
From a distance, it looked like one of those folding pole-
and-clothesline contraptions you hang laundry on.

This Strandbeest stood there for a while, unnoticed.
The shiny, wet sand held its reflection. Some new custom-
ers arrived and sat at one of the restaurant's outdoor tables.
A minute later, a stronger gust came up, and the apparent
clothes-drying rack suddenly went tiptoeing across the sand.
The people at the table did a triple take and began pointing and laughing, and talking in Dutch. "Dat ding is aan
het lopen!" (That thing is walking!) they cried.

September 5, 2011

The Toll: Sandy and the Future

When the storm hit, on October 29, all the Staten Island ferries on the water were on the Staten Island side. One ferry was in drydock; the seven others had been tied to piers near the St. George ferry terminal. At about five fifteen in the afternoon, the hawsers began to snap as the surge lifted the boats above the piers. Soon the piers could not be seen, and the boats' crews, at full strength, maneuvered them back and forth with the engines so they wouldn't go aground or crash into pieces of debris or each other. Fully lit, the seven ferryboats—the *John A. Noble*, the *Spirit of America*, the *Guy V. Molinari*, the *Andrew J. Barbieri*, the *Sen. John J. Marchi*, the *John F. Kennedy*, and the *Alice Austen*—hovered in the rising waves. Just down the shore, old dock pilings thirty feet long with two-foot-long rusted iron spikes that showed the marks of a blacksmith's hammer were floating in and smashing the lower windows and doors of a luxury apartment complex called Bay Street Landing. A few hundred yards beyond the apartments, a 184-foot-long tanker ship, the *John B. Caddell*, washed up on a small stretch of undeveloped shoreline and stayed there.

Staten Island has the shape of an ankle boot. The sole

runs along a channel called the Arthur Kill, and the upper heel and back border the Kill Van Kull; on the other side of those waterways, connected by three highway bridges and one railroad bridge, is New Jersey. The ferry terminal occupies the point at the top of the boot where you sometimes find a tab for pulling the boot onto your foot. From the terminal it is five miles across the harbor to South Ferry, in lower Manhattan. At the top end of the boot's tongue, the Verrazano-Narrows Bridge gives the island its only highway connection to the rest of New York City— and not an ideal one, because the bridge deposits incoming traffic on the Belt Parkway or the Gowanus Expressway in distant Bay Ridge, Brooklyn. The front part of the boot, where the lacings would be, faces southeastward, toward the Atlantic Ocean. Flooding did a lot of damage to the island north of the Verrazano Bridge, but south of it, on the island's ocean side, was where all but one of the fatalities occurred. The storm killed twenty-three on Staten Island, the highest number of storm-related deaths in any borough. Twenty of them drowned.

• •

Four days after the storm, I drove to Staten Island from my house in New Jersey to see some people I know. Kenny Myers and his girlfriend, Leah Venditti, live on Lipsett Avenue, which dead-ends at the ocean, and theirs is the last house on the street. From their windows, you could see a rock where harbor seals sometimes hauled out and lay in the sun. Leah used to call and tell me when the seals were around. I had lost her phone number, and I hated to think what might've happened to them or to the house.

When I got there, the street was about ten feet shorter. A fire hydrant dangled by its pipe in empty air, pieces of pavement crumbled downward, the traffic barrier and the sign saying END had washed away,' and the house's lawn had been eaten back. Just down from the lawn, the enlarged beach was muddy and raw, and filled with so much debris that I put off looking at it until later. The house still stood, with plywood on the windows. Leah answered when I knocked, and she asked me to come in. Kenny was leaning back in a recliner armchair. "Yes, we're fine, thanks for asking," Leah said. "We made it through, thank God, and the house is okay, and there wasn't even any flooding in the basement! For some reason, the water went right around the house. We knew we were supposed to evacuate, but we stayed, and my daughter kept calling, saying, 'Ma, how're you doing, how's the storm?' At seven o'clock that night, the water was coming over the road. The whole house was shaking. At nine o'clock, Kenny tells me to look out on the porch and I saw black water all around the house, and I screamed."

Kenny: "When she screamed, I said, 'That's it, we're goin'.'"

"We took flashlights and some clothes in a bag and we were wading up the streets, no streetlights, the trees were falling, forget it. We made it to Tottenville High School, and they already had cots laid out in the gym, and blankets and food and everything. I think it was the Department of Transportation had set it up. They did a very good job. Maybe a hundred or a hundred and fifty people stayed there, and some had lost everything. All kinds of ordinary people were bringing cakes, pizzas, Dunkin' Donuts. There was more stuff donated than they could even handle. On Halloween, the kids there trick-or-treated, going from family to family in the gym. I've never seen that many people come together that fast to help. It was a good feeling. After three days, the power was on again, and some volunteers gave us a ride back here."

When I left, I finally looked at the debris on the beach.

In the nearest heap of chaos, wooden playground equipment lay in a splintered jumble. From a two-by-four, draped
over it like an exotic pelt, hung a roll of commercial lawn
sod. Its grass was still green.

•   •

My friend Frank Crescitelli is a Staten Island fishing guide
who kept his boat in Great Kills Harbor, about midway
along the island's Atlantic coast. Luckily (or not, depending
on what the insurance would have paid), the boat was in
the shop during the storm. Great Kills Harbor is an oval of
water about two-thirds of a mile wide, with a spit of barrier
beach between it and the ocean. Frank e-mailed me photos
of what the storm did: docks gone, vast sprawls of debris,
hundreds of boats left on land. A sixty-two-foot Viking fishing yacht sat on the roof of Cole's Dock Side Restaurant.

I drove to Great Kills to check it out. The harbor is
among the quick-transition places of the city—one minute
you're in the unpromising everydayness of Hylan Boulevard, and the next baitfish are jumping in the shallows and
gulls are crying and lanyards are tapping against the masts.
This morning, the main sound was from the generators for
the antilooting floodlights. Police cars with their lights
flashing idled or cruised. From nearby came the warning
beeps of construction vehicles backing up. Where Frank's
boat dock used to be, and in every direction around it, bare
pilings stood in the calm water above their reflections' bar
codes. Empty patches of water showed where docks had
disappeared, pilings and all. A dock that had broken in the
middle and lost its other half sloped down toward the water,
its support pipes and wires leaning forward like when you
open a box of linguine and it slides out.

Most of the boat wrecks in the shallows had been removed. A small salvage vessel under coast guard supervision

was going to the remaining foundered hulks and draining them of oil and other pollutants. On the far side of the harbor, a thousand-horsepower push boat, like a flat-face tractor, was herding reefs of flotsam toward dump trucks on the shore. All the marinas on that side were completely gone. Trees and shrubs on the barrier beach all inclined in the same direction—inland—as if frozen in mid-kowtow. Everywhere, like dirty snow, little clumps and crumbs of Styrofoam congregated in the rocks and covered the matted ground. The storm surge, or maybe several huge surges, had overtopped the barrier beach and sucked the pilings from their twenty-foot-deep seatings in the harbor's bottom and hurled the docks, with large boats still tied to them, clear across the harbor until they heaped and jumbled into a cove-like pocket and crashed against a condominium building.

A man named Mark Nanos was going into one of the Great Kills boatyards. He wore a canvas porkpie hat and a green windbreaker and had lively dark eyes. "For two weeks after the storm, I had no idea where my sailboat was," he told me. "I was docking it at Nichols Marina, across the harbor, and everything there, every boat, every piece of dock, was *gone*! All I knew, my boat could be sunk or in New Jersey or Ireland. Then, incredibly, a friend of mine recognized my boat in a video on YouTube. It was in a pileup near the Port Regalle condos, next to some other boats. I went there and I asked the cops who were up in one of those mobile police towers if they were identifying boats, and they said, 'We're still trying to identify people. We just found two bodies under a dock.' At that point, a woman walked up and said, 'I hear you found my parents.' After that I had no more problems. Boat, no boat—didn't matter. I live next to the water, and by the grace of God my house and my family were spared. And then, when I did find my boat, and got a crane to pull it out, it had relatively no damage! Just some small holes in one side."

The couple whom the police had found were Walter and Marie Colborne. Apparently, they had tried to escape the storm in their car. He was eighty-nine and she was sixty-six. News reports gave their address as 23 Harbour Court, in the Port Regalle condominiums. When I looked online, I saw that the average price of condos in that immediate neighborhood seemed to be about half a million dollars. A promotional video taken from the air on a sunny morning highlighted Port Regalle's terra-cotta Mediterranean-style buildings against the blue of the harbor.

..

The College of Staten Island, part of the City University system, has about fifteen thousand students and an array of mainframe computers that's among the most powerful in the Northeast. CSI is in the Willowbrook section of the island, or (to continue my footwear analogy) roughly where the round white label would be in the middle of a high-top tennis shoe. The campus is new and large, and the computers are there because it has the space for them, plus dependable access to electricity for them and for their air-conditioning.

Dr. William Fritz, the college's interim president, is a geologist specializing in volcanology and geologic hazards. He has done a lot of work on coastal storms and sea-level rise associated with global warming. After Hurricane Irene, Dr. Fritz began a study of what would happen to Staten Island in bigger hurricanes. With Dr. Alan Benimoff, a CSI professor of geology, who had been examining the changes since 1898 in housing density along Staten Island's Atlantic shore, Dr. Fritz and other colleagues used the CSI computers to analyze millions of data points. They included factors like the contours of the seafloor, the geology of the coastline, the location of drainages and buildings, and the action of waves and tides. The finished study provided a model of what would happen to Staten Island in a hurricane surge of twelve feet. Last summer, Dr. Fritz and his colleagues submitted an abstract of the study to the Geological Society of America, and they were scheduled to present their findings at the society's annual convention, in Charlotte, North Carolina, in November. The storm arrived about a week before the event. The CSI study had predicted the extent of the flooding uncannily—the projected flood zone proved to be accurate to the street, and almost to the house. In Charlotte, the CSI contingent drew an admiring crowd.

I had hoped that Dr. Fritz could explain to me why this storm hit Staten Island so hard. He is a tall, slim man with a round face, unaggressive glasses, and an unbureaucratic gift for clarity. He grew up on a cattle ranch near Libby, Montana, and believes that the experience of living in that area—for years, most of America's vermiculite came from asbestos-contaminated mines in Libby, causing the town to have a high rate of asbestos-related cancer, as did parts of Brooklyn, where workers in the Navy Yard installed the vermiculite in ships for insulation—may have disposed him to think about environmental catastrophes. On a polished wooden table in his office, he laid out a coastline map from the hurricane study and pointed up its details with a sharp pencil. Deeper ocean water, indicated by dark blue, tapered toward the inland waters like an arrowhead. The shallow water was light blue or leaf green. "Down south, off the coast of Georgia, the continental shelf goes out twice as far as our shelf," he said. "Here, in a storm like Sandy, we have water being pushed by the winds with less seafloor resistance to slow it down. A hurricane's very low atmospheric

pressure builds up a bulge in the ocean it crosses—as if
you held a vacuum cleaner over a bathtub—and that alone
can lift the water twenty feet, although here the effect was
probably more like a foot or two. And you also had a full
moon on the twenty-ninth, and one of the highest tides
of the year; and on top of that, of course, you had all the
water that was piled up by the very strong counterclockwise
winds.

"In places like the Bay of Fundy, a tidal surge is focused
by the geography and its height is increased. The same is
true here—so the incoming water had no place to go. It was
funneled through the stretch between Sandy Hook, in
New Jersey, and the Rockaways, in New York"—his pencil
outlined those long, inward-pointing fingers of sand—"and
then there's this very short ramp of shallower water before
the surge gets to shore. In the protected water of New York
Harbor above the Narrows, you had a rapid rise without
the violent waves. But at the Staten Island shoreline nothing
much had interfered with the storm's energy before the
surge (or surges) hit, so the land had to absorb it. The Staten
Island shoreline functioned as a crumple zone, like a bum-
per on a car. The full force of Sandy hit there."

• •

I drove and walked along the shore for miles. Police cars sat
with their flashers going, and heaps of debris lined the
sidewalks and accumulated in the streets. Inch-deep mud
slicks made parking lots slippery. Even confining myself to
debris items of only one syllable, I compiled a long list: caps,
cups, pipes, tarps, boards, pails, planks, pots, rugs, sinks,
straps. Close study of the piles defied the urge to categorize:
wet plasterboard, bale of straw, caulking gun, claw-foot chair,
black Hefty bag, picture frame, white vinyl siding, decaying
jack-o'-lantern, soggy cushion, twelve-hole muffin tin. The

storm debris that had been hauled from many places and piled two stories high in a parking lot beside Father Capodanno Boulevard in Midland Beach was said to weigh 275,000 tons. A chain-link fence that ran along Bobby Thomson Field nearby had caught the flood's smaller pieces of debris. Mostly they were grass stems and vine tendrils, combined with plastic shreds, zip ties, coffee stirrers, cup lids, swizzle sticks, plastic cutlery, and plastic drinking straws. In the fence, they glittered like minnows in a net.

Somewhere not far away a heavy vehicle was backing up, beeping. I continued to Grimsby Street, where two women had drowned in houses on the same block. At 164 Grimsby, Beatrice Spagnuolo, seventy-nine, was found dead on the day after the storm, while at 158, first responders discovered Anastasia Rispoli, seventy-three. Bunches of red plastic roses now mourned on the white picket fence in front of 164. The house is a one-story bungalow, like most others in the island's low-lying zones. A small lake of water stood in the street, which dead-ended in tall reeds.

Farther down the shore, the community of Oakwood Beach is mostly marsh. Four roads there cross the marsh and go almost all the way to the ocean: Tarlton Street, Fox Beach Avenue, Fox Lane, and Kissam Avenue. Houses on these streets were swept off their foundations. Perhaps because of a streambed that the waters followed, some of the houses ended up in the marsh in a curved line, like traffic on an off-ramp, with only their roofs showing above the reeds. Three people died in their houses on Fox Beach Avenue. Leonard Montalto, fifty-three, a postal worker who lived at 176 Fox Beach, had stayed behind to make sure the pump was working. At 72 Fox Beach, John Filipowicz, fifty-one, and his son John, Jr., twenty, were crushed by debris. The father was a bus driver and a retired corrections officer, and the son attended the College of Staten Island.

The father's brother found them in the basement in each other's arms.

The beaches themselves showed how crumpled a "crumple zone" could look. Shrubs and saplings had been cut off at the roots—not cleanly, but as if scratched away by fingernails. Deep gouges in the banks undercut fences and asphalt biking trails, and the scrubby trees far above the usual high-tide line hunkered down as if some massive creature had slept on them. Shreds of plastic bags hung among the branches everywhere, while the ocean, distant and calm at low tide, offered its quiet wavelets and asked, "Who, me?"

Toward the southern end of the island, the destruction was intense. From the foot of Yetman Avenue looking east, past the Rockaways and Sandy Hook, I could see the oceanic runway the huge waves had come down. In the dark, with the power out everywhere, waves had blasted through the houses here and swept some away so thoroughly that few traces were found. The street's last two houses on the left as you faced the ocean were now just foundations and front-door steps. Waves had blown out houses from front to back. At 687 Yetman, George and Patricia Dresch and their thirteen-year-old daughter, Angela, had stayed in their house to protect it, because they had been burglarized during Hurricane Irene. At some point that night, all three were carried off in the waves. They were found blocks away. Only Patricia survived, seriously injured.

Several houses on Yetman Avenue had their windows boarded and red stickers on the front doors indicating that the houses were unfit for occupancy. From somewhere I could hear the beeping of a heavy vehicle backing up, and the whine of a power saw. The house across from 679 Yetman was so damaged that the overhanging roof appeared to be supported by nothing but the staircase. In the absence of a front door, or even a front, that house's red sticker had been posted on the wall above the mantelpiece. Many tributes of flowers and gifts covered the Dresches' doorsteps. There was a small statue of Jesus and a candle with the Virgin Mary. Patricia Dresch had taught a weekly religious-education class to elementary and junior high students at Our Lady Help of Christians Church, in Tottenville. When my friend Frank Crescitelli and his daughter, Julia, were walking on the beach about a mile away, Julia found a quilt that one of Mrs. Dresch's classes had made for her. Frank's wife washed and pressed it and took it to the church.

··

The saddest story of the hurricane occurred on Father Capodanno Boulevard, when a mother got out of her stalled SUV and took her two young sons from their car seats and tried to reach high ground and the waves swept the children away. They were Brendan Moore, two, and Connor Moore, four. If there were a typographic equivalent of a moment of silence, I would put it here.

After the storm, the police could not find the boys' bodies. Finally, they asked the Parks Department for help, and a Parks Department employee named Alex Summers, who knows the Staten Island wetlands, directed police divers through a marsh called New Creek, between Father Capodanno Boulevard and McLaughlin Street. The divers recovered the bodies near the place where McLaughlin Street comes to a dead end. According to the *Times*, the bodies were found "in the cattails." I doubted this description and went to the end of McLaughlin Street to see. Probably it did not use to be a benighted, wretched spot, but this dead end has become one, and will remain so for a long time. Big rocks prevent vehicles from going past the turnaround, and wood chips and trash and stems litter the ground.

Undisclosed sadness hangs heavy in the frowsy marsh and in the vines on the trees. Someplace in the distance a piece of heavy machinery was backing up, beeping.

As I suspected, there are no cattails in the marsh at the end of McLaughlin Street, or none that can be seen. We see a swampy place, we think "cattails," but there aren't very many cattails around anymore. Instead, in this marsh and others, and along shorelines, and in wet ground all over the Northeast and beyond, there is now an invasive, extremely competitive, highly adaptive reed whose scientific name is *Phragmites australis*, usually referred to simply as "phragmites" (pronounced "frag-*mighties*"). These reeds can be twenty feet tall, they have brushlike seed heads, their leaves grow on only one side of the stalk, and they reproduce both by seeds and by clones—that is, by underground rhizomes as well as by runners above the ground. Phragmites reeds have amazing resilience, surviving climatic and chemical changes of many kinds, and colonizing areas disturbed by development before other species can get established. Their invasion has been what ecologists call "cryptic," that is, the prevailing phragmites type moved in long before people realized it wasn't the native plant but a nonnative variant.

The native phragmites is able to coexist with other species like cattails and spartina grass. The invasive phragmites creates a monoculture. Because of its rhizome reproduction, a single huge expanse may represent only four or five phragmites plants, while other species are driven out. Today, in the Northeast, the native phragmites appears to have declined, itself a victim of the invader. The invasive phragmites now plays the role of ubiquitous Zelig-like fauna in images of the outdoors. Especially at outdoor crime scenes, and in places like McLaughlin Street, where bodies are found, phragmites reeds are often in the background, bend-ing their floppy seed heads above the trench coats and yellow tape.

Almost everyplace I went along the shoreline in Staten Island after the hurricane, the chaos of junk and drift and wrack contained mats of dead phragmites stalks. Standing in a soggy no-man's-forest near a beach, with invasive Japanese honeysuckle and bittersweet and greenbrier vines dragging down the trees, and shreds of plastic bags in the branches, and a dirty snow of Styrofoam crumbs on the ground, and heaps of hurricane detritus strewn promiscuously, and fierce phragmites reeds springing up all over, I saw the landscape of the new hot world to come.

••

A few years ago, when I was hiking the Staten Island beaches looking for seals, I used to find strange sculptures made of piled-up stones. Below the bluff where the old Mount Loretto lighthouse stands, a small city of these heaps stretched beside the waves like a lost rock-pile Atlantis. Asking around, I learned that the man who made them worked at the Staten Island Zoo. That tip led eventually to a zookeeper, Doug Schwartz. He is one of the zoo's groundhog wranglers, who sometimes appear on TV at Groundhog Day observances. He has worked at the zoo for twenty years and has been building his beach sculptures for sixteen. He does the sculptures for no reason but to do them, and almost never goes a week without working on them.

I met him at Conference House Park, at the southern tip of the island. He had told me to be there at 7:00 a.m.; I arrived at 6:45 and found him pacing in the dark. He said, "It's cold! I hope you're warm enough. I don't like to abuse my journalists. I live a few blocks from here. Most places where I make my sculptures or cairns or whatever you call them are within walking distance of my house. I have never driven a car. On the night the storm hit, the wind and waves were going crazy, and we live just a few blocks from the shore. But we weren't there—over the weekend, my wife's blood pressure had shot up, and her heart started to fail, so we took an ambulance to a hospital with a cardiac unit, and after ten hours of surgery they replaced two artificial valves in her heart. She was fine, as it turned out, but I had to walk home, and I kept getting stopped by National Guardsmen who were looking for looters. When I went to visit her the next day, all public transportation was out of service and there were no cabs, so I walked the ten miles there and ten miles back again."

We plunged into the brush. "Oh, great, the Parks guys didn't tear this one down!" he said, stopping at a construction of driftwood and rocks and mandala-like strips of pale-orange cloth set back in a storm gouge in the bank. His friend and dedicated helper Eric Alter appeared in the dimness beside us. A red sun rose. This part of the island is a city park and has no buildings, but the scattered foundations show that houses once stood here. The storm's huge waves had spent themselves among the park's trees and brush, leaving Port-o-Sans and other debris, most of which had been removed. Somewhere, heavy equipment had started working; there was diesel noise, and the beeping of a vehicle backing up.

Doug checked on a cairn they had erected atop the rusted engine block of a vestigial car, and did some touch-up on a driftwood pile shaped like a rickshaw carriage. It included a small bench with found stuffed animals—Scrappy-Doo, Curious George. I asked what had happened to his stone Atlantis on the shore by Mount Loretto. "It's all been destroyed by now, I'm sure," he said. "The state decided it was a hazard and told us to get out of there, so

we went. When officials give me an order, I comply. That's
what I did at the Groundhog Day press conference with
Mayor Bloomberg in 2009. The mayor said, 'Give me the
groundhog'—so I gave him the groundhog, even though I
knew it wasn't a good idea, and he bit him on a finger of
his left hand, right through his good dress gloves. I almost
got fired for that, but somehow by patience and nonresis-
tance I survived."

Kevin Norton, another close friend and helper, showed
up. Long, skinny tree trunks were added to the rickshaw
pile, and then we walked back along the beach. In the Arthur Kill, big tanker ships that Doug recognized passed by.
A few of them recognize him, too, he said, and blow their
horns at him sometimes. The four of us went to a diner for
breakfast; afterward, at Doug's house, he showed me photographs of sixteen years of beach constructions. All of
them had eventually been destroyed. I asked him what the
sense was in rebuilding—a practical question on many
people's minds these days. Would he reconstruct his stone
Atlantis? "Oh, of course," he said. "I'll never stop doing this.
I'm constantly facing obstacles. The *Staten Island Advance*
speculated years ago that my sculptures were satanic altars—
without knowing who had made them—and the article reduced my loving wife to tears, but even that didn't stop
me. I'll rebuild the cairns by Mount Loretto when the
political winds change and I get the opportunity. We've
rebuilt there after storms a bunch of times."

••

If all the ice on the planet melts and the oceans rise ac-
cordingly, the Statue of Liberty will be submerged up to
her waist, but parts of Staten Island will still be dry. The
top of Todt Hill, in the center of the island, is 409 feet
above sea level, the highest coastal point south of Maine.

The Wisconsin glaciation, which covered much of north-eastern North America twenty-two thousand years ago, did not extend far beyond Todt Hill in this area. The upper boundary of the glacier's outwash plain (the expanse of rocks, gravel, and sand left by its melting front) corresponds roughly to the line made by Hylan Boulevard. On the lower side of Hylan, the outwash plain descends to marshes, beaches, and the ocean.

When people first built houses on Staten Island, they usually put them on the high ground. The island had a small population for 250 years. In 1960, it was about 220,000, by far the smallest of any borough. The opening of the Verrazano-Narrows Bridge, in 1964, led to development all over the island, which has almost half a million residents today. As development will do, it kept expanding even after the more likely sites were taken. In the 1970s, it began to move into wetland areas, paving over streambeds and bogs and putting affordable bungalows on them. Almost all the Staten Islanders who died in the storm were on the out-wash plain—that is, in neighborhoods to the south of Hylan Boulevard.

Dr. Fritz and his College of Staten Island colleagues know the flooding pattern, which their study foresaw. To the question of rebuilding, their answer is that we should give it a lot of thought. "We can learn a lesson from the hurricane of 1938," Dr. Fritz told me. "After that storm, coastline land was so cheap that it tempted people to build on it. We don't want that to happen after Sandy. Now, should we simply zone all areas south of Hylan so they can't be built on, or so all the houses have to be elevated? I don't know. Maybe. That is the kind of thing we have to decide. As a college here in Staten Island, we want to start the conversation. We care about this personally. CSI lost a student and the husband of a faculty member in the storm.

Even now, this long afterward, the college still has fifteen hundred students and faculty who are virtually homeless because of Sandy. People are living out of their cars, and we even hear of some who have moved back into condemned, red-tagged houses because they don't have anywhere else to go.

"Following up on our hurricane-surge study, we're suggesting a five-point plan to protect Staten Island in the future," he went on. "First, protect the natural barriers we already have, the dune fields and the beaches. Second, build them up so they can absorb even bigger surges, and plant the dunes with the right vegetation to hold them in place. Third, rezone in the flood areas. Buy low-lying property of people willing to be bought out and turn it into parkland. Certain kinds of use can be fine in those places—baseball fields, for example, like they have in the Ohio River flood zones in Cincinnati. Fourth, reengineer intelligently, so you don't protect one area at the expense of another. A sea gate like they've been talking about to protect the narrows would probably be bad for Staten Island. Finally, educate people so they know the elevation of their houses and their risk in terms of flooding. Don't go into your basement if your house is in a marsh, for example. Hurricane Irene was relatively mild and it made people complacent. One certainty is that we are going to have more big storms. The college will be holding a daylong forum to discuss all these issues in our Center for the Arts on March eighth, and we hope everybody who has an interest will attend."

••

Staten Island is more island-like than Manhattan. It's a maritime place. As you approach it on the ferry (all the ferries survived the storm undamaged, thanks to the skill of their crews), the island rises above you and draws your eyes to the sky. From its Todt Hill summit, the ground slopes downward—sharply in some places, gradually in others—with the pleasing variety of a classic pirate island. You need altitude—a hilltop, a crow's nest—in order to appreciate the sea. More than that of other boroughs, Staten Island's geography provides sweeping ocean views. From an eminence just north of the Verrazano Bridge, you can look down upon the ship traffic coming through the narrows. A house that stood on that spot a hundred years ago loomed so prominently that it got mail addressed to "First House on the Left, America." At the island's other end, a house built of beach stones more than three hundred years ago commands a similar view of the Arthur Kill. It's now known as the Conference House, because John Adams, Benjamin Franklin, and Edward Rutledge met with British emissaries there in an unsuccessful attempt to call off the Revolutionary War. The house, one of the city's oldest, has hardly changed since then. And no Staten Islander ever had a better view than Paul Castellano, the mobster, who could observe the spires of Manhattan, on his left, and the western tower of the Verrazano-Narrows Bridge, on his right, all reduced to the size of garden whimsies from the backyard vantage of his white marble mansion, which he left one day for a meeting at Sparks Steak House.

Go downhill in any direction and suddenly the water is right before you. My favorite seaside place to stop and ruminate is still the cove at the end of Lipsett Avenue. Since the storm, a certain amount of debris has been removed, and some serenity restored. Recently, I stood at the end of the street and watched the water for a while. Three cormorants were sitting on the seal rock, minding their own business. I knocked on Leah and Kenny's door to say hello, and Millissa, Kenny's daughter, answered it. She was visiting from Queens. I had talked to her on the phone about seals but had never met her in person. Millissa is in her twenties and works as an airbrusher in a Manhattan tanning salon. Things had settled down in the household since the storm. They brought me up to date on Kenny's brother, who lives in nearby South Beach. He had stayed in his house while the waves wiped out everything on the first floor, plus his brand-new Lexus. Now he had rebuilt his downstairs almost completely. "Yeah, Uncle Butchie," Millissa said. "He trooped it out. Butchie never left and now he says he's never leaving." "To be honest, I've been thinking we should move out of here," Leah said. "Find another place not so close to the water."

"I don't know," Kenny said. "I like it here, it's quiet, you see the ocean, it's different every day, it's beautiful. Maybe some kind of new bulkhead can be put up to protect us here. I was talking about that with the guy next door. A while after we moved back, pretty soon after the storm, I was walking on the beach and I found two hundred-dollar bills. Then, two days later, I had this feeling, I just knew there were more bills where I'd found those two. I went back and looked again, and almost in the exact same spot I found three more! I don't know how I'd missed them the first time. Five hundreds! They're all spent now, though."

"Guys from Environmental Protection who were working on the beach told me that people have been finding money all along the shore," Leah said.

"So I decided to look on the beach for more coins and stuff, and I ordered a metal detector," Kenny said. "I'd always wanted one, for exercise, but finding those hundreds gave me inspiration. It's supposed to come tomorrow."

February 11 and 18, 2013

Hidden City

For baseball games, Yankee Stadium seats 50,287. If all the homeless people who now live in New York City used the stadium for a gathering, several thousand of them would have to stand. More people in the city lack homes than at any time since . . . It's hard to say exactly. The Coalition for the Homeless, a leading advocate for homeless people in the city and the state, says that these numbers have not been seen in New York since the Great Depression. The Bloomberg administration replies that bringing the Depression into it is wildly unfair, because those times were much worse, and, besides, for complicated reasons, you're comparing apples and oranges. The CFH routinely disagrees with Mayor Bloomberg, and vice versa; of the many disputes the two sides have had, this is among the milder. In any case, it's inescapably true that there are far more homeless people in the city today than there have been since "modern homelessness" (as experts refer to it) began, back in the 1970s.

Most New Yorkers I talk to do not know this. They say they thought there were fewer homeless people than before, because they see fewer of them. In fact, during the twelve years of the Bloomberg administration, the number of homeless people has gone through the roof they do not have. There are now 236 homeless shelters in the city. Imagine Yankee Stadium almost four-fifths full of homeless families; about eighteen thousand adults in families in New York City were homeless as of January 2013, and more than twenty-one thousand children. The CFH says that during Bloomberg's twelve years, the number of homeless families went up by 73 percent. One child out of every hundred children in the city is homeless.

The number of homeless single adults is up, too, but more of them are in programs than used to be, and some have taken to living underground, in subway tunnels and other places out of sight. Homeless individuals who do frequent the streets may have a philosophical streak they share with passersby, and of course they sometimes panhandle. Homeless families, by contrast, have fewer problems of mental illness and substance abuse, and they mostly stay off the street. If you are living on the street and you have children, they are more likely to be taken away and put in foster care. When homeless families are on the street or on public transportation, they are usually trying to get somewhere. If you see a young woman with big wheeled suitcases and several children wearing backpacks on a train bound for some far subway stop, they could be homeless. Homeless families usually don't engage with other passengers, and they seldom panhandle.

• •

One Saturday afternoon, I was standing at the corner of Manor and Watson Avenues, in a southeastern part of the Bronx, waiting for a woman named Christina Mateo. I had met her and her then partner on the street the day before. She had said she would show me what a shelter was like—I had never been in one. They were living in a nearby shelter for homeless families. No shelters say "Shelter" on them in big letters. This one looked like an ordinary shabby apartment building, with a narrow entry yard behind a tall black iron grate whose heavy iron door did not lock. People were going in and out. Two young men, one in a hoodie despite the heat and the other in a clean, tight white T-shirt and a black do-rag with the tie ends dangling, leaned into the open windows of cars that pulled up. In between doing that, they looked at me. I am past the age of being a prospect or a threat. I nodded back genially.

Christina came down the sidewalk pushing a stroller. With her were her nineteen-year-old daughter, her seventeen-year-old son, her fifteen-year-old daughter, and two grandchildren. They had just picked up the younger grandchild from a shelter where she was living with her other grandmother. We all went in, lifting the strollers, and crowded into the small elevator. The security person at the desk asked Christina if I was with her and she said I was. At the door to her fourth-floor apartment, she took out a single key, unattached to any chain, key ring, or other keys, and opened the door.

Uncheerful interior, and an air of many people having recently passed through; the floors were like the insides of old suitcases, with forgotten small things in the corners. Bent window blinds; tragic, drooping, bright-green shower curtain; dark hallway opening onto two bare bedrooms. Christina is forty-one and has pained, empathic dark-brown eyes. She wore blue denim cutoffs, a white blouse, sandals, ivory polish on her fingernails and toenails, and her hair in a bun. Sitting on the only chair in the larger bedroom while I perched on the bed, she told me how she came to be here. She was a home health aide. After the deaths of patients whom she had grown close to—one of them a four-year-old girl with AIDS—she had a breakdown and was given a diagnosis of PTSD. In shelters, out of shelters; for a while she enjoyed her own apartment, with a rent subsidy from a program established by Mayor Bloomberg. The program was cut. She lost the apartment, complicatedly, somehow without being evicted right away, although if she had been, she said, she would have qualified for other, preferable housing.

An accordion file of documents leaned at her ankle. Everybody has documents, but the homeless must keep theirs always close by. She showed me letters with letterheads and foxings and pencil underlinings, and a sheaf of certificates attesting to her success in various programs: Parenting Skills, Anger Management, Women's Group, Basic Relapse Prevention ("I was smoking a lot of marijuana, and this course taught me how to recognize my triggers. Boredom was one of my triggers"), Advanced Relapse Prevention, and My Change Plan. "What I'm waiting for is the paper saying that we have been declared eligible to stay in this shelter. Right now my case is under review. This place is adequate, but it's not hygienic—but I don't want to move. Stability is very important. They will decide if we can stay or not, and then they'll slide the paper under the door." She pointed to the end of the dim hallway as if this paper might appear at any moment, sliding in silently like the checkout bill in a hotel room.

As it happened, the news Christina was expecting arrived late that same night, in the form of a shelter employee who knocked on the door and presented the paper by hand. It said that she had been declared ineligible for shelter and would have to go to the PATH center before eight thirty the next morning to reapply.

••

Some of the things people have said to me outside the PATH center:

"I came here first when I was eighteen, when foster care maxed me out. I been in the system for fourteen years, and I don't know how many times I've had to come back here. When you go to PATH, they always want to deny you. They don't believe you really homeless."

"You know what is the best shelter? Covenant House. But it's for homeless kids, and only has about two hundred beds. There they max you out at twenty-one."

"This new place, PATH, is better than what used to be here, the EAU"—the Emergency Assistance Unit. "The EAU was horrible."

"Here they treat you more horrible than a drunk bum."

"The food here is not too bad, the bag lunches they give you. The baby likes the animal crackers."

"Hey, yo, you a writer—do you know Denis Hamill?"

"We left PATH at twelve twenty-six last night and they bused us to a shelter in Queens and we had about three hours of sleep and then they brought us back here at seven this morning to be reassigned, and my kids was falling asleep in the chairs, and a security guard hit the chairs with his radio and made them jump out they sleep, and I told him not to do that because they tired, and he yelled at me and wrote me up, and I filed an incident report, and I'm sure it ended up in the wastebasket."

"They spend *so much money* on us. It costs three thousand dollars a month to put one family in a shelter! Why don't they just *give* us part of that money so we can afford our own place to live?"

··

To get to the PATH center, you take the No. 4 train to Grand Concourse–149th Street, in the Bronx, walk two blocks to 151st Street, make a left, and continue for a block downhill, to 151 East 151st. Of all the places in the city's shelter system (aside from the Department of Homeless Services offices on Beaver Street, in downtown Manhattan), the PATH center is probably the most important. PATH stands for Prevention Assistance and Temporary Housing. All families seeking shelter start out here. When their numbers increase, PATH fills up. Night and day, year in and year out, weekdays and holidays, city shutdown or hurricane disaster, PATH never closes.

Often, it is a parking lot of strollers, a basic part of life for homeless families: these rolling miniworlds are the single unchanging point of reference that many homeless kids know. The strollers proceed awkwardly through the security scanners, they queue up in a caravan going back and forth in lines in front of the admission desk, they occupy the middle of the floor of the building's elevators while standees press themselves against the walls. Plastic bags of possessions drape the stroller handles, sippy cups of juice fill the cup-holders, Burger King paper crowns ride in the carrying racks beneath. Kids sleep peacefully while consultations and long waits go on around them. Some lean back and watch with a numbed, listless patience that suggests how much of their childhood has already been spent like this. Others hunch and squirm and scream their heads off.

The old Emergency Assistance Unit, which formerly stood on this site, is remembered fondly by nobody. Staffers, city officials, advocates for the homeless, and clients who had to make their way through it are all glad it's gone. The EAU was a windowless brick building with small, bare, ill-smelling waiting rooms. Hundreds of people, including the very old and infants, routinely spent the night there. In 2002, a sixteen-year-old boy killed himself when he learned that his family had to go back there. Linda Gibbs, now the deputy mayor in charge of Health and Human Services, which includes the Department of Homeless Services, was

Mayor Bloomberg's first DHS commissioner. She took the new mayor on a tour of the EAU one Sunday morning in 2002. "He was literally stepping over the sleeping kids all over the floor," she told me.

Bloomberg's eventual response was to tear down the EAU and build the PATH center in its place. Where the EAU was grim, PATH is gleaming and efficient—if not exactly welcoming. The land it sits on is oddly shaped and comes to a wedge point. The building fits the shape, so that its end makes an acute angle like the prow of a ship. Points and angles and big windows that expedite the sunlight from one side of the building through to the other define this place as a tool and not a zone for relaxation. Even the low walls around the building and next to the long, stroller-friendly entrance ramp are sloped, so that they can't be sat on. Inside it's clean and well run, and the social workers I talked to on a DHS-led tour of the place seemed serious and enthusiastic. The Bloomberg administration holds up the PATH center as a rebuke to its critics and as a symbol of its humane yet businesslike approach to homelessness.

The "PA" in PATH's acronym—Preventive Assistance—comes across forcefully in the Bloomberg policy, which tries hard to keep applicants out of the "TH," Temporary Housing. PATH will expend great energies in preventing you from being homeless, if other options can be found. If you have no home in New York but own a cabin in Alaska, PATH may give you a plane ticket to Alaska. To save scarce and valuable resources for those who truly merit them, PATH searches out every possible alternative to city-funded shelter. Usually, its efforts focus on finding relatives with whom the family seeking shelter can stay. Patiently and firmly and with endlessly bureaucratized persistence, it makes walking away and giving yourself up to fate seem the easier solution.

••

The families lining up at PATH, and the single adult men at their intake point, in the Bellevue Men's Shelter, on East Thirtieth Street, and the single adult women at the women's intake at the HELP women's shelter, on Williams Avenue, in Brooklyn: from a legal standpoint, these people are not asking for charity. They are exercising a right. Since 1938, the right to shelter has been implicit among the rights guaranteed by the constitution of the State of New York (though court action had to confirm it). No other city or state in America offers this right as solidly and unambiguously as does New York.

Advocates love the right to shelter. Most mayors hate it. Referring to it on one of his weekly radio shows last March, Mayor Bloomberg urged the city's taxpayers "to call their representatives in Albany and say, 'We ain't gonna do this anymore.'" Had he elaborated, he could have put the blame on literature. New York City has always been a place where reformers have scouted around in poor neighborhoods and written books about what they saw. In *American Notes* (1842), Charles Dickens affectingly described the squalor of the Five Points slum in what became Chinatown. Jacob Riis, a Danish immigrant, read Dickens and later filled his own exposé, *How the Other Half Lives*, with heart-wrenching Dickensian details, backed up by documentary flash photographs, among the first in history. Teddy Roosevelt read Riis, practically hero-worshipped him, and, as police commissioner, set about reforming the city's housing. Sometimes poetry does make things happen. If you declare, in a famous poem affixed to the Statue of Liberty, in New York Harbor, "Send these, the homeless, tempest-tossed, to me," you might consider that a certain commitment has been made.

Another Riis admirer was Fiorello LaGuardia, by general consensus the greatest mayor the city ever had. He loved *How the Other Half Lives* so much that he put a copy of it in the cornerstone of one of the nation's original low-cost public-housing projects, part of a series he built downtown and in Brooklyn. In 1938, with the Great Depression ongoing and his mayoralty in its fifth year, LaGuardia persuaded the state's voters to pass a constitutional amendment to help those in need. The amendment, Article XVII, reads, in Section 1:

> The aid, care and support of the needy are public concerns and shall be provided by the state and by such of its subdivisions, and in such manner and by such means, as the legislature may from time to time determine.

New York City's system of housing homeless people and caring for them, as it has evolved, rests mainly on this passage.

The upset-victory story of the *Callahan v. Carey* lawsuit, the right to shelter's first landmark case, gladdens advocates' hearts to this day. Demand for manpower in the Second World War absorbed most of the city's unemployed, largely solving the problems that Article XVII had addressed. In the prosperous decades following the war, very few in the city were without a place to live. Homelessness meant a small population of older, mostly white men along a few blocks of the Bowery. In 1964, a team of researchers looking for people spending the night in the city's parks found only one homeless man.

Then, all at once in the mid-seventies, homeless people seemed to be everywhere. Even today, nobody knows for sure why the problem became so bad so fast. Between 1965 and 1977, more than a hundred thousand patients were released from state psychiatric hospitals, and perhaps forty-seven thousand of them ended up in the city. At the same time, hundreds of single-room-occupancy hotels, or SROs, were shutting down; the SROs had provided low-income individuals with housing that was a step up from nothing. In 1972, the Supreme Court decriminalized vagrancy. Police became less aggressive about rousting those who were sleeping in public. The number of middle-class people in the city went down, which led to a decrease in the supply of livable and affordable apartments, leaving even fewer available to the poor. Whatever the cause, by the late seventies many thousands were "sleeping rough" (as the phrase had it) in the city's public spaces.

Robert Hayes was a twenty-six-year-old lawyer who worked for the Wall Street firm of Sullivan & Cromwell. Like others who became involved in advocacy for the homeless, he had a Catholic-school background—Archbishop Molloy High School, in Queens, and Georgetown University. After getting his law degree from NYU, he stayed in the neighborhood, and he began to wonder about all the homeless people he saw around his Washington Square apartment. From personal observation and from conversations with his friends Ellen Baxter and Kim Hopper, students at Columbia University who had spent hundreds of hours interviewing homeless people in the city, he concluded that the city and the state were neglecting their legal obligation.

Working pro bono, Hayes filed a class-action lawsuit in state court in October 1979 on behalf of three homeless men whom he met at a Catholic mission. These men claimed that they had been given nowhere to sleep but the so-called Big Room, a dangerous, unsanitary, and crowded overflow area in what had formerly been a municipal shelter; and that they had sometimes been denied shelter entirely. The lead plaintiff's name was Robert Callahan. He was a longtime fixture on the Bowery. His opposite number—the Carey in *Callahan v. Carey*—was Hugh L. Carey, then the governor. Hayes based his case on one word in Article XVII: "shall." When I talked to Hayes not long ago, he quoted, " 'The aid, care and support of the needy et cetera SHALL be provided.' " Then he said, "In our presentation before the judge, we simply argued that 'shall' means 'shall.'

"I dug around in the NYU law-library basement and found speeches given by the amendment's supporters and drafters back in 1938 that showed the intent," he went on. "These proved that the amendment was supposed to apply in hard times as well as in good. I kept the story simple because I'd never tried a case before and didn't really know what I was doing. Sometimes the judge had to instruct me in the rules of evidence." Arguments ended in late October, and the plaintiffs asked for an expedited verdict because winter was coming on. While awaiting the decision, Hayes let Callahan stay at his apartment; with some companions they made a big Thanksgiving dinner. Later, after Callahan moved out, Hayes noticed that his Archbishop Molloy High School class ring was missing.

On December 5, 1979, Justice Andrew Tyler, of the New York State Supreme Court, issued a ruling in favor of the plaintiffs. Finding that the state and the city were not in compliance with state law, he ordered them to provide emergency shelter for homeless men immediately in consideration of the weather. Attorneys for the state and the city were stunned. Plaintiffs had requested 750 beds; the city, caught short, asked that the number be left flexible. Plaintiffs willingly agreed. Hayes knew that city officials had no idea how many homeless men there actually were. Soon, more than a thousand men were seeking shelter every night, and the city had to scramble to keep up. The judge's ruling was of small use to Robert Callahan, however. He was found dead of alcoholism on a street near the Bowery not long afterward.

The decision that bears his name created the right to shelter, based on state law that had existed for forty-one years. In practical terms, *Callahan v. Carey* also established the courts as the de facto overseers of the city's shelter system. Dozens of court proceedings having to do with city shelters and their management followed, until details as small as the acceptable distance between beds and the prescribed amount of toilet paper in the bathrooms became the subjects of court orders. A consent decree in 1981 between the state and the city and the plaintiffs agreed on guidelines to manage the requirements of the *Callahan* decision, but other suits continued, including those which eventually confirmed the right to shelter for women, families, and people with AIDS.

Another result of *Callahan* was the beginning, in 1981, of the Coalition for the Homeless, founded by Robert Hayes, Kim Hopper, and Ellen Baxter. Relying mostly on private donors for financial support, the CFH disturbed and enraged the mayors of the nation's richest city regularly from then on.

••

On a recent Saturday, I set out to see how people were doing at some homeless shelters I knew about, and on the streets. First, I took the Lefferts Boulevard A train to the end of the line and walked three or four miles to a shelter called the Saratoga Family Inn. It is on Rockaway Boulevard by JFK Airport, across the highway from one of those long-term parking lots that elevate cars two- and three-deep. The shelter used to be a Best Western motel, and it houses about 250 families. Fencing topped with barbed wire surrounds the building on several sides, and large banners advertising a slip-and-fall attorney and an auto-leasing place hang from its windowless six-story front.

Two women were talking by the main entryway. Shirley, the older one, sat on her walker, while the younger, Diana, leaned against the wall. "We are living out in the boom-docks here," Diana said, when I told her I was a reporter. Breakfast had just ended and a smell of syrup lingered in the air. "I been in this shelter three years, and I don't care if I never see pancakes, French toast, or waffles again for the rest of my life," she remarked. "I don't even eat the breakfasts here no more. My stomach is too precious to me. And those artificial eggs—what do you call them—Egg Beaters."

"The food here ain't even real no more," said a woman named Kiki, who was returning with breakfast from a nearby deli. "Hey, y'all, this man is from the newspaper!" she called to some people coming out the door. Kiki had many long braids and an antic manner. People gathered around, and at each new complaint—playground is closed too much, kids have nothing to do, out here the travel is so long you have to get up at five in the morning to get your kids to school, kids see too much when they live in a single room with their parents, kids get sick more here, the $8-an-hour wage for in-house work will never get you out of here—Kiki whooped in affirmation. "Bloomberg put us in a corner and said fuck us!" she whooped. Pointing at the long-term lot across the highway, she said, "Those are parked cars, and we are parked people!" She let out a wild laugh.

"Every month, I get a paper from Welfare saying how much they just paid for me and my two kids to stay in our one room in this shelter, and I can tell you the exact amount," Diana said. "Three thousand four hundred and forty-four dollars! Every month! Give me nine hundred dollars of that every month and I'll find me and my kids an apartment, I promise you."

By foot, bus, and subway, I backtracked to Brooklyn, changing at outlying stops. Broadway Junction, near the Queens-Brooklyn border, was jumping like Times Square. In Bedford-Stuyvesant, I got off a C train at Nostrand Avenue and walked a few blocks to the vast old armory building that is now the Bedford-Atlantic men's shelter. People in soup-kitchen lines have told me that this is one of the worst shelters in the city. Sunlight glinted on its acres of gray slate roof, and its crenellated tower stood out against the sky. The guy I met here is Marcus "Country" Springs, originally from Lake City, Florida, who prefers to sleep on the street near the shelter—"Under that pear tree," he told me, pointing to a Callery pear up the street.

"In this shelter they treat you like an inmate," Springs said. "I stay in it only in inclement weather. It is not doing me no good, being in there. In a shelter you get what they call situational depression, but if you remove the person from the situation sometimes the depression goes away. These other guys you see on the corner are like me, hoping to meet someone who can help us. Sometimes contractors or movers come by with day jobs. Families visit and bring food. But the DHS—man, they have forgot us. The last person from this corner that got housed was like two years ago."

Next, I made a stop at the Bellevue Men's Shelter. For gloominess of aspect, Bellevue is unique, with its high columns near the entryway surmounted by the words PSYCHIATRIC HOSPITAL (the building's original function). Bellevue has 850 beds and is also called one of the worst shelters in the city; in general, the smaller shelters are said to be much less bad, and some are even nice. Ellis, the dollar-apiece

Newport cigarette seller on the street out front, suggested I go to Intake and register myself if I wanted to see what the place was like; I took his word for it instead. Then I subwayed up to 103rd Street on the Lexington line and walked across the footbridge to Wards Island, where a three-hundred-bed men's shelter occupies another former psychiatric hospital. That shelter, called the Charles H. Gay Building, is a lonesome place; constantly you hear the tires bumping on an approach ramp to the Robert F. Kennedy Bridge up above it. I asked a guy sitting on the curb in front of the shelter what he thought of it. He considered for a moment and said, "Jail's worse."

Nearby, a young man named Angel was helping a woman from Access Wireless hand out cell phones that were paid for by Medicaid. He called them "Obama phones," because they were free. A man in the background was being evicted from the shelter, cursing out the DHS police all the way. Angel told me that he had lost his job in a towel and linen warehouse about six weeks ago and that he wanted to get a job more than anything. He was wearing a pair of trousers that appeared to be riding very low, as the style now has it, but actually they were an optical illusion. The boxer shorts at the top of the trousers were a part of the garment itself.

An M-35 bus from Wards Island dropped me off at 125th Street in East Harlem along with a lot of guys from the shelter. Almost none of them paid their fare, but the driver looked the other way. Police had just concluded a sweep of makeshift dwellings under the Metro-North bridge at 125th and in front of a clothing store on Lexington between 125th and 124th. Cardboard lay scattered here and there and some ring-billed gulls were picking up french fries. A young policeman whose name tag said CHAN told me that some of the homeless who congregate here smoke a synthetic marijuana known as K2, which is sold as incense and causes lots of trouble. Just then a bearded guy ran up shouting, "Arrest that bitch!" He pointed at a woman. The cop asked what he should arrest the woman for and the guy said, "She just worked some voodoo on Maria's cart!"

As darkness fell, I took a bus downtown and looked for a man named Rick, who has slept on or near the steps of the Fifth Avenue Presbyterian Church, at Fifty-fifth and Fifth, intermittently since the Giuliani administration. Rick has told me that he prefers the streets to any shelter. Throngs of people were passing in the rush of a midtown Saturday evening, but Rick was not around. In the Village, I found a few small homeless encampments under construction hoardings, but the only person I recognized was a guy who used to attend a writers' workshop I taught a few years ago at a soup kitchen in Chelsea. The guy had been a problem because he would come to class and then just stand there and look at people. Tonight he was among all his stuff and reading a very small book held close to his face in the dim light. I tried to get his attention but failed.

In the warm Saturday-night air the city was hive-like, humming, fabulously lit, and rocking with low, thrilling Daisy Buchanan–like laughter. A young couple slept under a blanket beneath the hoardings at the Twenty-fifth Street Armory; the boy still had his baseball cap on. Meanwhile, attendees at a gala going on inside the armory took breaks on the sidewalk just around the corner and smoked and made phone calls. I ducked into the subway and rode a crowded No. 4 train uptown and went back to the PATH center. I had never seen it after dark. Up here, the night was quieter, and the building with its pointed end and five brightly illuminated floors rose up like an ocean liner, or the yet unsunk front of one.

Two school buses and a black van waited by the building's sidewalk-level door. A PATH employee in a blue T-shirt swept up under the streetlights and by the curb, and a guy wearing a fringed scarf wandered around muttering. The vehicles started up and began to idle, and a narrative of nighttime journeys seemed to take hold. For a while nobody came from the PATH building's door. Then a few families emerged with strollers and suitcases. Sleepy kids held pillows and stuffed animals. A tall woman with a shorter man and a teenage girl came to the van, and the tall woman asked me if I was the driver. The actual driver came up and opened the van's back doors and began to stow the family's stuff, quietly and taking care with it.

The van's interior light shone on him. A young mother with a baby in one arm had some trouble folding up her stroller and the driver helped her fold it and then he put it in the back. "We've been here at PATH since ten thirty this morning," the tall woman told me. "Twelve and a half hours. Now we'll go to a shelter for ten days while they decide if we're eligible. I don't know how this all happened. We were staying with my sister. Now we're wondering what this shelter we're going to will be like. A year ago we had to stay in a shelter for a week and it was kind of bad."

More families came out, accompanied by a woman with a clipboard. People got sorted out into the right vehicles. Kids slept on people's shoulders, except for a toddler named Jared, who was stagger-walking to and fro. He bumped against the legs of the man who was sweeping and a woman watching him picked him up and said to the sweeper, "Sorry, my bad." Soon all the passengers were aboard, the vehicles' doors closed, and the red taillights came on. Slowly the buses drove off, followed by the van. Nighttime departures and arrivals occupy the subbasement of childhood memory. The guy sweeping and the muttering man and the woman with the clipboard and the reporter taking notes existed in a strange, half-unreal state of being part of someone else's deepest memories a lifetime from now. An orange had fallen from a bag lunch and lay beside the curb. The muttering man picked it up and looked at it and rubbed it and put it in his pocket.

••

Deputy Mayor Linda Gibbs, the Bloomberg administration official most significantly involved in its policies for the homeless, is a trim, gray-haired woman in her mid-fifties whose father was the mayor of Menands, a village north of Albany. She grew up there and came to New York City right after getting her degree at SUNY Buffalo Law School. Intricate questions of public policy that would confuse and baffle most people intrigue her. Her blue eyes often have an expression that can only be described as a twinkle. I've seen this look in other Bloomberg staffers' eyes, and in photos of the mayor himself. It reminds me of the twinkle in the eyes of the Santa Claus in the Coca-Cola ads from the 1950s (inappropriately, given the mayor's feelings about soft drinks).

I think the contagious Bloomberg twinkle comes partly from the mayor's role as a sort of Santa figure. He works for the city for a dollar a year, he gives away his money by the hundreds of millions, and he manifestly has the city's happiness and well-being at heart. Every rich person should be like him. His deputies and staffers twinkle with the pleasure of participating in his general beneficence, as well they should. "You can't make a man mad by giving him money"—this rule would seem to be absolute. And yet sometimes people in the city he has done so much for still get mad at Bloomberg and criticize him. At the wrong of this, the proper order of things is undone, and the Bloomberg twinkle turns to ice.

Mary Brosnahan, the president of the Coalition for the

Homeless, has worked for that organization for twenty-five years. She grew up in Dearborn, Michigan, and got her undergraduate degree at Notre Dame. Dark-haired and soft-spoken, she seems to enjoy the complications of public policy as much as Gibbs does. Patrick Markee, the CFH's senior policy analyst, is a graduate of Saint Ignatius High School in Cleveland, and of Harvard. He has a high forehead, a short ginger-and-gray beard (sometimes), and a voice that jumps into its upper registers when he is outraged. That two such earnest, unassuming people can get our multi-billionaire mayor so upset seems a remarkable thing. Gibbs generally refers to them and to others in advocacy groups as "the litigants." The term applies, because the CFH and others have been bringing suits against the city, with the help of the Legal Aid Society, in an ongoing sequence ever since *Callahan.* She pronounces the word "litigants" with an air of careful neutrality that is somehow frightening.

One afternoon, I sat in the offices of the CFH on Fulton Street, downtown, while Markee and Brosnahan told me of the many things the Bloomberg administration had done wrong. On another afternoon, in a small conference room at City Hall, not far away, I met with Gibbs and two of her colleagues while they told me of the things it had done right.

"People have no idea what a mess the Department of Homeless Services was when we came on board," Gibbs said. "The litigants probably never saw the confused mass of court orders and directives that had piled up at DHS in folders *this thick,* not even cataloged in any usable way, as a result of all their lawsuits. And that mass of court orders was what the DHS had to constantly refer to in running the shelter system! Finally, in 2008, we were able to bring some clarity and structure to that. This gave demoralized DHS staffers hope, and a new sense of empowerment."

Markee: "The agreement worked out with the DHS in 2008 to resolve all the preceding court orders with regard to shelter management was obviously a good outcome for the homeless and for the city. But the CFH and other advocates accomplished it only in the face of constant opposition from Linda Gibbs and the city's lawyers."

Gibbs: "The 2008 agreement we finally reached with the litigants vacating all preceding court orders and replacing them with a coherent, mutually acceptable framework for running the shelters is an achievement we're very proud of. But the litigants fought us on it every step of the way."

Brosnahan: "The most amazing mistake the Bloomberg people made was that they were supposed to be this results-oriented, data-driven team, and they paid no attention to their own data! From the beginning, they ignored decades' worth of experience showing that homeless people who receive permanent housing with rent subsidies almost never go back to being homeless."

Markee: "So, ignoring all that data, Bloomberg ended homeless people's priority for subsidized public housing, and for Section 8, a federal subsidy that pays the difference between thirty percent of a renter's income and the market rent of his apartment. Section 8 is permanent once you've been approved for it, and studies show that nearly ninety percent of the people who get it are still in their own apartments five years later. A certain number of homeless people annually had been given priority over other applicants to receive Section 8. The policy had worked forever, and they ended it."

Gibbs: "We discontinued Section 8 priority because of its dwindling availability, and because we discovered that the chance of getting Section 8 was operating as a perverse incentive, drawing people to seek shelter who otherwise would not have done so."

Markee: "The theory of the 'perverse incentive' has been disproved over and over again. Most people who become homeless do not get themselves in that predicament in order to receive a rent subsidy. If a small number actually do take that unlikely route, the net effect on the shelter system is greatly outweighed by all those who leave homelessness permanently after getting a subsidy."

Gibbs: "We did not end Section 8 priority with nothing to replace it. In fact, we came up with a far superior subsidy plan, called Advantage, to be funded by the city and state, which was particularly targeted to homeless families and individuals. The litigants say they want rent subsidies, but they were opposed to Advantage from the beginning."

Brosnahan: "Actually, we were glad when we heard that the Bloomberg administration wanted to start a new rent-subsidy program. But when they announced, almost immediately, that the subsidies would have a short time limit, we flipped out. Short-term subsidies obviously were not going to be enough to keep people from again becoming homeless."

• •

The Advantage program went into effect in the spring of 2007. It was incremental, paying all but $50 of the rent to start; then, like Section 8, it paid the difference between an apartment's market rent and 30 percent of the renter's income. When asked about the program by the *News*, Markee predicted that it would be "a revolving door back into shelter." Within the next year and a half, some nineteen thousand people, including individuals and those in families, signed up for Advantage. Soon, they had moved from shelters into their own apartments and were paying rent.

In 2008, Rob Hess, the DHS commissioner, announced that no Advantage recipients had gone back to being homeless, and he quoted Markee's earlier prediction derisively, without mentioning him by name. But in 2011, the state, facing a budget shortfall, withdrew its funding for Advantage, and the city, unable to afford it without the state, ended the program. As the loss of the subsidy took hold, thousands of newly installed renters couldn't pay their rent, and many of them eventually returned to the shelter system.

The collapse of Advantage contributed greatly to the rise in homeless numbers during Bloomberg's third term. Most of the heads of households in shelters whom I've met, like Christina Mateo, say that they became homeless because they lost Advantage subsidies. Some say that getting their own apartments only to lose them again was worse than not getting them in the first place.

Bloomberg and his administration had set out to do something about homelessness. At the time he took office, he feared that New Yorkers had come to accept homelessness as a condition of city life, and the possibility alarmed him. He said, "We are too strong, and too smart, and too compassionate a city to surrender to the scourge of homelessness. We won't do it. We won't allow it." He assembled advisory groups by the score, called meetings, took recommendations. A blueprint emerged, titled "Uniting for Solutions Beyond Shelter: The Action Plan for New York City." The administration's businesslike, can-do ethic infused the effort, providing goals and charts and tables, and deadlines by which this or that would be accomplished. The mayor said that in five years he planned to reduce homelessness by two-thirds.

In this instance, he probably would have been better off if he had left office after his second term. His new homeless policy seemed to work for a while; by the middle years of his mayoralty, homeless numbers had leveled off. But by his third term the homeless population was climbing every year, exacerbated by the '08 market crash, and continuing upward even after the crash's effects on the city had begun to abate.

Faced with questions about these numbers—evidence of what was shaping up as the worst failure of his administration—the mayor grew peevish. He blamed "the advocates" for Advantage's failure, saying that they had lobbied to end the Advantage program (they supported ending it only because they wanted to replace it with something better, they countered). He reported that the New York City shelter system was being inundated by people from out of town, and, on one of his radio shows, he gave a skewed example of the city's long-standing legal obligation, claiming, "You can arrive in your private jet at Kennedy Airport, take a private limousine and go straight to the shelter system and walk in the door and we've got to give you shelter." He didn't mention that the DHS's stated determination to keep applicants out of city shelters whenever possible would have sent this hypothetical traveler back to her airplane forthwith, perhaps with a one-time subsidy for jet fuel.

Criticisms passed on to the mayor from the CFH seemed to make him especially touchy. On one occasion, he referred to the CFH as "not a reputable organization."

••

The difference in philosophy is fundamental, and it goes way back. In the years after the Civil War, a Massachusetts woman named Josephine Shaw Lowell wanted to improve the living situation of the thousands of postwar "vagabonds" then at large in New York City. Her husband, Charles Russell Lowell, had died in the war, as had her brother, Robert Gould Shaw, the famous commander of an all-black regiment. In her good works among the vagabonds, the young, high-minded New England widow considered charity to be corrupting. Soup kitchens enraged her. Rather than give handouts, she preferred to teach the indigent "the joy of working." Despite or because of her ardor, she proved a bad fit for the charitable organization where she served as the director, and she resigned.

That is one philosophy. To some degree, though perhaps not as much as Mrs. Lowell, the Bloomberg administration has subscribed to it. The mayor's plan to reduce homelessness has always stressed "client responsibility." In an interview in 2003, Linda Gibbs talked about the new outlook at the DHS. She said that a lack of standards had helped to create "passivity" among shelter users, and that the new goal was to "manage this in a way that people change their behavior." For the services homeless people were being given, conscientiousness and diligence were asked of them in return. To begin with, they had to look for jobs and apartments, attend regular meetings with social workers, and obey all shelter rules. Their homelessness was mostly their fault, and so their behavior had to change.

Then, there's the other philosophy, which says that it's not their fault. What the homeless need, this other philosophy says, is a stable place to live, not a system telling them what to do. Once stable housing is achieved, changes in behavior, if necessary, can follow. The problem is not the poor's lack of character but a lack of places in the city where they can afford to live and of jobs that pay a decent wage. The problem is not inside but outside. No change in personal behavior is going to make rents cheaper. According to this philosophy, the PATH center's relentless search for relatives with whom applicants for shelter can double up or triple up just crams more bodies into the too short supply of moderate- and low-income housing in the city, and sends people into unhealthy or even dangerous situations.

Manhattan is now America's most expensive urban area to live in, and Brooklyn is the second most expensive. Meanwhile, more than one in five New York City residents live below the poverty line. Nearly one in five experiences times of "food insecurity" in the course of a year—i.e., sometimes does not have enough safe and nutritious food to eat. One-fifth of 8.3 million New Yorkers equals 1.66 million New Yorkers. For people at the lower-middle and at the bottom, incomes have gone down. The median household income in the Bronx is about $33,000 a year; Brooklyn's is about $44,000. Meanwhile, rents go steadily up. A person working at a minimum-wage job would need 3.1 such jobs to pay the median rent for an apartment in the city without spending more than 30 percent of her income. If you multiply 3.1 by eight hours a day by five days a week, you get 124 hours; a week has only 168 hours.

The number of market-rate rental apartments available to those of low income is extremely small. A metaphor one often hears about the homeless is that of musical chairs: with such a small number of low-income-affordable apartments, the players who are less able to compete, for whatever reason, don't get chairs when the music stops. Every year, more and more chairs are taken away. The existence of so many people who are homeless indicates that a very large number of renters are close to that condition. Housing advocates in the Bronx report that some of the people they try to help are paying 70 percent of their income in rent and that others are living doubled up and tripled up and in unimproved basements and in furnace rooms— conditions that recall the days of Jacob Riis.

Patrick Markee has said that any real attempt to take on

these problems will involve the restoration of Section 8 and public-housing priority, creating a new rent-subsidy program, passing living-wage laws, and building more low-income and rent-supported housing. Given the unsuccess of Bloomberg's homelessness policies, and the comparative authority the CFH has gained thereby, its suggestions are likely to be more listened to. Joe Lhota, the Republican mayoral candidate, wants to amend Article XVII so that it limits the right to shelter to New York residents only; according to DHS statistics, 23 percent of shelter residents listed their previous dwelling as an out-of-state address.

Bill de Blasio, the probable next mayor, wants to ease the DHS restrictions determining who qualifies for shelter, set aside public-housing vacancies for the homeless, come up with a new rent-subsidy plan involving a voucher system by which rent-challenged tenants can afford their own apartments, and build a hundred thousand new units of low-income housing. Campaign contributions he has received from slum landlords who profit from running crummy shelters worry some observers, and should; the condition of the homeless can always get worse, while the financial reward for housing them can be enormous. De Blasio and his defenders say that he has always stood up to slumlords and wants to get rid of the expensive shelter housing they provide. In any event, the near future will likely bring a major revision of Bloomberg policies and another shake-up of the world of the homeless will occur.

• •

Over time, I lost touch with almost all the homeless people I talked to. There was Richard, a quiet, humorous man with disabilities I met at a soup kitchen. He had been in the care of friends until they took him to a subway station one day and left him there. He spoke of the friends without resentment, as if by accepting homelessness he had finally been able to do them a favor in return. Richard has not been seen at the soup kitchen for a while.

A young man named Jay was carrying a rabbit outside the PATH center when I met him one day last spring. He made a call on my cell phone because he thought I might take the rabbit off his hands (most shelters don't allow pets). The rabbit's name was Queen. A family member of Jay's was about to show up with Queen's cage and food when I finally declined. Jay and I talked on the phone a few times after that—the family member's cell phone had my number. He and his mother and brothers were in a shelter in Brooklyn and the rabbit was with a cousin. Later, Jay's or his relative's cell-phone number stopped working.

Michael, who was sitting by the road to the Charles H. Gay Building, told me he had lost his job when the dock where he worked was destroyed by Sandy. He said, "Bloomberg thinks we low-down, but we ain't—we just poor." In 28 percent of the families in shelters, at least one person has a job. Erica, who lived in a shelter despite working for an energy company in Connecticut, listed her rage-filled complaints in a burst like a ratchet gun, with swift, dramatic gestures. Her shelter apartment, which she showed me, was spotless. Paul, an older West Indian man, waited in line at a CFH food-distribution van by Battery Park while we talked. He said he had been laid off from his job as a furniture handler and shipper in Staten Island and was sleeping on the couches of friends. Shenon, a home health aide who lived in a family shelter on Junius Street, in Brooklyn, said that "grown-ass men" walked its hallways nearly naked in front of her kids. She offered to show me the shelter, and told me a cell-phone number, but, like most of the others I was given, it turned out not to work.

Soon after Christina Mateo received notice of her ineligibility for shelter, she called me in a frantic state. She was on her way to PATH to reapply. When I called her two days later, she sounded calm. It had all been a mix-up; she was back in the same shelter. Two days after that, we spoke again. A new problem with her eligibility had come up, and she was going back to PATH. I tried to find out what happened but wasn't able to reach her again.

Homelessness is a kind of internal exile that distributes people among the 236 shelters around the city and keeps them moving. In this restlessness, the homeless remind me of the ghostly streaks on photos of the city from long ago, where the camera's slow shutter speed could capture only a person's blurry passing. Of all the homeless people who gave me their cell-phone numbers, only two—Marcus "Country" Springs and a woman I talked to briefly named Rebeca Gonzzales—could still be reached after a few weeks had passed.

••

Robert Hayes, the young attorney who brought and won *Callahan v. Carey* and cofounded the Coalition for the Homeless, remained involved in homeless advocacy. He won other important class-action suits, kept up with the city's management of the shelter system, and continued to clash with the powers in city government. At times, the work overwhelmed him with its pressures and strident controversies. He thought the future of the city depended on him, he felt the weight of the suffering poor on his shoulders. When it became too much, he would get in his car and drive to Maine and not stop until he was in some uncrowded, remote place, and then after a short while he would drive back.

During the administration of Mayor Edward Koch, the city found itself more than usually strapped for places to house the homeless. Koch was among the mayors who hated the right to shelter and the onus it imposed on the city, and he and Hayes had many exchanges that ranged from bitter to nasty. Low-income and middle-income housing also was in short supply under Koch, and as these problems intensified his administration adopted a plan of setting aside buildings that had been seized in tax default and rehabilitating them for housing. These buildings are called "in rem" buildings, from the name of the legal action that transfers ownership to the city. By fixing up in rem buildings, Koch began a process that eventually provided 150,000 new units of affordable housing, much of it subsidized for low-income tenants. Of those units, 10 percent, or 15,000 units, were set aside for the homeless.

Colorful and witty as Koch was, the success of his in rem housing added gravitas to his reputation. When he died, last February, the fact that his in rem program had provided housing for many tens of thousands of poor and middle-income people ran at the top of his obituaries.

As for Robert Hayes, after ten years with the CFH his trips to Maine became longer, and his weariness at his job greater, until finally he decided to quit. He did a stint with the prestigious Manhattan firm of O'Melveny & Myers, and then moved with his wife to just north of Portland and set himself up in private practice. They had three daughters. In Maine, he represented Exxon as well as local people fighting paper mills, and he became less "us versus them" in outlook, partly because the legal community was so small that the people he went up against in court were the same ones he ran into at the supermarket. After nine years, he moved back, to Hartsdale, New York, where he is now a senior vice president at a company that provides health benefits for people covered by Medicare and Medicaid.

In 2003, he happened to cross paths briefly with former

mayor Koch in a TV studio. Afterward, Hayes decided to give his old adversary a call. His experience in Maine had led him to think about his battles of the past, and he wanted to make peace with Koch if peace needed to be made. Koch accepted the invitation and the two went out to lunch.

Hayes, a self-possessed, slim, sandy-haired man of sixty, looks like what he is—someone who has seen a lot, won some big games, and now levelly watches the world. "We met in the Bryant Park Grill, behind the library," Hayes told me recently, at his White Plains office. "The place was full, and everybody recognized Koch, and he was pleased by the attention. We talked—or he did, ninety-five percent about himself, of course, although I was happy to listen. After a while, the subject moved to our old disputes over homeless issues and the right to shelter. Koch said that if it hadn't been for the pressure from us advocates to do something about housing for the homeless he might not have been forced to undertake his in rem program. Now he was an old man, and he knew that the in rem housing was going to be his legacy.

"He told me he knew that, and then he did a very un-Koch-like thing," Hayes said. "He thanked me."

October 28, 2013

The Antidote

Joseph D'Agosto, a paramedic with the Fire Department's 23rd EMS Battalion, on Staten Island, is the best person in New York City. During his twenty-four years on the job, he has saved many lives—"hundreds, probably," he says. D'Agosto is known throughout the department as an instructor in emergency medical techniques. When I went looking for him the other day at battalion headquarters, near the southern end of the island, one of his colleagues said he was out, called him on the phone, and told me an address where I could find him. Somehow I had the impression that D'Agosto would be conducting an instructional session, but he turned out to be getting a tattoo of an owl ("for wisdom") on his left forearm at Contemporary Tattoo and Gallery, occasional workplace of his friend and EMS colleague Josh Fitch, who was washing down D'Agosto's arm for stenciling when I came in.

Staten Island has a lot of tattoo parlors, Italian delicatessens, two-story office buildings with empty spaces to rent, massage therapists, car services, Italian restaurants, places that give rock-music lessons and host children's birthday parties, Laundromats, liquor stores, tire shops, nail parlors, foot spas, pet-grooming salons, hair salons, barbershops ("buzz cuts, fades, tape-ups"). A small-business miscellany, sprung from the borough's abundant middle-class life, lines the bigger roads like Hylan Boulevard from one end of the island to the other.

Most Staten Island enterprises are as their signs describe them. Occasionally, one or two storefronts that look no different from the rest also do a steady word-of-mouth business in the illegal sale of OxyContin, oxycodone, Percocet, and other prescription painkillers. A neighborhood ice-cream truck playing its jingle might also be selling pills, according to police, who keep an eye on ice-cream trucks. A window-blinds and drapery store sold oxycodone pills until the NYPD arrested one of the owners and the store closed. At a barbershop called Beyond Styles, on Giffords Lane, in the Great Kills neighborhood, police arrested the owner and two accomplices in October 2013 for selling oxycodone and other drugs—two thousand pills a week, according to the Drug Enforcement Administration.

The silent sniper fire of overdoses from pills and heroin that has been picking people off one at a time in increasing numbers all over the country for almost twenty years has hit Staten Island harder than anyplace else in the city. For a number of reasons, this borough of 476,000-plus people offers unusually good entry routes for the opioid epidemic. In 2012, thirty-six people on Staten Island overdosed on heroin and thirty-seven on prescription opioid pills, for an average of almost exactly one overdose death every five days. Many of the dead have been young people in their late teens to early thirties. In this self-contained place, everybody seems to know everybody else, and the grief as the deaths accumulate has been frantic and terrified.

I wanted to talk to Joseph D'Agosto because he had recently appeared in the *Staten Island Advance* for saving an overdose victim. That alone would not have got him in the news, because he saves overdose victims with some frequency. What made this rescue different was that he used a nasal-spray syringe of a drug known as Narcan, whose name comes from the first syllables of "narcotic antagonist," a term for opioids that reverse the action of other opioids. In Narcan, the antagonist drug is an opioid called naloxone. Like heroin, naloxone is highly soluble in the blood, and it acts almost instantly, reversing the effects of heroin or pain-relief opioid pills often in one or two minutes. Formerly, D'Agosto and other paramedics administered an intravenous dosage of naloxone to revive overdose victims; general use of the nasal-spray injector is something new.

Josh Fitch traced the outline of the owl tattoo on D'Agosto's arm, which D'Agosto extended as if getting an IV himself. "We received a call for an unresponsive person in the courtyard of an apartment building, early morning, around three or four o'clock, on a night shift last February," D'Agosto told me. "The unresponsive person, a lady in her sixties, was slumped over on a bench, in like a robe or a housecoat. Near her we found a pill bottle for painkillers, almost empty, and I saw on the label that it had been filled only a week before. She was not breathing, lips blue, pupils miotic—pinpoint-size—all symptoms of opioid OD. We put her head back, secured a breathing passage. I took the Narcan injector and sprayed a milligram of the naloxone solution in each nostril, and about a minute later she coughed and started breathing again. My partner that night, Henry Cordero, and I were, like, 'Okay! We figured it out!' We put her on the stretcher and brought her to the hospital, and they took over from there.

"In the past, when we used the naloxone with the IV, that worked, too. But finding a vein for the IV can be difficult. Maybe the person was an IV drug user and he's got collapsed veins in his arms. Maybe you're in a dim hallway, family members around you crying and screaming—there it's not as easy finding a vein as in a well-lit hospital room. Also, you have the problem of when they come to, sometimes they get agitated and want to fight you, and with the IV there can be a danger of a needle stick from someone who may have a disease. With the Narcan atomizer, none of that is a problem, and anybody can use it. You don't need a special skill—you just spray it in the nose. And everybody's got a nose."

The Narcan nasal-spray program began in Staten Island's 120th Precinct in January. All first responders—police and firefighters, along with the EMTs—received Narcan syringes and instruction on how to use them. Including the police was important, because they usually get to the scene first, and speed counts; when an overdose victim stops breathing, brain damage begins in four to six minutes and death soon follows. By March, responders with Narcan had saved three overdose victims in the precinct. City higher-ups decided to extend the program to the rest of the borough and, soon afterward, to the rest of the city. More Narcan-produced rescues followed. In June, Governor Andrew Cuomo announced that the Narcan kits would be given to every first-responder unit in the state.

••

It used to be that the medical profession undertreated pain. Doctors didn't want to create opioid addicts, and the consensus was that patients should suffer rather than risk addiction. That started to change in the seventies, with the rise of the pain-management movement, when pain came to be seen not only as a symptom but also as an illness in itself. Now the worry was of "opiophobia." A widely used pharmaceuticals textbook advised, "Although many physicians are concerned about 'creating addicts,' very few individuals begin their drug addiction problems by misuse of prescription drugs . . . Fear of producing such medical addicts results in needless suffering among patients with pain."

Strong opioids like morphine and oxycodone already existed for patients with intense, short-term pain from healing trauma or end-of-life illnesses. Long-term, chronic pain was another matter—no existing drug was ideal for that. Seeing the need, Purdue Frederick, a pharmaceutical company in Norwalk, Connecticut, developed a long-term pain reliever called MS Contin, which was a morphine pill with a time-release formula. When the patent ran out on MS Contin, Purdue introduced a time-release oxycodone pill, OxyContin.

The pill entered the market in 1996 and quickly became an iatrogenic disaster. OxyContin's purpose was merciful—to provide pain relief at a steady rate over a ten- or twelve-hour period, so a pain sufferer could sleep—and millions benefited from taking it. But for its effect to last that long, the pill had to contain a lot of oxycodone. People discovered that the capsules could be crushed, then swallowed, snorted, or injected for a powerful high. Purdue marketed the drug aggressively to general practitioners who accepted the company's claim (untested and untrue) that OxyContin was difficult to abuse. Overdoses involving OxyContin soon became horribly routine in places like Maine and West Virginia. As the epidemic of "Oxy" addiction and overdose spread, Purdue did not take the drug off the market. Several states and many individuals sued the company, which fought with tobacco-company-like determination but eventually gave in. In 2007, Purdue pleaded guilty in federal court to misbranding the drug by not stating its potential for causing addiction—a felony—and paid a fine that totaled $634.5 million. It also introduced a version of OxyContin that was more tamperproof. By that time, the drug had made the company many billions of dollars.

Even with the fines and the deaths, OxyContin showed the profitability of long-term opioid pain relievers and contributed to the enormous proliferation of pain pills nationwide. Therein lay the beginning of Staten Island's opioid problem. More Staten Islanders work in health care than in any other industry. Health-care workers often know about and have access to pills, and their insurance generally pays for them. Many other Staten Islanders are police officers, firefighters, and sanitation workers, with health insurance from the city. If they get injured on the job, they see their own doctors, who can write prescriptions. Staten Islanders receive the pills, in short, because they are prescribed them and can afford them. In 2012, doctors and hospitals on Staten Island prescribed painkillers at a rate about twice that of the rest of the city.

Kids who abuse pills usually get them first from friends or the family medicine cabinet, but then they have to buy them. Illegal pills sell for as much as $40 or $50 apiece; $6 or $8, however, will buy a packet of heroin, for a high that's the same or better. Most people who come to heroin get there by way of pills. New York City is the heroin capital of the country; 20 percent of all the heroin confiscations and arrests nationwide happen here. When I talked to Agent James J. Hunt, the head of the New York Division of the DEA, he said that 90 percent of New York's heroin originates in South America and Mexico. Poppy fields in Colombia grow the raw opium, labs hidden in the jungle process it, Mexican drug cartels smuggle the heroin through the Caribbean or across the U.S.-Mexico border, and dealers, who are often Dominicans, package it, stamp it with brand names like Breaking Bad or Government Shutdown, and sell it to street dealers. Heroin confiscations at the border have increased from about 556 kilos in 2008 to about 2,100 kilos in 2012. In New York in 2014, 200 kilos had been seized by July, more than twice as much as during all of 2013.

Agent Hunt's office chair at his big desk in DEA headquarters in Manhattan is black and high backed. He wore a black shirt and a muted tie. His blue eyes and his blond, wavy hair parted almost in the middle made his face stand out as if in an Old Master dark-background oil portrait. I asked if the plan to push large quantities of cheap heroin and undersell the illegal pill market had been the idea of a particular person—like El Chapo Guzmán (the Sinaloan cartel leader). Hunt thought a minute and said, "Yes, it probably was his idea, or the idea of four or five cartel leaders like him.

"In Yonkers recently there were some dealers who were mixing heroin with fentanyl, a very dangerous opioid, and selling it on the street," Hunt went on. "Four people died from using it, and the dealers kept on selling it even after they knew that. Anybody who would sell heroin is evil."

· ·

The opioid epidemic may seem to be a crisis that simply happened, but actual people set it in motion, and other actual people make it worse and keep it going. The cartel leaders and the smugglers and the dealers belong to the second category. In the first category must be included the former management of Purdue Pharma, three of whom pleaded guilty to a nonfelony misbranding charge. Purdue Pharma is the huge drug company that grew from Purdue Frederick, whose owners, Dr. Mortimer Sackler and Dr. Raymond Sackler, were not charged in the case. Their older brother and mentor, Dr. Arthur Sackler, known as the founder of modern pharmaceutical advertising, served as the inspiration for the company's ambitious OxyContin marketing strategy. The Sacklers made many philanthropic gifts and many things are named after them, such as the Sackler Wing at New York City's Metropolitan Museum, with its famous Temple of Dendur.

Staten Island's special misfortune is to exist at a point where somewhat ambiguous but real corporate crime helped to provide a market opportunity for straight-ahead drug-cartel crime. In the years since Purdue Pharma pleaded guilty, the company has tried to make its product safer and to draw more attention to problems of abuse. During the early years of the OxyContin rollout, Purdue ignored the physician's basic rule, *Primum non nocere*—First, do no harm—with terrible consequences.

• •

Johnathan Charles Crupi is buried in Triangle 63, Lot 66, Grave 3, in Staten Island's Ocean View Cemetery. He died in March, at the age of twenty-one. A photograph of him— blue eyes, affectionate smile, gold-colored earring in one ear—looks at you from his marker. The grave is still fresh, the dirt reddish, next to a gravel lane that wanders by. Purple and white impatiens, a pot of campanula, and a circle of white stones brighten the plot. The ocean is difficult to see from the cemetery and impossible to hear. The main sounds are birdsong, a lawn mower, and the nearby buzzing of a Weedwacker.

Johnathan Crupi's parents, Barry and Candace Crupi, did not want his obituary in the *Advance* to say he "died at home"—a newspaper formula sometimes used for overdose victims. The write-up described him as a "wonderful kid until drugs came" and said he died of a heroin overdose.

In May, the Crupis took part in a New York State Senate Joint Task Force Panel Discussion on Heroin and Opioid Addiction at a community center near the middle of the island. The gathering was one of many held by the New York State legislature to get public comments on the problem at various locations around the state—the Senate held eighteen such forums, the Assembly held three. For this event, the room, a high-ceilinged conference space, seated two hundred or more, with many standees along the side. Before the proceedings started, a chatty, neighborly cheeriness overlay the nerve-racked, sometimes desperate mood underneath.

All stood for the Pledge of Allegiance. A state senator, the task force's head, spoke, followed by other senators. Then Brian Hunt, a panelist identified in the program as "Father of deceased Adam Hunt," stood up. (He and Agent James Hunt are not related.) Brian Hunt's voice was in a register almost beyond pain. He said that Adam had been in rehab for two months and came home to look for a job. In February, at a Super Bowl party, he took a drink. Soon afterward, someone sold him heroin. He died on March 2 of acute heroin intoxication. Some of the people he had bought drugs from, as Hunt later learned, lived in the Hunts' neighborhood, on the next block. Sellers of heroin hide in plain sight and may be friends and neighbors; sellers of heroin should get life in prison, he said.

Candace Crupi spoke next. Her voice was small, quiet, and almost devoid of intonation. She talked about a time when Johnathan was four and she lost him briefly at a Costco. She said what a sweet boy he was. She said no one was ever beyond redemption, because "every angel has a past and every sinner has a future." She added that the pharmaceutical companies should help pay for drug treatment, because they're reaping all the profits and suffering none of the sorrow.

••

Several young men who stood up at the meeting said they were addicts in recovery and praised a rehab program called Dynamite, in Brooklyn. When I called Dynamite's number, its executive director, Bill Fusco, and associate director, Karen Carlini, offered to show me around. Dynamite is the short name for Dynamic Youth Community, a rehab program with residential facilities in the town of Fallsburg, upstate, and outpatient services and main offices on Coney Island Avenue, in a distant neighborhood of Brooklyn.

Fusco, who cofounded DYC more than forty years ago, has the heft and the large hands of a blazing-fast softball pitcher, which he is. Karen Carlini, who's slim and pretty, began as a patient and then a volunteer at the center, in the seventies. DYC is for young people between the ages of sixteen and twenty-four. The program begins with a year's residence at Fallsburg and continues with a year of daily outpatient attendance at the Brooklyn center. At the moment, seventy-five members—"They're not clients or patients, they're members of the Dynamite family," Fusco said—were here on outpatient status, with an almost equal number in residence at Fallsburg. Seventy-eight percent had entered the program because of addiction to heroin.

Fusco and Carlini and another staffer and I sat and talked with a group of members in a circle in a high-windowed top-floor room with easy chairs and couches. Some of the young women got comfortable with their legs folded under them, as the incoming daylight of sobriety set the atmosphere. There was a moment of everybody looking at one another. A lot could go unsaid—how they got here, the nightmares that went before. Every sentence carried a freight of experience and accomplishment. They had built houses at Fallsburg, and gone without cell phones or Internet, and visited the county fair, and attended religious services in the town, and written letters, and hiked to the waterfall on the property, and played softball, and painted the scenery for the graduation ceremony, and sat on the lawn, and, as one young woman said, "learned how to have sober fun again."

They all said that they had thought pills couldn't be so bad, because doctors were prescribing them. "I never thought they could create an addict in me," one said.

Fusco repeated that they had worked hard to get where they are today and they should be proud, because they did the hardest parts themselves. Later, he told me that the program costs about $28,000 a year per member. Parents pay a portion, on a sliding scale depending on income, and New York State picks up most of the rest. "I think the taxpayers are justified in expecting that the state will contribute when their kids need this kind of help and the health insurance won't cover it," he said.

"Up to now, insurance has allowed for only seven or ten days of rehab, twenty-eight days at most," Carlini said. "That might work for adults who have families to support and a limited amount of time. But for kids who are addicted, rehab takes years, not weeks. The good news is that kids are more resilient than older people. They can recover fully, both physically and mentally."

••

Some of the Dynamite members said that at one time or another they had overdosed and naloxone had revived them. To a few this had happened more than once. Though the drug may have saved their lives, none said they enjoyed the experience. Naloxone is like the bouncer of the opioids; it stops the high of heroin or morphine or opioid pills so fast that the user does a 180-degree return to reality and undergoes the familiar miseries of detoxing in a sudden, intense onset. The reversal is of short duration, though, and after thirty to ninety minutes the person usually slips back into a milder opioid sleep. If the original opioid was in the system in such an amount as still to be a threat, the naloxone must be used again. Most overdoses involve multiple drugs; naloxone works only on other opioids. Alcohol, cocaine, and benzodiazepines like Valium are unaffected by it.

With a minor asterisk, one can say that naloxone was invented in Queens. (A Japanese pharmaceutical company received an earlier patent for the drug but seems not to have known what it had.) Dr. Jack Fishman, a young biochemist with a PhD from Wayne State University, first developed it in a small lab under the elevated tracks on Jamaica Avenue in the late 1950s. Ever since morphine was synthesized from opium, in 1803, chemists had been searching for a drug with morphine's good qualities but none of its bad. Mostly what they'd come up with was other addictive drugs—heroin, for example, invented by an English chemist in 1874 and developed commercially by Germany's Bayer Company as a cough suppressant aimed mainly at patients with pneumonia and terminal TB. Opioids with antagonistic properties had been discovered before naloxone, but they presented serious problems. Nalorphine and cyclazocine both reversed the effects of pain-relieving opioids but also caused severe dysphoria (the opposite of euphoria), hallucinations, and psychotic episodes.

Dr. Fishman worked at the Sloan Kettering Institute for Cancer Research and had taken a second job at the private lab in Queens because he was going through a divorce and needed the money. Dr. Mozes Lewenstein, the head of narcotics research at a company called Endo Laboratories, oversaw the private lab. A colleague of his at Endo, Dr. Harold Blumberg, proposed that a change in the structure of oxymorphone, a recently synthesized morphine derivative ten times as strong as morphine, might produce an opioid antagonist of comparable potency. Following Blumberg's idea, Fishman began to work with oxymorphone and, by replacing an N-methyl group in its structure with an allyl group, synthesized naloxone. Tests showed it to be more potent at reversing the effects of opioids than any other antagonist synthesized so far. In 1961, Lewenstein and Fishman applied for a U.S. patent for naloxone, called only by its chemical name, N-allyl-14-hydroxydihydro-nor-morphinone. Five years later, they received patent 3,254,088.

The drug turned out to have all kinds of uses. First, as an opioid antidote, naloxone comes with almost no contraindications—it does not combine to bad effect with other drugs. Its serious side effects are rare and few. (A study found that in 1.3 percent of cases where naloxone was administered, seizures and pulmonary edema occurred.) Though naloxone displaces other opioids, no other opioids displace it. During the period before it wears off, it has the final word. It produces no analgesic effects and is itself non-addictive.

Naloxone's invention led to important discoveries about the chemistry of the brain and the nervous system, such as the discovery of endorphins. These endogenous opioid peptides—chemicals in the body that provide pain relief and pleasure like pain-relieving opioids—revealed hints of their existence when it was found that electronically stimulated pain relief could be reversed by naloxone. If naloxone could reverse pain relief when no drugs were present, researchers guessed that the body must have its own pain-relief systems. "Endorphin," the word, comes from "endogenous morphine." A number of such natural chemicals were later found, along with receptors in the brain upon which they and the opioids acted. Other studies showed that naloxone may block the pain-relieving effects of acupuncture and placebos, temporarily suppress the urge to eat, and reduce the body's shock and stress reactions.

The drug must be injected or administered intranasally, because it's not absorbed well by digestion. This is fortunate for drugmakers who want to put safety brakes on drugs meant to be taken only orally. Suboxone, a methadone-like drug used in the treatment of addiction, consists of naloxone combined with an analgesic opioid called buprenorphine. The Suboxone pill releases its buprenorphine under the tongue, but if you try to grind up the pill and inject it for a stronger rush, naloxone's usual downer effect kicks in.

Naloxone is given to newborns whose mothers have had opioid painkillers during childbirth so the opioid won't suppress the babies' breathing. Postoperative patients sometimes are brought out of anesthetic with naloxone. Patients suffering from dissociative disorder, which often causes everything around them to seem unreal, can be treated with naloxone; the drug's true affinity seems to be with reality. Naloxone has no dysphoric or psychotomimetic effects and no obvious potential for abuse. Anybody can use it to revive an overdose victim with little fear of causing injury. Thebaine, the Tasmania-grown, opium-derived raw-material precursor of oxycodone and other legal opioids, is also the precursor of naloxone; the harmless drug comes from the same stuff as the dangerous ones for which it is the antidote. If there ever was a *primum non nocere* drug, naloxone is it.

..

Our Lady Star of the Sea, a Catholic church serving forty-
one hundred families, occupies a rise above Amboy
Road, in the Huguenot neighborhood. Weekly, the church
offers fourteen Masses and a dozen twelve-step-program
meetings—seven of Alcoholics Anonymous, two of Pills
Anonymous, and one each of Gamblers Anonymous, Adult
Children of Alcoholics, and Al-Anon. Cars come and go in
the ample parking lot all day. Some guys were leaving an
AA meeting at the rectory and having an earnest conversation as I went in one afternoon to see Monsignor Jeffrey P.
Conway, at that time Our Lady Star of the Sea's pastor (he
has since moved to St. Patrick's, in nearby Richmondtown).
Conway is a tall, narrow-faced, soft-spoken, cerebral man
who even in civilian clothes looks set apart. The blue polo
shirt, blue slacks, and blue sneakers he was wearing somehow evoked monastic garb.

He had been pastor at this church since 1993 and had
watched the opioid problem grow in the area, he said.
As an AA member himself for thirty-five years—in a kind
of apostolic succession from one of AA's founders, Bob
Smith, whose nephew was the doctor at a rehab clinic for
priests that he attended in Michigan—Conway instituted
the church's various addiction programs. In 2010, two
young brothers said they wanted to start a chapter of Pills
Anonymous here. Only about five people came to the first
meetings, but fifty or sixty attend regularly now.

An assistant brought him a black-bound ledger with
DEATHS on its front cover in gold Gothic letters, and he began to turn its pages slowly. "I wanted to look at this. I've
presided at a lot of funerals for overdose victims," he said.
"Here's one . . . March ninth, 2011 . . . He was eighteen
years old . . . Another, April tenth, 2011 . . . twenty-two

years old. I remember he joined AA as a sixteen-year-old, and later stopped coming to meetings. I heard he was doing pills and I tried to get in touch with him but he wouldn't take my calls . . . May of 2012 . . . He was thirty-one. His family said it wasn't drugs, but I'm not sure of it . . . It's hard to know what to say in your funeral homily, almost impossible to give consolation. The families feel guilty, bereaved, angry at the kid, angry at themselves . . . Here's a fifteen-year-old boy . . . A young woman, May of '13 . . . And here, June of '13 . . . This young man was in rehab in Georgia and got out and was found dead a few days later in a motel room . . . Another, November thirteenth, end of last year . . . twenty-three years old."

He laid the book aside. I asked if Scripture has any verses that apply to this situation. "Second Corinthians, chapter 12," he said, and then he recited, " 'In order that I might not become conceited by the abundance of revelations, a thorn was given me in the flesh, a messenger of Satan, to harass me, to keep me from being too elated . . . The Lord said to me, "My grace is sufficient for you, for my power is made perfect in weakness." I will all the more gladly boast of my weaknesses, that the power of Christ may rest upon me . . . For when I am weak, then I am strong.'

"That's the twelve-step idea of admitting your weakness in the face of addiction and giving yourself up to a higher power," he continued. "Alcoholism takes a while to ruin your life, but opioid addiction can happen in a week. It's almost instant. And the physical addiction of opioids is much harder to fight. Once you're off the drugs, you still have to maintain your sobriety by going to twelve-step meetings. The programs that get kids off drugs are wonderful, but some don't emphasize the follow-up enough. At meetings, you have the fellowship of older participants who know about sobriety day to day and year to year. Stopping drugs is the beginning. Then you must keep getting the power in order to stay stopped."

••

I wandered all over Staten Island but saw very few outward signs of the opioid crisis. On July 8, police arrested a pharmacist named Anthony D'Alessandro at his house in a new development for stealing almost two hundred thousand oxycodone pills while he was head of the drug dispensary at Manhattan's Beth Israel Medical Center (he pleaded not guilty). When I walked through his neighborhood soon afterward, it seemed untouched, with kids playing baseball in a little park and women watering yards. In the pharmacist's front window was a vase with a bouquet of pussy willow.

I checked behind a high school, where a footpath rumored to be a drug hangout dozed, empty of hangers-out, in the suburban fragrance of newly mown grass. By a shopping-center alley in which drug deals supposedly occur, a young man in a yarmulke was handing out campaign literature to passing shoppers. At a park entrance where, according to police, an undercover cop bought four oxycodone pills for $30 each from a young woman drug dealer, an Uncle Louie G's Italian Ices truck was playing "I Can't Stop Loving You," "The Battle Hymn of the Republic," and "O Come, All Ye Faithful."

As I drove by Silver Mount Cemetery, on Victory Boulevard, suddenly a shirtless young man with tousled blond hair and wild eyes was walking toward me in my lane. I veered. His face was weirdly red and he held a clear plastic water bottle in one hand. By the time I pulled over and looked back for him, he was gone.

••

The plague's silence and invisibility on Staten Island kept it from public attention for a long while. Deaths from overdose do not tend to happen on the street. As a veteran rehab counselor said at the Senate Joint Task Force meeting, "The kids would come home by curfew, say good night to their parents, and leave their bedrooms feet first the next morning." Then commuters started noticing kids nodding out on the ferry and on the Staten Island Railway. Neighbors heard from neighbors about kids who had overdosed, and the bad news spread. Daniel Master, the chief assistant district attorney of Richmond County (Staten Island's coextensive county), remembers going to a wake for an older person and observing that the other part of the funeral home was filled with weeping teenagers.

Staten Island is not the healthiest place. It has the highest rate of smoking in the city and shares the highest rate of obesity with the Bronx. More teenagers here, per capita, use alcohol and binge-drink than in the other boroughs. "Kids drinking is just a part of the culture here," explained Diane Arneth, the president and CEO of a nonprofit called Community Health Action of Staten Island (CHASI). "Staten Island is a mostly blue-collar community, and drinking on the weekend is a normal way to relax. When kids are around, sometimes they drink, too. The parents say they'd rather have the kids drinking at home than out somewhere on the street. I know people who play drinking games with their underage kids and their kids' friends at family parties. It's not seen as a big deal.

"Staten Islanders generally work in other parts of the city, and they have the longest average commuting times in the United States," Arneth went on. "So the kids are alone a lot. The parents accept that, because this is a supposedly 'safe' place. Staten Island kids have cars, they use social media, they're mobile, looking for the party. Pills fit right into that world. And then, when substance-abuse problems come up that the parents can't handle, they hate to ask for help. A lot of them are cops, firemen, they've done military service. They give help, they're not used to asking for it. Help is for 'those people'—families in the projects, Latino immigrants, poor people—not for them. When we went to community boards back in the nineties trying to set up local needle exchanges to stop the spread of AIDS, some of the responses were so cruel. Nobody thought it was their problem. They said, 'They're just junkies—let them die.' Now some of the same people who used to yell at me about why I cared about the junkies are asking for help for their addicted kids."

Community Health Action of Staten Island works closely with a larger nonprofit called the Staten Island Partnership for Community Wellness, which in 2011 responded to the youth opioid problem by founding a coalition called Tackling Youth Substance Abuse. TYSA's enterprising director, Adrienne Abbate, brought together many groups and agencies to look for solutions, and the idea of giving Narcan kits to all emergency personnel came from one of TYSA's meetings in 2013.

••

If you want a Narcan kit of your own, Community Health Action of Staten Island will provide you with one at no charge. You have to attend a training session at a CHASI office, where you watch a PowerPoint presentation, hear some facts (drug overdoses recently overtook car accidents as the leading cause of accidental death in the United States; most victims of drug overdose are between the ages of thirty-five and fifty-four), answer questionnaires having to do with your knowledge of opioids, and do a hands-on assembly of syringes from kits that are past their expiration dates. You leave with a small blue nylon zip-up bag that contains a prescription for the drug signed by a doctor or a nurse practitioner, two syringes and two capsules in small cardboard boxes that say "Naloxone Hydrochloride" on them, two "Intranasal Mucosal Atomization Devices" that fit onto the syringes, a pair of rubber gloves, two alcohol wipes, and a mouth-to-mouth-resuscitation face shield.

Joshua Sippen, a vice president of CHASI, led the session that I attended. Before he began, he pointed me out and said I was a reporter, in case anyone in the group objected on the ground of privacy; a number of the attendees were the mothers of addicts. Nobody did. Afterward, a woman named Melissa Forsyth, who had been sitting a few rows up, introduced herself to me as Missy. I was glad to meet her. She has a good laugh—the kind that's full-throated and infectious, an intact survival from a younger self. She said her son had been addicted to heroin. Like others there, she wanted the naloxone kit in case she ever had to save her child. Data show that as many as 85 percent of overdose victims are with other people at the time of the overdose; if there's naloxone in the vicinity and someone to administer it, they could be saved.

A few days later, she and I met at a bagel place on Bay Street. She was on a break from her job as a YMCA peer counselor working with families of addicts, she had a four-month-old girl she was taking care of in a stroller, she was getting lunch for herself and her seventeen-year-old daughter, Leanne, and her phone kept ringing. Missy Forsyth is forty-six years old. Her husband, a New York City firefighter, is forty-seven. Her brown hair was pulled back in a clip, and she wore a patterned top and rectangular glasses, lightly tinted purple.

"My addict is my oldest son, Joe," she told me, jiggling the baby on a knee. "He had a horrible experience—his cousin Amanda, who he was close to, was hit by a car and killed on Richmond Avenue coming out of a sweet sixteen party in 2006, and he blamed himself. He was supposed to come home and take care of his younger siblings so his father could pick her up. Of course, the accident was not his fault, but he started drinking heavily, then doing pills, and eventually he went to heroin. We understood how bad it was when we found he'd been taking money out of a family member's bank account."

She answered a phone call, got a bottle of water for the baby, and told her daughter what sandwich she wanted. "Joe says he's clean now," she said. "He's been in three re-hab programs. I hope that's finally true. But, really, it never ends. He went to college at Oneonta, left after a year. Worked at a café, got a job as an exterminator, went to College of Staten Island, dropped out. Did a year of treatment at a residential rehab, came back, started working at a brand-new hotel in Brooklyn, lost that job. Now he lives with his fiancée. The disease is hard to fight, and he kept getting sucked back in. I support him when he's in recovery, at arm's length when he's not."

A young woman she knew came in and stopped to talk to her. (People in Staten Island seem constantly to run into friends and acquaintances when they go out.) "I used to try to control what my kids do, but I've stopped that," she said, turning back to me. "I was a helicopter parent, but my helicopter landed long ago. Now I'm working on a certification in counseling at CSI, I volunteer for the YMCA, and I do presentations at schools about drug addiction. I want to give people a face they can put with the addiction crisis. I was very involved with my kids' lives, coached their sports teams, drove them to lessons, and still this happened to us. I tell the high school kids again and again that opioid pills can make them addicts in five days. I say, 'Don't drink, but if you do, whatever you do, DO NOT take any pill. Stick to alcohol!'" She laughed; she was kidding about the last part.

"Joe is a loose, tall, gangly sort of kid," she said after a moment, readjusting the baby in her arms. "As a little boy and a teenager, he was always kind of flopping around and tripping and falling down, and then he'd get right up again and be fine. It's a reality I've accepted in my life that Joe may one day be dead. But so far he's still alive. As long as he's still breathing, I've got hope."

· ·

In 2012, New York State passed a law called I-STOP/ PMP, for Internet System for Tracking Over-Prescribing/ Prescription Monitoring Program, and it went into effect in August 2013. I-STOP requires that most prescribers of painkillers and other drugs with the potential for abuse check the state's Prescription Monitoring Program to see what the patient's prescription history has been during the previous six months before giving out a prescription. The idea is to make it difficult for people to go to a series of doctors and get repeats.

Within a few months, evidence seemed to show that I-STOP had reduced the amount of illegal opioids on the market. Critics said the law would create a greater demand for heroin, and that seemed to have occurred. According to NYPD Captain Dominick D'Orazio, commanding officer of Staten Island Narcotics, seizures of pills had gone down 44 percent, while seizures of heroin had gone up by the same amount. D'Orazio said he saw this as a good sign for the long run, because virtually everybody who tries heroin nowadays begins as an opioid pill abuser; fewer pills out there may mean fewer heroin addicts in the future.

Diane Arneth took a similarly positive view of what sensible laws and public-health policy can accomplish. She

noted that AIDS needle-exchange programs, which met resistance not only in Staten Island but all over the country,
reduced the number of needle-transmitted AIDS cases in
New York from 50 percent in 1992 to 4 percent today. Programs that are now handing out naloxone kits in Chicago
and San Francisco and other cities started, like her own
CHASI, as providers of AIDS services and needle exchanges.
Reducing overdose deaths will be their next victory, she
believes.

An August 28 press release from the New York City
Department of Health and Mental Hygiene announced
that the citywide rates of drug-overdose deaths had gone
up 41 percent between 2010 and 2013. Now the city's average for such deaths is two a day. The Staten Island overdose
death rate, however, is starting to come down after its
fourfold increase between 2005 and 2011. The department
said that the aggressive approach to Staten Island's overdose
crisis would now be applied elsewhere in the city.

On Staten Island, the new Narcan program had resulted
in thirteen overdose reversals by July, adding to the thousands naloxone has already rescued nationwide. Dr. Jack
Fishman could be proud. When he invented naloxone, he
was only in his twenties; I wondered if he might still be
alive, and what he thought of his invention now. It turned
out that he died in December 2013, but his oldest son,
Howard, lives on the Upper West Side. Howard remembered the storefront lab, the el tracks overhead, the smell
of chemicals, and the drugstore next door where his father
used to buy him a pistachio ice-cream cone after his visits.
After his father and his father's parents escaped from Poland,
in the thirties, they were penniless, Howard told me. His
father's pharmaceutical discoveries and career eventually
made his fortune. He did important work on breast cancer,
headed a pharmaceutical company, served as a consultant

to the World Health Organization, and was director of research at the Strang-Cornell Institute for Cancer Research until shortly before his death.

I asked Howard if his father took satisfaction from the fact that his invention had saved so many lives. "He was a complicated man," Howard said. "Like many superachievers, he thought he had never really achieved anything. He shied away from the spotlight. He didn't talk about himself; he talked about other people—like when he met Kissinger, he talked about that. Originally, he had wanted to be a rabbi. He was very generous to his family members around the world. He was a good father. I'm happy just to bask in his glow. His was a well-lived life."

..

A woman whom naloxone revived more than a decade ago, when she was in her twenties, now works for a national nonprofit that fights drug addiction and its dysfunctions. She is married, with two small children, and her official job-related manner is bright and hopeful. When I asked her what being revived by naloxone had felt like, she hesitated. Her voice changed; a particular quiet bleakness filled it. "When I overdosed, I was with some other people, and one of them had a naloxone injector kit he had bought from his dealer," she said. "I guess this dealer was kind of conscientious, if that doesn't sound too strange. Maybe he wanted his clients to be safe, so he wouldn't be hit with drug-induced-homicide charges. Anyway, he sold naloxone kits sometimes. Back then, there were no naloxone distribution programs where we were.

"So we did heroin, and I overdosed, and the guy with the naloxone injected me with it, and all I remember is waking up and feeling so horrible that I thought the people I was with were being mean to me. I didn't thank anybody for saving me—I was only angry and upset that they had made me feel like this. The withdrawal came on immediately and it was very, very painful, like twenty times worse than the worst flu I ever had. But without the naloxone I don't know what would have happened. The thought of being left passed out where I was still scares me. We were homeless junkies. Nobody who saw me would have bothered with me. No way anybody would've called nine-one-one."

She talked about her recovery and what it still involves. I asked her what she imagined would be the best possible result of the work she's doing, and she said, "I love that question!" Her voice brightened completely. "We're going to stop this opioid pandemic!" she said, and began to explain how.

September 8, 2014

The Cabaret Beat

During my senior year in college, forty-two years ago, I spent a lot of time reading old issues of *The New Yorker*. My purpose was to write an English honors thesis about them, if possible. I had no real focus; my brother, who had been sick for a while, died soon after I started. I sat in a remote study carrel in the library's stacks, next to a narrow, dim window with an interior view, and idled through the brittle pages in bound volumes. In the end, I turned in the thesis (such as it was) too late and graduated in General Studies. The one success I can point to is that I read every issue, more or less cover to cover, from the magazine's first three years—from February 21, 1925, until sometime in 1928.

Harold Ross, *The New Yorker*'s founding editor, envisioned it as a magazine of sophisticated humor. According to the historic marker on a building where he lived on the West Side, Ross once said, "If you can't be funny, be interesting." What I found in the old issues may have been both or neither, but I couldn't really tell. Humor tends to evaporate with time, and what is interesting in 1925 will probably be less so almost half a century later. The first piece I came across that connected with me—in fact, the only piece I still remember from my reading—appeared in the issue of

November 28, 1925. It was called "Why We Go to Cabarets: A Post-Debutante Explains." The byline at the end was Ellin Mackay.

I didn't understand it much better than the other articles, but somehow I kept rereading it. The piece was a personal essay—a telling-off, essentially—centered on an Upper East Side, high-society problem. The young woman essayist was saying that social events involving debutantes and the "stag lines" of suitable young men who asked these young women to dance were oppressive and boring. The young women preferred the far more exciting and democratic experience of dancing with their dates in cabarets, she said. I didn't get some of the language. To prove she was not unfastidious, Miss Mackay wrote, of the people one met in cabarets, "We do not particularly like dancing shoulder to shoulder with gaudy and fat drummers." I wondered why the guys in the cabaret's band would be on the dance floor, and why the band would have such a large percussion section. Years later, I learned that "drummer" also meant "traveling salesman."

Miss Mackay was so scathing about the young men in the stag lines, so confidently snobbish. "There is the gentleman who says he comes from the South," she wrote, "who lives just south of New York—in Brooklyn. There is the partner who is inspired by alcohol to do a wholly original Charleston, a dance that necessarily becomes a solo, as you can't possibly join in, and can only hope for sufficient dexterity to prevent permanent injury to your feet." I identified with the stag-line duds and winced for them. At that age, you think that when a woman you want to like you calls you boring or pompous or stiff or idiotic, the verdict is final. Later, you learn that those all can serve as positive attributes in the right circumstances. I now see that what chimed with me, beneath the essay's apparently rarefied subject matter, was the anger. She was twenty-two when she wrote the piece; I was that age when I read it. At twenty-two, I was confused and stressed-out. At that age, as I later learned, so was she.

••

Ellin Mackay made her debut in society in 1921, when she was eighteen. Her father, Clarence H. Mackay, the president of the Postal Telegraph-Cable Company, gave her a dance at the Ritz-Carlton Hotel attended by more than a thousand guests. She had blue eyes and blond hair and a face that could be cute, beautiful, or interesting, depending on the light. Debutantes in New York in those days rose to movie-star levels of celebrity. The unusual spelling of her first name, combined with the cool, Irish-tough pronunciation of her last—"Mackie"—made her what today might be called a brand, though the concept would have repelled her.

Her coming-out was covered in the *Times*, which led with her name in the headline. During her years of fame, it and other papers—the *New York Herald Tribune*, and tabloids like the *Daily News*, *The Sun*, and the *New York Mirror*— ran many stories about her, while *The Wall Street Journal* focused on the business dealings of her father. Later books about *The New Yorker* and its beginnings almost all mentioned her, especially Ralph McAllister Ingersoll's autobiography, and *Ross, The New Yorker, and Me*, by Jane Grant. The book that describes her best, and the one I learned the most from, is *Irving Berlin: A Daughter's Memoir*, by Mary Ellin Barrett.

Ellin Mackay, deb extraordinaire, married Irving Berlin, the most famous songwriter in the world, six weeks after her article on cabarets appeared. The ceremony took place in the Municipal Building, downtown, with Berlin's longtime business partner and his wife for witnesses and none of Ellin's family present. A call she made immediately afterward, at a pay phone in a nearby drugstore, was a heads-up to Harold Ross. When he answered and addressed her as "Miss Mackay," she replied, "Oh, no, it's Mrs. Berlin. I'm not a Lucy Stoner. The fact is I shan't be able to get my piece in on time. I'm leaving town in about twenty minutes."

Lucy Stoners were women who kept their maiden names after marriage, following the example of the woman suffrage leader. The piece that Ellin referred to, the one that she did not have time to get in, remains a mystery. Two weeks after the cabaret article, Ross had printed another essay by her, called "The Declining Function: A Post-Debutante Rejoices." After that, she never published anything else in *The New Yorker*, though she wrote about a dozen short stories for *The Saturday Evening Post* and other magazines, as well as four novels, all under the name Ellin Berlin.

••

My father was a chemical engineer who read *The New Yorker* every week and paid close attention to the articles whether he understood them or not. When John McPhee visited my high school and I even talked to him, my father was powerfully impressed. Other *New Yorker* regulars had less appeal. To my announcement, after college, that I intended to be a writer, he replied, "Whatever you do, don't write like that guy Barthelme." (Of course I then did try, unsuccessfully, to write like Donald Barthelme.) My father often said funny things without cracking a smile and could listen to them just as inexpressively. Try as I might, I rarely got him to laugh. Once I came upon him sitting in a chair in the living room reading a book and laughing out loud. The sight so shocked me that I had to see the title—*The Years with Ross*, James Thurber's memoir of the editor.

After reading that book, Dad seemed to think of Ross

as someone he knew personally. He referred to him simply as "Ross," following the lead of Thurber and of Ross's other *New Yorker* colleagues, and I needed to remind myself that Ross was long dead and he and my father had never met. Later, when I came to the magazine, I learned with surprise that people there did not like *The Years with Ross*. Robert Bingham, then the executive editor, told me that the book made Ross look like a buffoon when he was in fact a brilliant and sensitive editor, the greatest of his day.

In fairness to Thurber, Ross's contemporaries often did regard him as a comical figure. Ralph McAllister Ingersoll, who was the managing editor in the magazine's early years, described him: "His face was made of rubber, which stretched in every direction. Out of the lower half hung a huge Hapsburg lip to which cigarettes stuck." He said that the editor was prone to making large, spasmodic gestures. During Ingersoll's job interview, Ross knocked a bottle of ink onto Ingersoll's suit. Portrait photographers emphasized Ross's hair, which grew straight up and which a famous actress said she would like to walk barefoot in. But the comic aspects served as mere distraction. In his deeper, less visible self, Ross was like the soul in the Bible that hungers and thirsts for righteousness.

He had the idea of doing a weekly magazine about New York when he was in France during the First World War, editing *The Stars & Stripes*, the newspaper of the U.S. military. After returning to the States, in 1919, he edited a short-lived version of *The Stars & Stripes* for veterans and became a New York nightlife figure known for carrying around a dummy of his still unnamed magazine and talking about it endlessly. When he finally published the first issue of *The New Yorker*, ninety years ago, he paid for it partly himself. Nearly half the magazine's original funding was a $21,000 stake put up by Ross and his wife, Jane

Grant, and their friend Hawley Truax. Raoul Fleischmann, a baking heir and almost millionaire whom Ross had met through mutual friends, supplied another $25,000.

••

One afternoon last fall, I went out to Green-Wood Cemetery, in Brooklyn, to see the Mackay mausoleum. The family's money came originally from John W. Mackay, Ellin's grandfather, and his name is carved in big letters on the top step leading to the walk to the mausoleum door. John Mackay immigrated to New York from Ireland in 1840, when he was nine. At twenty, he sailed for San Francisco to try his fortune in the California gold fields. Eight years of placer mining in that state produced little, so he went over the Sierras to Virginia City, Nevada, and worked in the silver deposits known as the Comstock Lode.

Mark Twain, who at the time happened to be a reporter for Virginia City's *Territorial Enterprise*, mentions Mackay in his autobiography, and says he once offered to trade businesses with him—Twain would take over Mackay's mining and his brokerage house, and Mackay would step into Twain's reporting job. Mackay asked what the *Enterprise* paid, and Twain said $40 a week. Mackay replied that he'd never swindled anybody in his life and didn't intend to start now—his business wasn't worth $40 a week. Twain goes on to note that, within ten years, "John Mackay developed suddenly into the first of the hundred-millionaires." With three fellow Irishmen business partners, Mackay persevered in mining the Comstock, through boom and bust, and in 1873 they hit one of the richest veins of silver ore ever found anywhere.

Great as Mackay's triumph was, his wife, Louise, a young widow whom he had met and married in Virginia City, outdid him. As the wife of one of the richest men in the world, she took on the world. When society in New York City rejected her, she moved the family to Paris, where she bought a mansion near the Arc de Triomphe, threw fabulous parties, and gave a ball for the visiting ex-president Ulysses S. Grant and his wife, which was the hit of the 1877 Parisian social season. Continuing on to London, she bought another home, met more nobility, entertained members of the royal family, and gained an introduction to Queen Victoria. New York ladies who had snubbed her began to angle discreetly for introductions. On one of the family's many ocean crossings, the Mackays' younger son, Clarence, met Katherine Duer, a beautiful young woman from an unimpeachably high-ranking New York family. After Clarence and Katherine married, John Mackay built them a fifty-room mansion on Long Island, and they lived there and in a town house in the city. Retiring from her overseas conquests, Louise eventually moved back to be with her son. By that roundabout route, the Mackays of Virginia City established themselves in New York.

John Mackay began construction of the Green-Wood mausoleum in 1895, after the death of his elder son, John, Jr., in a riding accident. He was interred there himself in 1902. The tomb is about three stories high, of mica-flecked gray granite, and topped with allegorical statuary. In the grass beside the back wall is a small metal cap that Con Ed removes when it wants to read the meter. The Mackays' is the only mausoleum in the cemetery that has electricity— in fact, it may be the only such in the country. Groundskeepers switch on its built-in heating coils when the family opens it for memorials. Ellin and Irving Berlin are not in the Mackay mausoleum. They were buried in Woodlawn, in the Bronx.

••

Katherine Barrett Swett is the head of the English Department at Brearley, a Manhattan private school for girls. Two years ago, I wrote a magazine piece about her husband, Benjamin Swett, the photographer. At the time, I didn't know that Katherine is one of Ellin and Irving Berlin's grandchildren. Recently, I asked her if we could talk about her grandmother, and she met me at a coffee shop on East Eighty-sixth Street near her school. Around the eyes she resembles pictures of the young Ellin, with the same combination of sharpness and gentility. She wore a blue silk scarf and teardrop-shaped crystal earrings and her brown hair in a French braid. "Granny didn't like reporters, after the terrible experiences she'd had with them," she said. "She told me never to deny anything to a reporter, because he'll put in his headline that you denied it and make you look bad anyway. She had a temper, and sometimes a sharp tongue, but she was wonderful with us grandchildren—affectionate and indolent and very physical. I remember snuggling with her on the couch when she would read to us for hours.

"Grandpa we saw less of, partly because of his work, but he was fun, too. My first memory of him is being at Luchow's and him telling me a story about Hansel and Gretel, how the witch's house wasn't made of candy but of wood, and they tried to eat it and their teeth all fell out. Living in the shadow of the career of Irving Berlin and of his fame was difficult, though, for her and for the rest of the family. In many ways it sucked. But I don't think Granny ever felt that she'd lived a thwarted life. She dedicated herself to being Mrs. Irving Berlin. At the same time, she kept a sense of who she was. In her later years, she returned to the Catholic Church, and she went to Mass at St. Patrick's often. When they married, she'd had to give up a lot more than he did. Marrying him and defying her family was an extreme move, an amazingly brave personal decision. And their marriage lasted for sixty-two years! They just really loved each other."

••

Ellin Mackay and Irving Berlin met on May 23, 1924, at a New York dinner party to which he had been invited as a last-minute replacement, a Plan B that Ellin later regarded as fate. The hostess, Frances Wellman, knew the Long Island crowd that Ellin's father, Clarence Mackay, socialized with, but her circle also included theater people. She had been a friend of the Mackays for years.

In Ellin's 1944 novel, *Land I Have Chosen*, she describes the moment when Anne Brooke, the main character, meets Marco Ghiberti, a young Italian who has just arrived in New York. The setting is a dinner party given by Mamie Winton, a family friend: "They stared at each other. This isn't meeting. This is recognition." Anne Brooke thinks, "You didn't fall in love like this, suddenly. Not at a dinner party—not with a stranger, in this familiar room . . . It was this party—this night—this time for which she had waited. There was, after all, a reason in your heart. A reason for the stars and the sea. A reason for all the beauty you had ever seen. An answer to all the questions . . . How queer that that long-remembered room should now forever be the frame in which she had first seen Marco."

Ellin was twenty-one, Berlin thirty-six. Slim, dark, always well dressed, he had a lightness of manner and he danced beautifully. At the same time, he was a genuine tortured genius who walked the floor all night and wrung songs from himself with main force and last-minute, out-of-nowhere inspiration. By the time they met, he had been through enough for several life stories. He was born Israel Baline, probably in Tyumen, a city in Siberia. His father,

Moses, moved the family around in his profession of itin-
erant cantor. Berlin's earliest memory was of lying by the
side of the road and watching his house and village burn in
a pogrom. Like hundreds of thousands of other Jews, he
and his family—his father; his mother, Leah; and his seven
older siblings—fled attacks in Russia's Pale of Settlement
and immigrated to the West. The Balines came to New
York in 1893 and settled on Cherry Street, on the Lower
East Side, where he attended P.S. 147.

At thirteen, after the death of his father threw the
family into near poverty, Israel quit school and left home
for good. He delivered telegrams, worked in sweatshops,
sang on street corners, slept in flophouses. "Berlin," an ap-
proximation of his last name, he acquired on the streets;
"Irving" he chose himself, for its dignity. Friends still called
him Izzy. Graduating to singing waiter in rough downtown
saloons, he learned how to balance trays, sing, and corral
tossed coins with his feet simultaneously. Improvising par-
odies of popular songs led to composing his own. He wrote
his first national hit, "My Wife's Gone to the Country
(Hurrah! Hurrah!)," when he was twenty-one; its sheet music
sold three hundred thousand copies. Soon afterward, a stint
in the army inspired his "Oh, How I Hate to Get Up in the
Morning," which became a marching song on two continents
during the First World War.

Songs possessed him, sometimes arriving three or four
a day. Ragtime, the new music invented by black musicians, was shaking up the straightforward rhythms of the
previous century and syncopating them irresistibly. Berlin
heard this culturewide change better, perhaps, than anybody. As rock and roll did fifty years later, he took the
era's insurgent black music and reframed it and widened
its appeal. According to Philip Furia's biography, *Irving
Berlin: A Life in Song*, he made ragtime "seem ingratiating,

not threatening." His "Alexander's Ragtime Band," written in 1911, became the biggest hit song ever composed until then and set off an international dance craze. By starting a music-publishing company and building his own Broadway theater (the Music Box, which still stands), he doubly secured his fortune. In the twenties, the *Times* estimated his income at half a million dollars a year. When Berlin was twenty-three, he married Dorothy Goetz, the sister of a writing partner, but she died soon afterward of typhoid fever, contracted on their Cuban honeymoon.

Through his rise to fame and later, he remained eccentric in many ways. He composed without writing down the music himself, played piano only in the key of F-sharp (using a special keyboard adapter to change to other keys), and sang in a high vibrato. Reinventing American popular song, he added a Yiddish accent, making it even more American in the process. He adored his adopted country; admirers of his enormously popular "God Bless America" wanted it to become the national anthem. In later years, when his daughter Mary Ellin asked her mother if she had ever entertained any doubts about marrying him, she said that she once saw her future husband under a streetlight chewing gum and wearing a hat she didn't like, and the hat was going up and down on his head as he chewed, and she wondered if this funny little man really could be the one for whom she intended to give up everything, and she decided that he was.

Berlin left no memoir or other account of what he thought when he first met Ellin, but he did write a song for her, "Always," which became a No. 1 hit in 1926. Everybody knows the dreamy opening: "I'll be loving you / Always . . ." He signed the rights to "Always" over to her in perpetuity as a wedding present soon after they were married and her father disinherited her.

••

For a rich man, Clarence Mackay suffered from excep-
tional bad luck. His older brother's death, when Clarence
was twenty-one, wracked the family. With his blue-blooded
wife, Katherine Duer Mackay, he had three children (Ellin,
Katherine, and Willie), but in his thirties he got throat cancer, and she ran off with Dr. Joseph Blake, his surgeon and
close friend, who had operated on him and saved his life.
Giving up claim to her children, she divorced Clarence,
married Dr. Blake, and moved to France; Ellin was ten
years old. The scandal got a lot of attention in the papers.
At its height, Ellin noticed that people sometimes stopped
talking when she entered the room.

John Mackay, the father, had built a transoceanic-cable
company to compete with Western Union, after his Virginia
City mines played out. Clarence took over the Postal
Telegraph-Cable Company when his father died. During the
First World War, the government requisitioned Clarence's
ocean cables in the interest of wartime efficiency and put
the head of Western Union in charge of them, a move that
Clarence objected to but could not stop. After he got them
back, he set about modernizing the company, but his
prediction, "Radio will never supplant cables," proved di-
sastrous. Over time, telegraph traffic kept going down. The
company went with it, suffering various further setbacks,
including bankruptcy. Eventually, Postal Telegraph was
split into parts and merged with other companies.

Newspaper photos show Clarence in a shiny black top
hat and with a well-trimmed white mustache, like the millionaire in the Monopoly game. He belonged to every important club in Manhattan and served on the boards of
the Metropolitan Opera and the New York Philharmonic.
Through a mutual friend, Ellin knew the conductor Leo-

pold Stokowski, and they had a flirtation. Clarence felt so strongly about his Catholic faith that—for example—he would not consider remarriage while his ex-wife was still alive, even though she herself was remarried. Stokowski, a divorced man and a showy, artistic type, was out of the question. When Clarence asked Ellin not to see him anymore, she complied. But after he found out about her romance with Berlin and made a similar request on the basis of incompatible backgrounds, she surprised him by refusing.

And yet she wavered. When Clarence gave a grand ball at their Long Island mansion for the Prince of Wales (Edward, later the king who abdicated), Ellin stood at her father's side to greet their guest, and he escorted her in to dinner. As she and the prince danced, she told him that the song the orchestra was playing had been written by her young man friend and she asked the prince to cover for her while she slipped away to make a telephone call. Berlin, of course, had not been invited. Clarence even instructed the guards to make sure he did not attend. Young Wales, the world's most eligible bachelor at the time, on whom rested every young lady's mother's eye, later said that he found Ellin's lack of interest in him "refreshing."

Newspapers ran photos of her arm in arm with her father; because of his continuing refusal to remarry, she was his key default companion. He and Ellin took a long trip to Europe with the hope (on his part) that she would get over her love. Musically, her songwriter chaperoned and pursued her even overseas; wherever they went, orchestras were playing his songs. On Ellin's return, reporters met the ship in the harbor to ask if she and Berlin were engaged. She said she was NOT ENGAGED TO ANY ONE, as the *Times* put it in its headline. She averred that she had not yet met the young man for whom she would leave her father. Berlin, too, denied the rumors, saying that he was not engaged to anyone except Sam Harris, with whom he was engaged to write a Broadway revue and a show for the Marx Brothers.

At some point during this back-and-forth period, Ellin wrote "Why We Go to Cabarets."

••

Meanwhile, *The New Yorker* began and almost ended. Forty-six thousand dollars was not enough to start a magazine, as it turned out. After less than ninety days, with subscriptions not increasing and too few ads coming in, Harold Ross and Raoul Fleischmann and other principals met at the Princeton Club and decided to suspend publication. The move devastated Ross. He and his wife had invested all they had; they would be ruined, she said.

The next day, May 9, 1925, Ross went to the wedding of Franklin P. Adams, the nationwide newspaper columnist, in Connecticut and New York. (Because of a technicality of his recent divorce, Adams could not remarry in New York. He found a place where he could have an outdoor ceremony in Connecticut, then walk across the state line, which ran between house and orchard, for a reception in New York.) The apple trees were blooming, the weather benign. The guests included many in Ross's set, among them Raoul Fleischmann, who saw Ross standing alone. In the atmosphere of contingency arrangements and new beginnings, Fleischmann went over to him and suggested they make another try with the magazine.

This time, Ross's plan was to lie low through the summer, continuing to publish each week while saving up ideas and material for a serious push in the fall. The enhanced fall issues would be accompanied by a big ad campaign, which Fleischmann said he would pay for. If this strategy did not cause circulation and advertising to go up, then the magazine would quit publishing at year's end.

Against his better judgment, Ross had listed some friends of his with journalistic or literary reputations—such as George S. Kaufman, Dorothy Parker, Alexander Woollcott, Hugh Wiley, and Marc Connelly—in a kind of masthead of "Advisory Editors" at the front of the magazine. The purpose was to give a sense of probity. Most of them provided Ross with little editorial help or actual writing, though a few began to contribute more after the magazine was securely on its feet. One of the advisers, Alice Duer Miller, a bestselling novelist and a poet known for her verses ridiculing opponents of woman suffrage, happened to be a first cousin of Ellin's mother. Alice became especially close to Ellin and helped her when she began to write; Ellin considered Alice her mentor.

Ross knew better what he didn't want for his magazine than what he did want. Sentiment, gag-book humor, and comfortable articles that people his mother's age might enjoy distressed him. He viewed most submissions with dour skepticism. Sometime during the magazine's early months, Alice Duer Miller gave him Ellin Mackay's "Cabarets" essay. Jane Grant recalled that Ross kept it at the bottom of the pile of manuscripts he brought home, procrastinating because he liked Ellin and expected he would have to reject it, as he often did with others. Grant urged him to run the piece. "It will make wonderful publicity," she said. Alexander Woollcott, the *Times*'s drama critic, with whom the Rosses shared a house, and whose relationship with Ross so closely fit the word "frenemy" one wonders that the word had not been coined back then just for him, also championed Ellin's piece. Woollcott knew her through Berlin, whose worshipful biography he had written.

At the office, the "Cabarets" manuscript went to Ingersoll. Ross had hired him partly because, as a great-nephew of the McAllister who had declared that there were only four hundred notable people in New York, Ingersoll would be up on the doings of high society. He was also young, just a few years older than Ellin. He read the essay and next to Ross's "What think?" wrote, "It's a *must*."

Plans for the rest of 1925 went forward. The thin summer issues grew even less confidence-inspiring. Staffers became used to seeing large numbers of copies returned from the newsstands. Circulation, which had been at about 8,000 in April, fell to a low of 2,719 in August; Woollcott, anticipating the end, asked that his name be taken off the list of Advisory Editors. But in September, as promised, Fleischmann bought full-page newspaper ads, spending $60,000, a huge amount. The issues that Ross had been preparing for during the summer began to appear. Circulation slowly began to climb.

Whoever edited the manuscript of "Why We Go to Cabarets" for publication did a skillful job, replacing its many breathless dashes with more accurate punctuation, indenting for paragraphs in several places, but otherwise mostly leaving the piece alone. It ran on page 7 of the November 28 issue, illustrated with a drawing of hapless-looking young men standing around in tuxedos.

••

When a piece of writing rocks the world, it's a glorious thing. Or, in this case, rocks *a* world; suddenly, all over, people of a certain sort were talking about "Why We Go to Cabarets." The *Times* covered the article on page 1, upper left-hand corner. Other papers in the city and across the country splashed stories about it on the front page. The president of the New York Junior League, Mrs. Pleasants

Pennington, said she had not formed an opinion about the article, but "it amused me very much." The Waldorf Hotel issued a statement promising to arrange dances in an exclusive setting that would solve the problems Miss Mackay had outlined. In Paris, American ladies with daughters told a reporter from *The Chicago Daily Tribune* that the stag-line situation described in the article was why they had left the United States. James Thurber, in Paris after having given up trying to write a novel, learned about the existence of *The New Yorker* for the first time when he saw the headlines. The Jazz Age chronicler F. Scott Fitzgerald offered his thoughts on the piece (pity the naïve Midwestern lads invited to such soirées, Fitzgerald said). For the first time in its young history, *The New Yorker* sold out on the newsstands.

The celebrated Miss Mackay had hit a weak spot in the social patriarchy. Basically, her essay intimated that non-society, non-white-shoe guys were more attractive—i.e., sexier. Instead of dancing with the tiresome authorized princes at the ball where she was supposed to be, she had metaphorically slipped away to meet a much more interesting guy in a cabaret. *The New Yorker*'s issue of December 5 carried a response. Written by William T. Adee, a young Yale alumnus, "The Retort Courteous" came off as both condescending and wounded, conceding that although the debs were charming and "a few can even carry on an intelligent conversation," it was unfair to criticize the young men for being inadequate, because the debs themselves had invited them. Adee blamed the debs' complaints on their "restless craving for amusement and an insatiable capacity for the stimulation of jazz." (In 1938, at the age of thirty-seven, Adee and his wife, Sally, who was twenty-four, died when their house, in Tuxedo Park, New York, burned down. Their baby's nurse escaped and saved the baby.)

In the follow-up essay, "The Declining Function: A Post-Debutante Rejoices," published in the December 12 issue, Miss Mackay talked about how social gatherings organized around musical performances and cultural "lions" had also become dreary. The subject allowed her to elaborate on the establishment bashing of the "Cabarets" piece. What her father thought of either article is not known. In the second, having argued that modern young women possessed the independence of mind to seek out entertainments on their own, she wrote, "Modern girls are conscious of the importance of their own identity, and they marry whom they choose, satisfied to satisfy themselves. They are not so keenly aware, as were their parents, of the vast difference between a brilliant match and a mésalliance."

Ross's fall push succeeded beyond expectations, increasing circulation by a factor of ten, to almost thirty thousand, and attracting some of the high-end advertisers the business staff had hoped for; both Saks and B. Altman's signed big contracts for 1926 on the day before Christmas 1925. In 1,076 words, the "Cabarets" essay had hit precisely the sophisticated young nightclub-going, speakeasy-patronizing, up-and-coming, unimpressed-by-their-elders readership Ross was aiming for. The grateful editor gave Ellin Mackay a lifetime subscription to the magazine.

• •

As all this was happening with her first published piece of writing, her romance with Berlin approached a crisis. The couple could not meet at her father's house, and going to Berlin's Forty-sixth Street penthouse risked the appearance of impropriety. Sometimes they met in company with friends (including Ross's crowd, at his and Jane Grant's place) or had dinner together at an Italian café on Houston Street where they thought they weren't recognized. At the beginning of January, Berlin planned to sail for Europe to work on theatrical productions that would occupy him for several months. He made his reservation on a ship leaving on Saturday, January 2, but was still in town that evening, distractedly playing cards with some of his poker companions. Early on Monday, January 4, he called Ellin and asked if she wanted to get married that morning. He already had the ring. Without changing into a nicer dress, she put on her coat and came to his place, and they took the Seventh Avenue subway downtown. She had never been in the subway before.

Anyone curious about the newspaper coverage of what followed—the couple's quick wedding, honeymoon in Atlantic City, return to New York, and departure for Europe on the ocean liner *Leviathan*—can get a sense of the popular reaction by the sheer arm strength required to scroll through the pertinent reels of old, streaky microfilm. Newspapers put out many editions every day back then, and Ellin and Irving, newly married and smiling blissfully, or running from reporters, flicker on front page after scrolling tabloid front page, next to unwed mothers who had poisoned their newborns and nearly naked showgirl companions of the playboy Harry Thaw. Clarence Mackay's refusal to give the couple his blessing provided the plotline. The papers kept printing his original statement: "The marriage comes as a complete surprise to me and was done without my knowledge or approval. Beyond this I have nothing to say." Publicly, that represented his position on the subject for the rest of his life. Many of the articles also mentioned the bride's recent essays in *The New Yorker*—an ongoing promotional windfall for the magazine.

Ellin had underestimated how angry her father would be. She wrote him letters and pleaded through the newspapers, but got no reply. His influence, or a more general and shared disapproval, chilled friends and relations. When the Berlins sailed for Europe, no one in her family saw her off, and only reporters greeted them when they returned, seven months later.

••

By then, Ellin was pregnant, and she had her baby in November. As with other events in the Berlins' life, the arrival of Mary Ellin, born on Thanksgiving Day 1926, made the front pages. Mary Ellin Berlin Barrett, now eighty-eight, lives in a building in the same neighborhood as the Mackays' former town house. With her late husband, Marvin Barrett, a journalist and teacher, she raised four children (Katherine Swett is their youngest), and she worked as a writer and editor. Besides her memoir about her parents, she has published three novels. She is a slim, well-spoken woman of erect carriage and humorous eye. When I visited her apartment recently, she had laid out some pictures to show me—of Mackays, Berlins, Duers, Barretts—and the themes were of reconciliation and family.

"I knew my grandfather Mackay only as a loving old grandpa with a white mustache," she said. "The previous estrangement between him and my parents was something I learned about later. He had softened toward them when Irving Junior, the baby after me, died in infancy. Grandpa's ex-wife, Katherine, the one who ran off with Dr. Blake, became part of their lives, too. She had never opposed my mother and father's romance, and she even became close to Grandpa again. After she died, he finally married Anna Case, the opera singer, who had been his mistress for years.

"In the Depression, Grandpa Mackay lost almost all his money," she went on. "But it's not true, as some writers have said, that Irving Berlin bailed him out. My father lost a lot in the crash himself. As far as I ever saw, Grandpa

Mackay always got along well with my father. Once Grandpa was reminiscing about the ball he gave for the Prince of Wales, and he said, 'Oh, Irwin, my boy, it was splendid! You should've been there!' He had forgotten that he had hired guards to keep him out. I wondered what my father thought about that, and about how he and my mother had been treated, but he didn't let on. He was a kind man and would never have been other than gentle and respectful toward his father-in-law."

Berlin was an agnostic, but Ellin thought that both his and her religious traditions should be honored in their family. Christmas, Hanukkah, Passover, Easter—the Berlins celebrated all. In the family's uniqueness they devised a blended culture of their own. Instead of placing themselves in the Long Island world of her father or the show-business society where Berlin moved, they divided their time between New York City and the house Berlin bought for them in the Catskills as a surprise in 1938. Their self-constructed family life probably contributed to his biggest and most enduring hit, "White Christmas," along with his other perennial, "Easter Parade"—both unlikely songs to have been written by a Jewish songwriter.

From a shelf Mary Ellin took an outsize book, *The Complete Lyrics of Irving Berlin*. Only about 35 of its 530 pages contain songs written after 1960. "Daddy kept writing his songs to the end," she said. "But in the sixties he turned more to painting, with works like those he did on artists' palettes, there on the wall. Mother wrote her novels and stories, and Daddy was always her number-one supporter. Everything she wrote, she read to him out loud, and he gave her editing suggestions. He used to tell me, 'Your mother's writing is *wonderful*.' After I read her second novel, *Lace Curtain*, I said to her, 'Mamá, if you hadn't married Daddy, you could've been a famous writer like Edna Ferber.'

She laughed and said, 'Have you ever *seen* Edna Ferber? No, thank you. I'm happy with my family, and no one has a husband such as I have.' "

The Berlins' marriage resulted in two other children (Linda and Elizabeth), nine grandchildren, and fourteen great-grandchildren. Irving Berlin's hair never turned completely gray, and he even outlived the seventy-five-year copyright limit on his early songs, dying in 1989, at the age of a hundred and one. Ellin lived to be eighty-five, predeceasing him by a year. "She continued to receive the *New Yorker* subscription Mr. Ross gave her, up to the end of her life," Mary Ellin said.

••

The original manuscript of "Why We Go to Cabarets" is now in the Library of Congress, among the Irving Berlin papers. Not long ago, I tracked it down in the Music Division and spent part of a morning with it. Books about the early days of *The New Yorker* say that Ellin had her manuscripts bound in leather. The manuscript for "Cabarets" is in an ordinary three-ring notebook, about ten inches by seven, on lined paper. The notebook is leather-bound; a label on it gives the name of a Fifth Avenue bookseller and stationer now long gone. The author wrote her piece by hand. Ellin never learned to type, make a bed, cook, or so much as boil an egg. The handwriting, in blue fountain-pen ink, has a breezy, assured style, with backward threes for *e*'s and big pedestals on the capital *I*'s.

Sometimes you can tell how alive a piece of writing is, and how alive the author, just by the physical look of the letters on the page. This piece appears to have been done in a headlong rush. The neat handwriting at the beginning becomes faster and less neat as it goes along, and the lines begin to slant. There's passion in the document's physical self as well as in what it says. I wondered if, when Ross took a second read of this piece and decided to publish it, he saw something new in it: an adventurous person not unlike himself, just starting out.

February 23, 2015

Blue Bloods

A few years ago, I went on a boat trip to Fire Island with some researchers who were doing a population survey of horseshoe crabs. Soon after I boarded the boat, on a hot spring morning at a slip in Patchogue, I overheard this conversation:

"Diane, did you have your conga-drum lesson?"

"No, I missed it today. Horseshoe crabs are the only thing that can take me from my congas."

"Did you bring your drums with you, at least?"

"No, they're very heat-sensitive. I'd bring them if you could air-condition part of your boat."

The conga drummer turned out to be a volunteer named Diane SanRomán. On that morning, she wore knee-high rubber boots, a bright-pink cotton shirt, and complicated turquoise earrings: an in-the-field style that became familiar. "My life was good before I discovered horseshoe crabs, but now it's even better!" she announced to me, adding that she was raising a thousand horseshoe-crab eggs in the bathroom of her apartment, in Manhasset, and that her husband, a doctor who specializes in clinical nutrition, kindly put up with them. Along with playing conga drums, she throws pots and is pursuing her second MA, in experimental psychology with a focus on marine biology. She looks enough like the late Bea Arthur, the star of the 1970s sit-com *Maude*, that it would be negligent not to say so.

Of all the horseshoe-crab people I've met, Diane is the most enthusiastic and devout. She watches out for horseshoe crabs constantly. If poachers are seen in New York City waters with a boatload of nine hundred horseshoe crabs taken from Jamaica Bay, where you're allowed to take almost none, Diane sends out a group e-mail with the story. Ditto if the price of horseshoe crabs used for bait by eel and conch fishermen goes up to $5 per crab, or if a shipping crate of horseshoe crabs of unknown origin and destination appears at JFK airport, or if the Zoological Survey of India expresses concern over the dwindling horseshoe-crab population in the Bay of Bengal. With no previous training as a scientist, Diane learned enough about horseshoe crabs to make a presentation at a marine-biology workshop in San Diego in 2013, and she is preparing a study on horseshoe-crab behavior for a gathering in Japan in 2015.

• •

That day on Fire Island, we saw very few horseshoe crabs. The waves were too high, Diane said. Among horseshoe crabs' main predators are seagulls, which tear out their insides if they get turned over on their backs onshore. In high waves, horseshoe crabs go through gyrations to keep their carapaces upward, and they generally don't venture toward shore when the surf is rough.

Sometimes I went looking for horseshoe crabs on my own in New York City. At a beach in Staten Island where I'd heard there were many of them, I saw a rippled sand bottom, seaweed fragments rocking back and forth, and a single horseshoe crab swimming through the shallows in a meandering, lonesome way. Diane had told me that she participated in horseshoe-crab population surveys at a place in Brooklyn called Plumb Beach. On a May evening, I drove there, taking the Belt Parkway to Exit 9, per her directions. I came off the Belt at the Plumb Beach parking lot and parked and walked down to the waves. Compared with other beaches, the place was hopping.

A moon as big and orange as a whaling float had just come up over the Rockaways, the sand peninsula that partly shields Plumb Beach from the ocean; the moon's reflection, a line of wavering dimples that increased in size as they got closer, stretched across the inlet, about a mile wide. This is the kind of sheltered embayment that horseshoe crabs like. They wait to spawn until the water temperature gets above fifty degrees, and they prefer a high tide that coincides with a full-moon or a new-moon night. Already a number of them were in the shallows. From above, a horseshoe crab looks like a somewhat rusty Second World War tin-pot army helmet. John Rowden, of the Audubon Society, which organized this survey in affiliation with Cornell University and the New York State Department of Environmental Conservation, wore green rubber boots and carried an aluminum clipboard. Eight or ten volunteers, most of them college age, stood around him for instructions. Diane carried a square plastic frame that measured a meter on a side. She wore a bright-orange shirt, round silver earrings that were circles within circles, and a headlamp.

A guy who said his name was Allen came down the shore right behind me. To the group at large, he said, "I just dropped my mother off at Sheepshead Bay, and I stopped at the parking lot to smoke a cigar, and somebody asked if I was here for the horseshoe crabs, and I said, 'No, but what the hell, I'll stick around!' I got my camera—maybe make some horseshoe-crab porno movies!"

"It can get pretty wild here during a spawning event," John Rowden confided, when Diane introduced me. "One night last year, we were doing the survey, and there happened to be three or four models in bikinis here for a fashion shoot just at twilight, and the moon was full like it is now. When the horseshoe crabs started spawning, the models got kind of giddy and tore off their bikinis and went running through the waves."

The dusk deepened, the moon rose higher. A few non-volunteering spectators showed up—a woman in a fur coat, her beautiful daughter, and a young man carrying a bicycle wheel. Farther along the beach, Russian fishermen stood beside their belled fishing poles, impassive and unimpressed as only Russians can be. They had lit fires of damp straw to keep the bugs away; the sharp-smelling smoke coiled around. Spawning was now in full flower. Male horseshoe crabs are smaller than females, and when they spawn, the male grasps the back of the female's carapace with boxing-glove-shaped front pincers and hangs on. The female works herself into wet sand at the waterline, lays a cluster of some thousands of eggs, moves a short distance up, and lays more. The attached male fertilizes the eggs, as do other males, sometimes four or five or more, crowding around the pair. Mating pairs and satellite males now filled the shallows, moonlight glistening on their carapaces. In places, the wet sand seemed to be cobbled with them.

Volunteers paced off sections of the beach, taking a certain number of steps along the shallows, laying down their meter-square frames, and counting the males and females in the frame. Then they took another so many steps and repeated the process. John Rowden followed, writing down the data. When the counting was complete, and the moon overhead, he used a battery-powered hand drill to make small holes in the carapaces of about a dozen horseshoe crabs so he could attach tags to them. The tags had a phone number to call if the animal was found, so the survey could study how far horseshoe crabs travel after spawning. A small cork on the drill bit kept it from going in too far, but one of the volunteers, an older Asian lady, could not bear to watch. She refused to hold the horseshoe crab. "That's okay, Mrs. Wu," Rowden said. "You don't have to. No pressure."

The tide started to go out, and the horseshoe crabs became fewer. Diane walked the high-water line looking for any that had got turned over in the fray. By the light of her headlamp, she showed me a small male. The front part of the horseshoe crab's helmetlike carapace, called the prosoma, attaches to a lower part, called the opisthosoma, which would be like the helmet's neck guard. The juncture of the parts is hinged, and the opisthosoma moves up and down, providing a swimming motion. The pointed tail resembles a file and is called the telson. It connects to the opisthosoma by means of an almost universal joint. If the animal becomes upside down, the telson moves all around in an attempt to lever it onto its legs. Diane held the horseshoe crab with her hands on each side of the prosoma. "*Never* pick up a horseshoe crab by the telson," she cautioned.

We looked more closely at the horseshoe crab's underneath. Six pairs of spidery, multijointed legs radiated from the center, where both the mouth and the brain are. The brain is doughnut-shaped and encircles the mouth. The legs did a kind of slow-motion random insectoid running-in-place as Diane lifted the animal to show its gills—called book gills, because they resemble bound pages—which are also underneath, below the legs. Turning it upright again, she pointed out the large eyes on either side of the prosoma. Horseshoe crabs have a lot of eyes, and the species name,

Limulus polyphemus, derives from some of them. The two large eyes can be construed as squinting; hence *Limulus*, which means "squinting or aslant" in Latin. A pair of smaller eyes on top of the prosoma are so close together they might be mistaken for a single eye; hence *polyphemus*, from the Cyclops.

Diane handed the wet, sand-covered male to me and I carried it to the water. Held upright, it felt like a closed cardboard box with something alive moving around inside. Meanwhile, she found a large female that had gone far up the beach and was headed in the wrong direction. "Why doesn't she know to go back, and out with the tide, like everybody else?" Diane asked, returning the female to the waves. "Sometimes these animals seem sharp as a tack and sometimes they have no clue."

The cars on the Belt Parkway, no more than fifty yards from the water in some places, sped as madly as before. Sirens passed and faded, the bass reverbs of car stereos went pulsing by. Along the shore, you could still see a few volunteers looking into the dark water with their headlamps, bent over the small pools of blue-white light at their feet.

••

Horseshoe crabs are aliens from another planet, if we allow that the other planet was Earth about 500 million years ago. Creatures much like horseshoe crabs go back that far or farther, to almost the beginnings of animal life. The earliest known horseshoe-crab fossils are 485 million years old. The land then was bare rock without plants, except for some algae and tiny mosses along the watercourses. All animal life was in the oceans; millions of years passed before any animals lived on land. The oldest fossils of land animals date to between 420 and 410 million years ago, and they are of the horseshoe crab's relatives—scorpions, spiders, and insects. All belong to the phylum Arthropoda, the most populous phylum, which has more than a million species. True crabs are also of that phylum, but their class is Crustacea, while horseshoe crabs are of the class Chelicerata. That is, horseshoe crabs are not crabs.

In the fossil record, the nearest ancient relatives of horseshoe crabs are the trilobites, a successful group for hundreds of millions of years. Because trilobites had shells made mostly of calcium carbonate, they fossilized better than horseshoe crabs, whose shells are composed of chitin. Most trilobites had ovoid, segmented bodies that would make good paperweights. The last species of trilobites disappeared in the Permian Extinction, between 252 and 250 million years ago. Horseshoe crabs survived that extinction and the others—at least a dozen extinctions in all. Having exoskeletons of chitin rather than of calcium carbonate may have helped during times when the oceans acidified. Horseshoe crabs can tolerate low-oxygen water and other life-killing conditions. Animal life probably began in the bottom of the sea. Horseshoe crabs still live in the mud and sand at the bottom of shallow inland waters, and on continental shelves out to about a hundred feet deep. They are like our old neighbors who never left our hometown.

In 2005, Dr. Dave Rudkin, a paleobiologist at the Royal Ontario Museum, in Toronto, found horseshoe-crab fossils in central Manitoba. At one site, on the shores of Hudson Bay near Churchill, he and his colleagues spalled off thin layers of rock with two-pound sledgehammers while keeping an eye open for polar bears. The fossil horseshoe crabs, to which he gave the name *Lunataspis aurora*, were no larger than two inches across. From tests of the rock's isotopes and by comparing index fossils, he could date the horseshoe-crab fossils to the late Ordovician period, about 445 million years ago.

Manitoba lies mostly on the Canadian Shield, part of the North American midcontinental core that has remained geologically stable for much longer than 500 million years. In the late Ordovician, it was in the subtropics, near the equator, and a shallow sea spread across its central region. It was moving away from Rodinia, the supercontinent it had been a part of. Eventually, it recollided with other continents to form the supercontinent Pangaea, which in turn split apart, about 210 million years ago. North America reached its present position on the planet about 20 million years ago, in the Middle Cenozoic. Unlike more recent arrivals, horseshoe crabs might have ridden North America here.

Lunataspis aurora did not fall prey to birds, because there weren't any, and wouldn't be any for hundreds of millions of years. Horseshoe crabs saw the aeons come and go. In the Carboniferous period, when most bacteria able to digest wood had not yet evolved, a planetary reservoir of plant carbon was buried and became coal. The remains of *Euproops*, another early horseshoe-crab species, have been found in fossilized feces in coal deposits in England. A species of horseshoe crab that scientists named *Limulus coffini* because of its close resemblance to the *Limulus* of today became a fossil in 80-million-year-old rock in Colorado. A horseshoe crab known as *Mesolimulus walchi*, whose fossils have been found in limestone quarries in southern Germany, preexisted by 50 million years certain formations of ocean algae that died and fell to the bottom and occupied deeper rock and cooked at the right temperature for millions of years and eventually turned into oil; the kin of *Mesolimulus* may or may not still be here when all the planet's oil is gone. Horseshoe crabs have been around at least two hundred times as long as human beings.

••

"The main problem for horseshoe crabs in Asia is people eating them," Dr. John Tanacredi told me. A big man with a gray mustache and (sometimes) a soul patch, who likes to wear Hawaiian shirts with palm fronds on them, he is one of the world's leading experts on horseshoe crabs. We were in Rockville Centre, Long Island, in a room at Molloy College, where he teaches marine biology. In 2004, Tanacredi began organizing the International Workshop on the Science and Conservation of Horseshoe Crabs, a group of scientists from America and Asia who hold conferences about the animal every two years. "You can buy horseshoe crab in seafood markets in Taiwan and Hong Kong," he continued. "People eat the eggs, too. A Japanese colleague tells me that in Vietnam there are snack carts that sell steamed horseshoe crabs on the beach. Protein is protein, I guess. As an experiment, some students and I tried to make a horseshoe-crab stew one time. It was the worst thing we'd ever tasted. We threw it out and ordered pizza."

For no reason that scientists can explain, horseshoe crabs are found only on the eastern coasts of North America and Mexico and on the eastern coast of Asia and near environs. Atlantic horseshoe crabs have a range from Maine to Florida, to the Gulf of Mexico and the tip of Yucatán. An estimated 19 million horseshoe crabs, by far the largest population in the world, live in Delaware Bay. Asian horseshoe crabs are of three species: *Tachypleus tridentatus*, in southern Japan, the Philippines, and on the central and southern coast of China; *Carcinoscorpius rotundicauda*, in the western part of the Bay of Bengal, on both sides of the Malay Peninsula, and on the island of Borneo; and *Tachypleus gigas*, in a range overlapping with that of *Carcinoscorpius* but in smaller numbers. All the Asiatic species are in severe decline. *Tachypleus gigas* seems to be the hardest hit of the three.

"In many parts of Asia, the other disaster is habitat loss, of course," Tanacredi said. "In Hong Kong, for example, there's almost no undeveloped shoreline left. On the coast of China, the pollution is becoming too much even for horseshoe crabs. But the numbers here in America are not reassuring, either. Since we started doing local surveys, back in 2001, we've seen a decline of about one percent in the horseshoe-crab population on Long Island every year, for a total drop of about twelve percent. It's a scary trend."

People's tastes in seafood affect Atlantic horseshoe crabs, too. Some local East Coast horseshoe crabs are exported for tables in Asia. More are consumed at one remove, when fanciers of eels or of scungilli (conchs, also called whelks) buy those foods in stores or restaurants. The best bait for conchs or eels is female horseshoe crab; you take a female, cut it in quarters, and put the pieces in eel pots or conch traps. Suppliers ship conchs and eels internationally, so the global market drives local harvests of bait. Over the past decades, many millions of horseshoe crabs on the East Coast went for bait. When their numbers seemed to be dropping alarmingly, the Atlantic States Marine Fisheries Commission, or ASMFC, to which New York and the other Atlantic seaboard states belong, set harvest quotas.

The ASMFC's horseshoe-crab directives require that each member state make an annual census of horseshoe crabs. Going all along the shoreline on spawning nights and counting horseshoe crabs is beyond the means of any state's department of environmental conservation or fish and game. Ergo: volunteers, or practitioners of "citizen science," that newly fashionable term. Now on any full-moon night in late May or early June, thousands of volunteer horseshoe-crab census takers like those I'd joined at Plumb Beach descend upon the coast.

Matthew Sclafani, of the Cornell Cooperative Extension in Riverhead, Long Island, oversees the New York State detachment of this army. In his office, he showed me a six-inch-high pile of applications for volunteer positions that he had received already in 2014. "We get hundreds of people who want to count horseshoe crabs," he told me. "Interesting types—they love horseshoe crabs, they come from all over, they're retired or they're young, they're willing to go out and collect data at one in the morning. The census program helps create local stewards, and it's great for us and for the state DEC, who we contract for, because it gives people an attachment to the resource. Our volunteers know that the data they gather will go directly to conservation. The horseshoe crab is the model species for citizen science. Most marine animals, you have to spend a lot of money and go to difficult or even dangerous extremes to observe them. But horseshoe crabs are easy. What other marine animal comes up by the thousands right onto the beach?"

••

When Diane walks local shorelines checking on horseshoe crabs, I accompany her sometimes, and try not to wince when she politely asks hard-looking fishermen pointed questions about the horseshoe crabs lying strewn at their feet. If she sees kids hanging out under a bridge, she tells them about horseshoe crabs, and if she comes upon horseshoe crabs tangled in fishing line or seaweed, she untangles them, and if she notices some that appear to have been mistreated, she documents the injuries by taking photos with her iPhone.

One of her recent photos shows a horseshoe crab that has likely been punctured in the heart and has bled out on the sand. Horseshoe-crab blood is blue. I had never seen it before; unless the heart is pierced, the structure of the animal's anatomy generally keeps it from serious bleeding. The blue comes from hemocyanin, a copper-containing protein that transports oxygen in the blood, like the iron-containing hemoglobin in red blood. Other animals, including snails, octopuses, and scorpions, have blood with hemocyanin, but you rarely see their blood in a big puddle.

Horseshoe-crab blood is said to be worth $15,000 a quart. It contains a unique substance known as limulus amebocyte lysate, or LAL, that responds dramatically to the presence of even the tiniest amount of bacterial toxin. LAL is used to test vaccines, IV fluids, surgical instruments, artificial implants, and any other medical item that goes under the skin. Some horseshoe-crab experts consider $15,000 to be too low an estimate, considering the amount of LAL that may be refined from a quart of blood. Biomedical companies take adult horseshoe crabs that have been caught in the wild, and then workers clean them, strap them to racks, stick needles in their hearts, drain them of about a third of their blood, and, eventually, release them. The crabs are supposed to be put back where they came from, but that doesn't always happen, according to reports. Mortality rates from the bleeding procedure are unknown; they may be as high as 30 percent. In 2012, the industry bled about half a million horseshoe crabs. From somewhere in my travels, I acquired a vial of LAL with the brand name of Pyrogent, made by a company called BioWhittaker, in Walkersville, Maryland. The vial, good for one test, contains a small dusting of a white powderlike substance that could fit on the tip of a finger.

The strength of the LAL reaction may be an adaptation related to the animal's shell. The ocean bottom breeds a lot of bacteria, and a chitinous shell punctures more easily than a mineralized, calcium-carbonate one. If a horseshoe crab's shell gets a hole in it and bacterial toxins enter, ame-bocytes, or blood cells, instantly attack the bacteria by spewing enzymes that clot the blood. For a better grasp of how this works, I called Dr. Norman Wainwright, the di-rector of research and development at Charles River Labo-ratories, a major manufacturer of LAL, with headquarters in Massachusetts. That is, I made calls and then exchanged e-mails with a series of public-relations people associated with Charles River, until a conference call was set up be-tween Wainwright and me, plus Charles River's director of public relations, who said that she would listen in and "provide insight where needed."

Dr. Wainwright, who worked with Dr. Jack Levin, one of the two discoverers of the LAL reaction, told me that watching the cells under a microscope is amazing—the way the granules in the amebocytes suddenly pop like popcorn and make a clot around the bacteria. He explained that en-zymes in the blood increase the reaction so that each step is a tenfold amplification of the one before, like a chain letter. Recently, he invented a handheld LAL-based device that can detect bacterial toxins chromogenically. You wet a sterilized swab with purified water and rub the swab on whatever you want to test. Then you put the sample in a well in the device and a display changes color if there is con-tamination. This will be handy for prelaunch testing of spacecraft, which by international treaty must be free of microbes before they are sent into space. (Another, more time-consuming assay is currently employed to test space-craft.) Wainwright said that someday the LAL test could be used to search for microbial life on other planets, and that for this ancient animal's blood to be a part of space exploration is a remarkable development. I asked, by the way, since the enzymes of the LAL reaction are so impor-tant to it, and since other natural enzymes have been synthesized in the lab, why couldn't the same be done with these enzymes? And might somebody be working on a synthetic LAL already? He began to answer, but the Charles River Laboratories director of public relations, who had said nothing so far, declared this subject beyond the scope of the interview. Brought up short, Wainwright and I fell silent, and the conversation petered out.

• •

Synthetic LAL does exist, and a biotechnology company called Lonza sells a version of it under the brand name PyroGene. Other synthetics have been developed and could, in theory, replace natural LAL entirely; for now, industry inertia and the cost of getting FDA approval remain in the way. The next time I saw John Tanacredi, I asked him if it didn't make sense to raise a lot of horseshoe crabs in captivity anyway, to have a reserve. "You know why I love to work with horseshoe crabs? Because they're the perfect research animal," he said. "It may sound silly, but they don't bite, they don't take your finger off. They're not slimy. They've got some sharp, nonpoisonous spines on their opisthosomas you have to look out for—that's about it. Horseshoe crabs don't harm anything except the small clams and worms they eat. That's partly why LAL was discovered in the first place. The animals were readily available and no problem to work with. Back in the sixties, a Nobel Prize for research in vision went to optic-nerve research done on horseshoe crabs. The photoreceptors in their eyes are large and easy to study.

"So, yes, it would be great if we could raise them outside their environment," he continued. "I have horseshoe crabs I'm raising in my lab right now. We've brought thousands past their first three or four instars—their first molts—and released them to the wild, but we have no way of knowing what happened to them. Scientists in Hong Kong and Taiwan have done the same. So far, though, nobody has raised a horseshoe crab to adulthood—to sexual maturity, which they reach at about ten years old. These animals can live to be twenty or even thirty. In an artificial environment, no one has kept them alive past the age of about five and a half. So what all this tells me is that we have to work harder to preserve them in the wild. Our international group has been trying to get the UN to declare the horseshoe crab a World Heritage Animal. We already have World Heritage Sites—natural and cultural places that UNESCO has declared worthy of preservation. Why not a World Heritage Animal? Giving that designation to horseshoe crabs would provide conservation groups, especially in Asia, with a lot more authority in working to preserve them. The first animals on Earth were invertebrates. It would be really cool if this invertebrate became the first World Heritage Animal."

• •

A spring day at Mispillion Harbor, on the western shore of Delaware Bay about twenty miles south of Dover, out-springtimes almost anyplace else. The beaches and the creeks and the broad flats of cordgrass and phragmites are a widespread racket of bird noise, the sky above the shoreline effervesces with fliers, the breezes send ripples over the water and through the reeds. Individuals go streaking by, and long skeins of birds, incoming or outgoing, cross the sky far away. Delaware Bay is one of four main staging areas for migratory birds on the continent, and the beaches of Mispillion Harbor are the bay's most important sites for migrating shorebirds. As it happens, the millions of adult horseshoe crabs that live in the bay usually are in their spawning phase when the birds arrive. This continental stopover is catered substantially by the horseshoe crabs.

One Memorial Day, on a long excursion, I visited the viewing deck at the DuPont Nature Center, overlooking Mispillion Harbor. Bird-watchers lined its railings with emplacements of telescopes and cameras. Some of the bird-watchers were talking on their cell phones and leaving excited messages for other bird-watchers. When the other bird-watchers called back, the ringtones were birdcalls. Jeffery Davis, a birder from near Philadelphia, offered me a look through his well-positioned 30-power Kowa telescope. Oystercatchers, stilts, dowitchers, willets, black-bellied plovers, dunlins, royal terns, ruddy turnstones, semipalmated sandpipers—along the sand and in the shallows, thousands of heads were going up and down as long, thin bills plucked up what probably were horseshoe-crab eggs. A single horseshoe crab swam nearby on the surface, on its side. Lenses turned to the odd swimmer for half a minute, then went back to the birds.

Jeffery Davis pointed out the red knot, the bird I had come to see. When birds flew up, they went by species—all the oystercatchers in a fluttering bunch, then all the dowitchers, and so on. A bunch of birds with rust-colored bellies and brown legs went up and then came down where the scope was pointed, and he said they were red knots. These are a famous kind of bird. Next to the nature center stood a seven-foot-high statue of a red knot known as B 95, which has completed round-trip migrations of eighteen thousand miles at least twenty times and often stops off here. Red knots spend our winter months in Tierra del Fuego, near the tip of South America, and begin to fly north when the South American winter approaches, at the beginning of

our spring. They cross great distances flying at forty or
fifty miles an hour and when they get here may have burned
off half their body weight.

For unknown millennia, red knots have been rebulking
up along Delaware Bay annually at this time in the spring.
During a span of about two weeks, they work the beaches
and eat many tons of horseshoe-crab eggs. Then they continue northward to the tundra above the Arctic Circle, where
they lay their own eggs in nests in the ground cover, raise
their young, then turn south again. Through the scope, some
of the red knots already looked plump as they stepped
among the other birds and moved their heads briskly. Red
knots used to stop off here every spring by the many tens
of thousands. Since the 1980s, their numbers have been
going steadily down. An estimated forty-four thousand
came in 2013. The U.S. Fish and Wildlife Service wants to
list the red knots as a threatened species, and the proposal
is now under public review. A drop in the horseshoe-crab
population may be part of the red knots' problem.

• •

Glenn Gauvry, the president of the Ecological Research
and Development Group, describes his organization as the
only one in the world whose goal is the conservation of
horseshoe crabs. He lives in the tiny town of Little Creek,
Delaware, a short drive up the shore from Mispillion
Harbor, in a frame house that is also the ERDG's headquarters. He came to horseshoe crabs by way of an army
upbringing, service in the air force as an air-traffic control-
ler, establishment of a business that made expensive wood
furniture for corporate boardrooms, closing of that business, involvement in animal-rescue groups, travel to oil-spill
sites all over the world for the rescue of oil-covered animals,
survival of a near-fatal illness caused by drug-resistant

bacteria, eventual burnout on animal rescue, and reconsideration of his life's purpose. He is a soft-spoken, limber, Zen-influenced man. We sat and talked in low chairs in his uncluttered living room.

"I had always known about horseshoe crabs," he told me, "but when I came across them again while cleaning oil off seabirds I was surprised to discover there was no horseshoe-crab advocacy organization—none. So in 1995 I started the ERDG. We have the broadest mission. We talk to the biomed industry and the fishermen and the birders, groups that mostly don't talk to each other. We establish local horseshoe-crab sanctuaries, try to reduce harvests, gather habitat data, and let people know about these animals. Getting people to care about horseshoe crabs is a hard, hard sell. Millions of people love birds, and you can read long, poetic descriptions of the journey of the red knots. The birders have the influence and the money. When the horseshoe crab enters their consciousness, it's only as a source of food."

Gauvry was wearing a loose white shirt, cargo pants, and sandals. He leaned back and took a moment, in a centered way. "As an industrial designer, I'm fascinated with horseshoe crabs," he said. "Their body plan is configured for success and yet they seem to be built on sacrifice. Look at their suffering. When they meet an obstacle, they overcome it by dying in enormous numbers. They lay billions of eggs but only a tiny percentage become adults, while the rest feed other animals. Fishermen use the bodies of horseshoe crabs, we take their blood for our medicine. I choose to be moved by that. There's a truth in horseshoe crabs that we must be attentive to. They've been around for half a billion years; the jury is still out on us."

..

Near Gauvry's house, a narrow paved road runs through fields of phragmites directly to the bay. I drove to the end of pavement and got out. The tide had receded; acres of dark-brown mudflats featured occasional stuck horseshoe crabs waving their telsons. On the horizon, seven oil tankers with identical silhouettes waited at regular intervals; Delaware Bay is the second-biggest oil-transport waterway in America. Wandering along trails in the shoreline reeds, I found horseshoe-crab fragments by the thousands, among paint buckets, tires, condom wrappers, bricks, Clorox bottles, bushel baskets, six-pack yokes, Sierra Mist cans, tampon dispensers, taillight fragments, shotgun-shell casings, butterfly-shaped Mylar balloons, and two-by-fours. Next to the carapace of a large horseshoe crab someone had set a battered yellow hard hat, perhaps as visual commentary.

Past an initial puddle, the gravel road going north along the shoreline looked drivable, so I took it. The road skirted the bay so closely that it required a barrier wall of riprap for protection. On the inland side, landing lights for Dover Air Force Base led away and out of sight. Dover is the military's largest mortuary base, and it appears often in news stories about the return of the bodies of soldiers who died overseas. As I watched, a C-5 transport plane came out of the clouds, so huge and slow it seemed it would drop from the sky. Glenn Gauvry had told me that there was a fuel dock up ahead, and now I saw it—a long pier set apart by barbed-wire fencing and studded with warning signs. Ocean tankers unload airplane fuel there, he said, and it flows through a pipeline system to the base.

The crumbling brittle of horseshoe-crab parts under the car wheels now became so thick it was unnerving, with uncrushed, whole horseshoe crabs all over the road as well. I pulled onto the left-hand berm to investigate. When I climbed up on the riprap wall, I saw throngs of stranded horseshoe crabs lying in the interstices among the rocks. The carnage stretched into the distance and had a major-battlefield air, reminiscent of the Mathew Brady photograph of the dead at the Sunken Road at Sharpsburg. Some of the horseshoe crabs seemed to be moving feebly. The ones on the road had evidently managed to make it past the rocks.

A blue car came driving slowly along the road and parked behind my car. A blond, crew-cut man wearing a short-sleeved shirt got out, followed by two boys. The boys bounded onto the rocks and went along them checking the horseshoe crabs, picking up any that showed signs of life, and carefully putting them back in the water. "This is an annual thing for my sons and me," the man said, climbing up beside me. "The air force built this rock barrier to pro-tect the road, because it's important to the fuel pier and to the base. The beach that used to be here was perfect for the crabs, so naturally I guess they keep trying to spawn here. We come out and try to save the ones we can. Most of the crabs here are dead. This beach is a total loss for them, and we keep hoping that next year they'll get the message, but so far they haven't."

••

Plumb Beach, where I'd first seen horseshoe crabs spawn-ing, looked different every time I went back. Because of its easy access from the Belt Parkway, I visited it often. It is a wild place—one of those ungovernable margins of the city where the wildness of nature coincides with human wild-ness and a sense of chaos prevails. Plumb Beach used to be an island. A neighboring barrier of sand called Pelican Beach, which shifted around at the eastern end of Coney Island, protected Plumb Island from sea currents incoming from Rockaway Point. In the late 1800s or early 1900s, Peli-can Beach disappeared—dredged up or washed away, no one today remembers—letting the currents in. Just west of Plumb Island, in Sheepshead Bay, some of the richest men in America built shoreline mansions. A nonrich, less presentable element inhabited Plumb Island. To get to it, you had to take a ferry across a tidal channel called Hog Creek, though at low tide you could walk.

In 1940, the city's parks commissioner, Robert Moses, made Plumb Island Plumb Beach by filling in Hog Creek with dredged-up sand. Evicting the locals, he then put a mile or so of the Belt Parkway on this stretch of dunes and added a city park beside the eastbound lanes. Moses believed that people should drive on parkways uninterrupted by stoplights to places set aside for the appreciation of nature and healthy outdoor exercise. At Plumb Beach, he created a habitat for chaos instead. A parking lot you could speed into and out of, with isolated dunes beside it, in New York City—what was likely to happen? Plumb Beach became a famous make-out spot, and later a cruising area for older men waiting alone in cars. Drug dealers liked the parking lot's drive-through convenience. There were murders; a man was stabbed to death in his car. People getting rid of their cats abandoned them at Plumb Beach and a feral-cat population spread through the windblown foliage. Dumped-out trash accumulated and blew here and there in windrows.

In 2006, a designer at the IKEA store in Nassau County drove to the Plumb Beach parking lot to have sex with a man he had met online. The designer brought a blanket so they could lie on the sand. When he arrived, the pickup and three confederates tried to rob him. Struggling with two of them, the designer ended up on the parkway, where an SUV hit him and kept going. One of the attackers went through his pockets before running away. He died a few days later in the hospital. The attackers were caught, tried, and sentenced to up to twenty-one years in prison. The designer's family and friends put a memorial bench beside the parking lot; his name was Michael Sandy.

Carl Kruger, the local New York State senator, declared Plumb Beach a menace and said it should be closed after dark. He later pleaded guilty to taking bribes in an unrelated matter and went to prison, where he remains. Nor'easters hit Plumb Beach hard and erosion ate so far into the beach that it threatened the parkway. Local citizens called for beach replenishment. They found a champion for their cause in their young congressman, Anthony Weiner.

Eventually, the pollution and trash at Plumb Beach became less bad. The park is part of the Gateway National Recreation Area, which includes most of Jamaica Bay and some of the Staten Island shoreline, so Plumb Beach is partly under federal management. John Tanacredi, who served as Gateway's ecotoxicologist for five years, remembers seeing horseshoe crabs spawning in the back of a drowned Volkswagen in precleanup days. Theresa Scavo, the chair of the local community board, who has lived in the area for all her sixty-two years, knew Plumb Beach when refuse filled the shallows. "Trash or no trash, made no difference to the horseshoe crabs," Scavo told me. "The horseshoe crabs have always been there."

••

When I stopped by Plumb Beach four days after the 2012 hurricane, it had been transformed. Blue plastic barrels and dock segments and huge unidentifiable objects—pieces of ships?—had washed onto the dunes and lay like giants' toys. Sand buried the groves of cottonwoods and ailanthus trees far up their trunks. Shreds of plastic filled their branches. Michael Sandy's bench sat in sand up to its arms. At the same time, a beach-replenishment project—the final result of Anthony Weiner's efforts—was going on, overseen by the Army Corps of Engineers and contracted by the Great Lakes Dredge and Dock Company, according to a posted sign. A concrete pipe three feet across extended into the water, where it inhaled sand from a barge offshore. Another set of pipes and hoses applied the sand to the most eroded parts of the beach. At the old suture where Hog Creek used to be, wide expanses of new white sand kept the waves two hundred yards or more from the parkway.

The next year on Memorial Day, I called Diane and asked if she had any idea what the hurricane had done to the horseshoe-crab population. She said she didn't know yet—spawning wasn't very far along and nobody had much new data. She suggested we meet at Big Egg Marsh, a beach by the bridge across Broad Channel to the Rockaways, and see for ourselves. When I got there, Diane's Toyota was already in the horseshoe-crab-shell-strewn parking area. Tonight, her outfit included red rubber boots, jeans, a purple T-shirt, and earrings that were small triangles depending from big triangles.

People of India-Indian heritage from Guyana who now live in Queens often spend time at Big Egg Marsh. At a certain time of year, they perform Hindu ceremonies that involve putting money, flowers, fruit, and little ghee-burning lamps on paper plates and setting them afloat to go out with the tide. Tonight, the Guyanese were only fishing for smelt. Their seine nets, blue and white and orange, flared against the bridge's tan concrete like silent fireworks when they cast them. Planes taking off from JFK went roaring above every few minutes, showing their wide white undersides. Diane and I walked the shore, but only a few horseshoe crabs appeared. She found one that had a tag and she made a note of its number. Another struggled with its legs in a tangle of bright-pink ribbon, perhaps a leftover from the

Guyanese ceremonies. Diane gently asked some Guyanese if they would please refrain from putting ribbons in the water, explaining the hazard it posed. The Guyanese nodded and smiled.

Hoping for more action, we then drove to Plumb Beach. The trouble-magnet parking lot had been gated and locked, so we had to park a mile or so away and walk in along the bicycle path. The near part of the beach, closest to the parkway, was now enclosed with orange plastic fencing, and construction equipment and piles of rocks for new breakwaters occupied the site. We continued farther down, to where we'd seen the most horseshoe crabs before, at the eastern end of the beach. In the little marsh between it and the highway, a stadium-size congregation of birds yakked and called. The lights of cars sped past. The sun set, the dusk deepened, a full moon rose. Horseshoe crabs began to emerge. One after another, and then in bunches, like the helmet tops of surfacing mermen, they came up in the outwash along the smooth wet sand.

• •

Horseshoe crabs in the Northeast seemed to have survived the big hurricane with no major change in their numbers. According to the Delaware Department of Natural Resources and Environmental Control, egg densities on horseshoe-crab spawning beaches on the Delaware side of the bay were about the same in 2013 as they had been in 2012. On Long Island, Tanacredi said, the numbers of horseshoe crabs continued to decline at about one percent over that period, following the recent pattern.

Not long ago, I went with Diane on a chilly walk at Big Egg Marsh—to collect winter data, she said, though there turned out to be nothing much to see besides a few horseshoe-crab parts and the concrete stumps of supports for a now vanished bridge sticking up at lowest tide, their rusted rebars like tousled dreadlocks. Afterward, we got pizza in nearby Howard Beach and then sat by the water at a little park by the Congressman Joseph P. Addabbo Bridge. Seagulls were flying over the parking lot and dropping clams to break them and get at the meat. The view to the west was of islands, with distant Manhattan just another one of them, distinguished only by its dim, vaulting skyline. I asked her how the thousand baby horseshoe crabs in her apartment were doing. "All but a dozen of them died," she said. "The biggest one I still have is about like this." She made a coin-size circle with her finger and thumb. "They molt four or five times in their first year, and that's the tough part. For some reason, when they molt they die."

I asked Diane why, after all, she was so interested in horseshoe crabs.

"My husband wonders that," she said. "Right after the first night when I went on a horseshoe-crab survey, I told him I had found my niche, and he thought I was being comedic. He assumed I would get over it. But my fascination with horseshoe crabs only grew. There's something about them—they have a deep purpose, a secret knowledge of their imperativeness. I want to understand how they perceive the world. For example, supposedly horseshoe crabs can't hear—but how do we know? We really have no idea what horseshoe crabs think or what they are doing. They're mysterious, and they're also adorable."

I remembered a famous horseshoe-crab fossil I'd seen pictures of. The horseshoe crab is in a matrix of rock that includes the fossilized imprint of the animal's final tracks. In some distress, it left a wobbly, winding set of tracks and, at the end of them, died. Its fossil lies at the conclusion of its preserved last pages. Perhaps it found itself in anoxic water and couldn't get out. But there is sense in what

happened to it, a one-thing-after-another set of consequences, as there was, in fact, to everything around it
and to all existence after and before. When no human consciousness existed, everything that did exist, including this
dying horseshoe crab, had its own story and made its own
sense.

Humans may drive horseshoe crabs to extinction, or
not. Sea-level rises may cause shoreline reinforcement that
wipes out their habitat. Or perhaps there will be even
more beaches for them when sea levels rise; probably we
won't be able to reinforce every foot of shoreline. In any
case, there will be a future where natural events continue
to make their own sense, as they've always done, as they will
whether we are still here to see the sense in them, or not.
Based on past performance, horseshoe crabs may well survive us. Next to the road, where most people never look at
them, they show how life goes about living on the actual
earth.

April 14, 2014